LET ME EAT

A Celebration of Flour, Sugar,
Butter, Eggs, Vanilla, Baking Powder,
and a Pinch of Salt

Leslie F. Miller

Simon & Schuster

New York   London   Toronto   Sydney

Simon & Schuster
1230 Avenue of the Americas
New York, NY 10020

First Simon & Schuster hardcover edition April 2009

SIMON & SCHUSTER and colophon are registered trademarks of
Simon & Schuster, Inc.

For information about special discounts for bulk purchases,
please contact Simon & Schuster Special Sales at
1-866-506-1949 or business@simonandschuster.com.

The Simon & Schuster Speakers Bureau can bring authors
to your live event. For more information or to book an event
contact the Simon & Schuster Speakers Bureau at
1-866-248-3049 or visit our website at www.simonspeakers.com.

Designed by Suet Y. Chong

Manufactured in the United States of America

1   3   5   7   9   10   8   6   4   2

Library of Congress Cataloging-in-Publication Data

Miller, Leslie F.
Let me eat cake : a celebration of flour, sugar, butter, eggs, vanilla,
baking powder, and a pinch of salt / Leslie F. Miller.
       p.   cm.
Includes bibliographical references.
1. Cake. I. Title.
TX771.M45   2009
641.8'653—dc22   2008025862

ISBN-13: 978-1-4165-8873-3
ISBN-10:   1-4165-8873-6

Acknowledgments

At the Oscars, when the winner for Best Use of a Font begins her award speech by saying "I have so many people to thank," we all groan. Fortunately, you can just skip to the dedication—unless you're looking for your own name. The list seems to be in order of physical contact; if I've touched you, you're probably closer to the bottom. (If I've cleaned wax out of your ears, you're in the last paragraphs.)

Without my sporadic running, I'd have gained forty pounds, instead of twenty, while writing this book. That I ran at all is thanks to the music on my iPod: cake lover Bob Schneider (whom I call Bahhhhhhhb), Willy Porter, Chuck Prophet, Marah, Ani Difranco, Jonatha Brooke, and Brandi Carlile. When I don't run, I sing their songs real loud in my kitchen, usually with Red Hook ESB, and now with my own guitar.

I consulted dozens of books, and thanks for the morsels I borrowed come in the form of endnotes. But the following people either led me to those books or assisted me when I needed more help: candy freak Steve Almond; Karen Ammond; Chowhound; Steve Ettlinger, author of *Twinkie, Deconstructed;* Joanne Larson, of dietician.com; Elinor Murray, customer care at Mr Kipling Cakes; Lynne Olver, a research librarian doing the brilliant Food Timeline; foodie Kirk Os-

born; Michael Pollan, author; Alice Ross, food historian; Fred Sauce-
man, author of *The Place Setting* series; Mark Scarbrough, Ultimate
Cook; Dr. Bruce Semon; Linda Stradley, who writes the brilliant
What's Cooking America books and Web site; Ann Thompson; and
Marsha Winbeckler.

Thanks to my interview subjects: Bunny Koppelman (who, I'm
sad to say, died of pancreatic cancer before we had a chance to meet
in person); Sarah Raley-Dale; Lindsay Reed; Philip Rosenthal; and
Roland Winbeckler; and thanks to the ladies at the Cake Cottage,
especially Susan Stahling, Rebecca Cook, and Carole Eaves.

Thank you to the chefs who gave their valuable time to speak
with me in person: Leslie Poyourow, Fancy Cakes by Leslie; Jamie
Williams, Sugarbakers Cakes; the adorable Warren Brown, owner
of Cakelove and host of *Sugar Rush;* Velma Haywood, baker of the
rainbow/ribbon cake at Gourmet Bakery; Sugg Eddings, Terry
Perkins, Pearl Floyd, Lawrence Crawford, Cleveland Milton, Nella
Mednikova, and the rest of the Gourmet Bakery bakers; and a very
special thank-you to Duff Goldman for his character and candor. He
is as whimsical and colorful as the cakes he creates.

Thank you to Ted Kunkel, of Capitol Cake Company, for ship-
ping twenty-one fruitcakes to New York in a big hurry, and to
Sammy Goldberg, who allowed me to spend a day at Gourmet Bakery stalking the cake that stalks me.

Thanks to all of my pals on Flickr, where I vented, whined, cried,
celebrated, and wrote, all to immeasurable support. And when the
suck voice exposed itself, Flickr became Squashr. Thanks especially
to Jennifer König (her step-great-grandfather invented the New
York–style cheesecake, which is really pie), Patrick T. Power, and
Rita Spevak, for reading portions and giving advice.

Big crumb-lipped kisses to Goucher College students and faculty,
especially program director Patsy Sims, who is magnificent; my
mentors Diana Hume George, Philip Gerard, Richard Todd, and
Joe Mackall—who is just one of the finest, most decent humans I

have known; and my close Goucher chums, especially Lisa Davis, Clinton Doggett, Richard Gilbert, Towles Kintz, and Traci Joan Macnamara. Also thanks to those I pestered regularly by e-mail and who often fed me tips: Barbara Benham, Sheri Booker, Gretl Claggett, Barbara Goodman-Shovers, Stewart Green, Betsy Kaylor, and Carrie Killman. Extra thanks and bouquets of flowers to Barbara Benham for saying, "Betsy Lerner would be the perfect agent for you!"

A huge debt of gratitude goes to *Crazy* author Pete Earley. The day after graduation, when we were gently pushed out of our comfy nests, I attended his lecture on proposal writing. After an hour of statistics and mysteries, he said to query an agent first, and she would help with the proposal. He was right on the money. I wrote that query in the car on the way home, and I only needed to send it twice.

Thank you to the good friends who compose my diet group, The Square One-ers (because one needs a diet group when one is researching a book about cake): Laura Boland; Lysandra Cook; Michele DeLuca; Beth Evander; Charlet Givens; Julie Hallberg; Cindy Rosenfeld; Dawn Rossbach; Ashley Simmons; Jane (Janer) Timleck; and Joy Turner. Special thanks to Joy for sending me a file with a cake with a file in it!

Grazie a Tina Cavaluzzi, Cindy Rosner, *e* Matteo Persivale for help with Italian.

Bless you, Dr. Howard M. Cohen, for the painless root canal (in two parts) during the compilation of my notes. You know how people say, "At least it's not a root canal"? I now say, "At least it's not endnotes."

Thank you to everyone at Simon & Schuster, especially my editor, Denise Roy, who has said some of my favorite things, like: "Oh, authors never pay for lunch!" When I submitted the first draft on a Friday, I warned that I'd be dancing naked with a dead chicken if I didn't hear something soon. By Monday, she'd sent the word *delectable*. She, too, does delectable work.

Thank you to my agent, Betsy Lerner, whose name should be *Besty*. How lucky could a girl be to get the absolute perfect match on the first try? Betsy is a real rock star. I named my guitar after her.

Love and thanks to my sister, Beth vonBriesen (and Rich, Graham, and baby Marcus), for their endless barrage of emotional and ego support. And to Steven Parke for the same and for the rockin' author photos. And to Dorothy Miller, my other mother for so many years, for her love. And to Aunt Margaret for so many cakes and so much fudge.

Thanks to my grandparents, Ruth and Marcus Weitz, rest their souls, for all the cooking and baking and force-feeding. Thanks to my parents, Sharon and Harvey Miller, for their emotional and financial support during tough times and for always allowing me to believe I could do anything, even when I wasn't actually doing it. And thanks for not making me feel like a loser when I wasn't. And to my dad for slipping me a Grant now and then. And to my mom for being my first proofreader all of my life. Having a smart mother and a generous father are two of my best blessings.

The other two blessings are my husband and daughter, for putting up with my endless hours on the computer, which was payback for all the doughnuts and cake they consumed in my presence. Thanks to them for listening to me read aloud. Thanks to my husband for backing up the car so that I could take an excellent picture, and to my daughter for being smart, beautiful, talented, and low maintenance and for helping me proofread the notes for this book and for raising her eyebrows whenever she tastes my cooking and for letting me clean the wax from her ears.

My dogs, Cleopatra and Chance, are very good dogs.

And cake is awesome.

To my parents, for their dough;
to my husband, for his sugar;
and
to my daughter, for her icing on my cake life

Contents

Third Tier: The Moist White Underbelly

Fourth Tier: Tiers

Fifth Tier: Competitions

Sixth Tier: Cake Fanatics

Seventh Tier: The U.S. of cAke

Eighth Tier: The Last Course

A Note to the Reader

You can't have everything. Where would you put it?
—Steven Wright, comedian

Lots of writers I know tend to keep their projects a secret, as if someone will steal the idea right out from under them. But it takes a long time to write a book. This one has been three years in the making, and something noteworthy about cake—a funny quote, a stand-up routine, a new snack cake—seems to unfold daily, like the coat of a serial flasher. You know it's freaky, but you just can't look away.

News finds me because I've told *everyone* about it.

Sometimes the responses go the way they did on a trip to New York. I duck into Desmond's, a seedy pub on Park Avenue near Twenty-ninth Street, to hide from the rain. Brian, the bartender, is celebrating his forty-second birthday without beer, cigarettes, or cake. Poor guy. If I had met him before this late afternoon, I'd swear he had aged from the stress of it. I order a Smithwicks properly (Smiddicks) and take out my notebook. A few guys want to buy Brian a drink, but that would weaken his resolve to quit smoking for good.

Brian moves from one customer to the next, switching places holding an empty, used pint glass, setting it on the bar ledge in front of me while he talks with the guy next to me, putting it in front of that guy while he talks to me. He does this several times before I ask. "It's an idiosyncrasy," he tells me, blaming it on the nicotine withdrawal. He looks like a movie star. He's smart. He has a good vocabulary. He knows more facts about politics and history than any of the twenty-something businesspeople he sets straight about them at the bar. I don't know why this surprises me. Bartenders often know more.

At least two guys near me are British, and the one beside me is on a Christmas-shopping holiday. He is in his forties, too, it seems, and wears a knit cap pulled down to his eyebrows; I have no idea if he has hair. He's just finished describing how his forklift flipped over while he was driving it, how he got back into the seat, how he was subsequently ejected, how the forklift kept going, and how it ran over three of his toes, which had to be amputated. He's having trouble getting around.

Because I asked him, he wants to know what I'm doing in New York, and I tell him I'm working on a book. In order to hear this properly in your head, imagine the bloke is folksinger Billy Bragg or some Bob Hoskins character—or whatever you think is Cockney.

"About what?" he asks.

"Cake," I say.

"Cake?" he asks.

"Cake," I say again.

"C-A-K-E cake?" He almost cocks his head like a puppy.

"Yes, cake!"

"About making it?"

"No, about eating it!"

"Well, all right then!" And with that, he offers to buy me a beer. Both he and a gentleman at the end of the bar start laughing about someone they and the bartender know as "Mr. Kipling." By way of explanation, they say, in unison, "Exceedingly good cakes!"

"Are they?" I ask.

It's the company's tagline (and, I discover, the name of a now-defunct band). They agree that the cakes are pretty good, but the pie! I'm a sucker for those mincemeat pies, the little ones that look like cookies, but I'd still choose cake.

My seven-toed English friend and I move on to other subjects, amputation among them. I show him where I chopped off my thumb tip a few years ago with a mat knife, and he shows me a similarly damaged finger.

Back at home in Baltimore, I visit their site on the Web and learn that Mr. Kipling's cakes are the "benchmark of quality and innovation in the ambient cake market place."

It *is* ambient, isn't it? Oh, how I long for some cake ambience right now!

My e-mails to the forty-year-old Kipling, a man who's as fake as Betty Crocker, yield little more than a lovely chat with a woman named Elinor about their pretty Battenberg cakes. I never even learn whether Rank Hovis McDougall, Mr. Kipling's parent company, has a Crying Room, like General Mills does for all the ladies who are reduced to crumbs when they discover that their beloved Betty was a marketing mirage.

So you won't find a visit to Mr. Kipling's in this book about eating cake. There's no appendix of every cake ever made, all the best cake blogs, or any cake supply companies. I don't even speak much of carrot cake, our household favorite. I hardly utter one of the biggest names in cake: Martha Stewart. I neglect to mention a late 2007 bobblehead cake topper recall (it contained lead), Eddie Izzard's "Cake or Death" sketch (cake, of course!), and when to use baking *soda* instead of *powder*. (Since you asked, for recipes with sour ingredients—sour cream, vinegar, buttermilk—use soda.) And though all of those ingredients are often found in cake, they aren't essential and wouldn't have fit on the cover anyway.

I set out to write a layered cake full of a little bit of this and that: some history for those who need to know, some folklore for flavor, some narrative. Every bite has a little bit of something, including nuts. And like cake, this book is light and fluffy. Don't look here for answers to poverty (and don't look at Marie Antoinette anymore, either) or a cure for heartache or ennui, though you may laugh a bit and forget your pain or boredom briefly. But I would be lying if I told you that *everything* about cake is here. It can't be here. Cake is just too big.

Even as I finish the last words, friends and acquaintances are calling me with cake news or e-mail links, or they show up at school dismissal with a newspaper article they've clipped for me. The other day, over coffee and a delicious breakfast muffin from the Red Canoe, a bookstore and café in my neighborhood, my friend Kim told me about moving her grandmother to a nursing home. She took a few things home with her, including her grandmother's cool old cake pan, and I was coveting it, remembering my grandmother's silver and black one. Talk of grandmothers usually turns to cake eventually.

"My uncle, Chris, always had a birthday cake from Fenwick's," Kim told me, "always the same cake from the same bakery—yellow pound cake with chocolate icing, a ring cake with a cardboard tube in the center—and she actually shipped that same cake to him through the mail when he was in the Marines, including once when he was aboard ship in the Mediterranean."

Kim reminisces about her grandmother's cigarette dangling, the kitchen fan swishing, and the cake she made from scratch each weekend, then sliced and kept in that square 1950s cake keeper, from which it diminished, a slice or two at a time, throughout the week.

The stories of cake are such important ones! Now that I have finished collecting all these hunks and slices and have carved something new out of them, I am loath to waste a crumb. I'd like to wrap them up in foil and stick them in here somewhere, like little surprises. It's actually considered bad luck to throw away scraps of bread or cake, so perhaps the rest of it will have to be baked into a second book someday. Or fed to the birds.

All the world is a birthday cake, so take a piece but not too much.

—George Harrison, musician, songwriter,
Beatle, "It's All Too Much"

LET ME EAT

Introduction

One morning, I was driving to the University of Baltimore, planning a lecture for my two composition classes about punctuation, not thinking at all about, you know, *it*, when I stopped at a traffic light behind a truck bearing a blue and gold logo and phone number. I stared at it for a few minutes, contemplating commas, before I realized what it said: Capitol Cake Co., 1-800-EAT CAKE. A cake company—in Baltimore—that I don't know about? And because I am, in addition to a cake junkie, a chronic chronicler, I took the truck's picture.

Before I discovered the truck, I hadn't noticed the brand name of the unglamorously packaged one-dollar pound cakes stacked in a freestanding display at the end of the bread aisle at Shoppers food market: Capitol Cake Company. The three Cs have been around since 1922, when Harry A. Kunkel (a cake name if ever there was one) and Edward J. Leonard realized their snack cake dream, just as Tastykake's Philip J. Baur and Herbert C. Morris did before them in 1914, and Little Debbie's O. D. McKee would do in 1960. (Whether initials are a requirement or a coincidence, I'm in!) But Capitol's Shirley Jean fruitcake, named for Harry Kunkel's daughter-in-law, would boldly go where no other cake—not even those of the imaginary Betty Crocker—had gone before: to the moon. Literally and not once, mind you, but several times.

"It's Out of This World," says the CCC Web site, quotation marks and all. The Web page displays photographs from a 1999 Hubble mission of the space shuttle *Discovery* (STS-103). Right there, on the dashboard, with a view of home out the window, sits the pink-and-green-wrapped traditional Christmas treat. Another photo shows the package by the joystick, "drivin' the bus." The last picture shows a smiling Commander Curt Brown with the fruitcake by his face. Each caption calls the snack "Old Fruity," a name I'd not be too keen on were I Shirley Jean.

An astronaut picked up the fruitcake at a Florida convenience store just before his 1994 Christmas mission. It's not clear whether he bought it to *eat* the traditional holiday treat while not home for Christmas, or whether it would simply provide the comic relief of a fruitcake in space. But, like most fruitcakes, it remained uneaten. At some point in the trip, the astronauts on the mission signed it. And then it went up again the following Christmas. Eventually, the package became so full of signatures that it was retired. It's now on display at the Cake—*Cape* Canaveral museum.

By the time Ted Kunkel, the founder's grandson, heard about his product's space exploration, it already had orbited the moon a few times, and NASA was on the phone wondering where they could get another one to continue the tradition.

I'm a bit of a fruitcake myself. There aren't too many things I'd rather have on my plate than something sweet and bready, preferably with frosting. Even the much-maligned fruitcake could make my heart flutter, though I confess that I haven't actually bought or baked one. My passion has taken me far beyond my own taste buds and deep into the moist white underbelly of the cake world, visiting pastry chefs, collecting trivia, and frequently tasting. Like a good cake, the folklore and history, the traditions and secret ingredients, beg to be celebrated and shared. (As long as I get the piece with the most frosting.)

Cake has an ancient and rich tradition, but it has never been more popular—as a hobby, a spectator sport, and a curiosity—than it is right now in the United States. *Martha Stewart Living* has a Cake of the Month; the Food Network hosts regular cake competitions, and two East Coast chefs—Duff Goldman and Warren Brown—have had their own weekly cake series, *Sugar Rush* and *Ace of Cakes;* decorating classes, in both the blue states and the red ones, are full; and books like Rose Levy Beranbaum's *The Cake Bible* and Anne Byrn's *The Cake Mix Doctor* sell like hotcakes.

Where did cake come from, and where, besides the moon, is it going? Who's using it, and who's abusing it? Who's credited with its rise, and who's going to make it fall? It's time we heard cake's story and learned who bakes it best.

Put on some elastic-waist pants and grab a fork.

Shrek: Onions have layers. Ogres have layers.
           Onions have layers. You get it? We both
           have layers.
Donkey: Oh! You both have layers. You know,
           not everybody likes onions. Cakes!
           Everybody loves cakes!
Shrek: I don't care what everyone likes. Ogres are
           not like cakes!

—Shrek

Cakelure & Cakelore
FIRST TIER

Lure

Cake is a close approximation of God. Isn't there something holy about the trinity of flour, sugar, and eggs (and butter, some salt, and vanilla)? Nothing earthly comes as close to being supreme. In that respect, it's *Gahhhd*.[*]

Cake is omnipresent around the globe, except in Asia, where the oven is only now appearing on the residential kitchen appliance landscape, which explains why you get no bread and butter at a Chinese joint. Cake is part of every major celebration, secular and religious, even where it may not seem appropriate, like the bris.

Nearly every victory is celebrated with cake. The 131st running of the Preakness was commemorated with a fifty-pound cake. Super Bowl XLI (Forty-one) VIP attendees (including Jamal Anderson, a former Atlanta Falcon) could eat a slice of football field—with

---

* Low-carb guru and blogger Johnny Bowden says that our Genome Organizing Device, or GOD (an idea developed by science writer Matt Ridley), helped us seek out the sweet taste of fruits so that we can get the necessary vitamin C our bodies are unable to make.

bleachers and benches, players and coaches, giant 3-D helmets, and team logos—or choose a bite from the giant Lombardi trophy on top of this cake, which stood nearly as tall as a short adult.

But those are nothing compared with the current Guinness record holder for world's largest cake: a 130,000-pounder made from 30,000 half sheets and 40,000 pounds of frosting.* The cake, for the Las Vegas centennial celebration, had to be edible and safe and contain the normal ingredients found in birthday cake. It had to look like one, too. When *cake* happens in Vegas, it probably doesn't stay there. It probably comes back in a bigger pair of jeans.

It's hard to think of an event since the signing of the Declaration of Independence that wouldn't have involved a cake. It's probably not too far-fetched to imagine a July 3, 1863, cake declaring, "Yea, Union! Congratulations on Gettysburg," blue plastic army men along the perimeter. After all, one of the first specialty cakes was invented before the American Revolution and was dubbed Muster Cake, because it was served to farmers called by the English for military training (mustering). They ate the cake at night, while not mustering, and it was hearty stuff, full of heavy nourishment for potential soldiers. By 1771, colonial women had begun baking these in their brick ovens, in fierce competition with each other, as offerings to those in town for the Hartford elections. These were yeast-leavened cakes, *English* cakes, filled with things that many feel ought not to be in cake, like spices and molasses and currants, and washed down with flagons of ale or mulled wine.

So cake is more than the just dessert at birthdays and graduations, retirements, showers, baby namings, confirmations, bar and bat

---

* Also at the Guinness Web site, you'll find the place for "World's Largest Waist" occupied by American Walter Hudson, whose girth measured an inch short of ten feet. Hudson's acceptance speech would have had to include thanks to his daily rations: ten bags of chips, two pizzas, a dozen doughnuts, and half a cake. *Half* a cake. There's gluttony, and then there's Gluttony.

mitzvahs, and funerals—petits fours, usually, but one time a shivah houseguest brought a Carvel ice cream cake, decorated with black balloons and inscribed with "Deepest sympathies on your loss." The heavenly angel food cake is a traditional postfuneral food in the black community. Historians have even suggested that early 1800s African slaves had to create it, because making it required such arm strength, which few delicate plantation ladies possessed. It makes a richly symbolic story that they would expend excess energy to really whip and beat those whites stiff. This revenge is sweet, and it makes *just deserts* (or desserts) more delicious.

If cake is everywhere, it is because few things are more associated with joy or more emblematic of the sweet life. Even pie, which so many claim to prefer (hot apple with ice cream is a favorite of my daughter and husband), cannot hold a candle to cake, probably, literally, because it cannot hold a candle! And it would be hard to get excited about a birthday tomato or a wedding latke. It's cake that is always a beloved and invited guest; sometimes it even seems as though it's a prominent member of the family. What photo album doesn't contain that picture of baby's first cake—all over baby's face, in baby's hair, on baby's clothing well beyond that tiny thumbnail of a bib? What wedding album doesn't glorify the many-tiered masterpiece before it is cut? Cake cutting offers a second photo opportunity; the ritual feeding, a third. Some of your guests aren't recorded *anywhere*, but your cake is in three shots.

My own wedding cake, a stack of fancifully wrapped packages of different flavors (maybe carrot, chocolate something, white something—just because it's in the couple's photo album doesn't mean they actually got to taste it), is in my album six times, at the photographer's whim. One is a solo portrait, centered, alone on a page. In my favorite picture, my father is bending over the cake, as if he is about to bite the heads off the cake topper. Another page shows three stages of the cake-cutting ceremony. In the first, I daintily cut a corner from the bottom package. In the second, my husband helps cut, as I am inept, while my grandmother's hand pushes aside the flowers I am about to hack. In the third, Marty and I feed each other, while my grandfather reaches for something. It's no secret what he's about to do, because his act is worthy of a giant solo shot. My grandfather can wait for cake no longer and slices himself a piece off our ceremonial plate with the enormous knife. While it was happening, I was oblivious, but all eyes were on the crazy, cake-deprived (hence, cake-depraved) old man. My uncle, our videographer, should have dubbed Bernard Herrmann's *Psycho* theme in the background.

For most people, the love affair with sugar begins at the first birthday. We spend the first year of our lives sucking down breast milk or formula, gumming whirled peas and puréed carrots—the green vegetables and then the orange and then the fruits last, so their comparative sweetness doesn't spoil us too early. And after a year of those tiny jars of bland, which we learn to polish off like pros, our prize arrives, laid before us on the high chair tray, while a family member waits, poised for shutter release, to capture the moment. Our mothers coat their index fingers with frosting and poke it in our mouths. Someone with a camera is nearby (unless you're the second or subsequent child), and if he is adept, the click will come between that moment and the next, when our faces bow to meet the treat, our mouths agape to receive the wonder that is cake. White sheet cake. With white, buttercream frosting.

Michael Pollan, author of *Botany of Desire,* captured that moment in his son Isaac's face: "Between bites Isaac gazed up at me in amazement . . . as if to exclaim, 'Your world contains *this*? From this day forward I shall dedicate my life to it.' (Which he basically has done.)"

My love affair with cake was inherited from my mother and began in the womb, where my daughter's also began. I have worshiped it from afar; I have knelt at the altar of birthday cake; I have put it on a pedestal. I've eaten it in bed, in other people's kitchens, in my car, and bent over in the refrigerator. Recently, in a girlfriend's kitchen, I pulled over a corner of the foil covering the remains of her husband's birthday cake and helped myself to a bit while she was in another room. I've put gentle forkfuls in my mouth in public and then made off to a private corner to shovel in more of it. I have eaten it stale from a box filled with party trash, and I've scarfed it down frozen a year later. *Frozen*.

I probably spend an inordinate amount of time thinking about cake: when I'll eat it next, when I'll have to work hard to avoid it, when someone may need me to make it—an occasion that comes more often than one might think. We are about to get new neighbors, and my daughter suggested I bake them a cake to welcome them to the neighborhood. I don't think of cake all the time, but I'm thinking of it now. And when you live in a city whose major celebrity is Duff Goldman, the *Ace of Cakes* reality show baker whose mug is blossoming like buttercream roses all over Baltimore billboards, it's always a peripheral thought. If you're me, anyway. I have a *cake jones*. It's that edge you get about the one thing you can't resist, be it potato chips or fancy cars or basketball, as portrayed in the famous Cheech and

Chong sketch *Basketball Jones,* an animated video about a kid whose life revolves around basketball. "I need help, ladies and gennlemuns," cries the fanatic. (Peter Sellers watches this video in the limo in *Being There*.)

I imagine I eat birthday cake much like some people have sex, grunting like a baboon, squealing like a leaky balloon, writhing, as if the methamphetamine were beginning to take effect. Though I am silent, these are the sounds I hear in my head. Though I am still, this is how I feel beneath my skin.

I eat cake mostly for the icing. When no one's looking, I snatch a taste before a cake is cut. I choose corners—hunks, not slices. I get there first, nudging the greedy fifth graders out of my rightful spot. I slide my fingers along the waxed cardboard, mounding the piped, sugary fluff, picking it up with my fingers, savoring the stickiness on the drive home.

I even judge people by the way they eat—or don't eat—cake. I cannot abide the skinny girls who stop after a bite or two, or leave a heap of frosting behind on the plate, frosting that I want to rescue and warm inside my mouth. "Too sweet for me," they say, the remark cloying. Children can be forgiven, their bellies often too full of pizza and pop to appreciate the purity of refined sugar versus high-fructose corn syrup.

Cake calls to me. It speaks my name in a smoky voice. I can smell its cologne. It goads me in Italian: *"Leslie, amore mio. Vieni da me. Voglio entrarti dentro."* (Leslie, my love. Come to me. I want to be inside you.)

Unlike the addict, I do not go in search of a cake fix. I don't steal quarters from my husband's change jar and hide on the side porch with my works, waiting for him to leave, like I used to do with cigarettes. But like the addict, I have a constant craving. I mark cake events on the calendar and plan my weeks around them. But it's under control. I can stop at just one—or two. And an extra blop of icing.

When cake makes a surprise appearance on a conference room table or someone's desk, I can sometimes overcome the temptation. On the day I decide a book can be written about cake, a partial cake has appeared, unexpected, in Towson University's faculty mailroom, just two doors from my office. Most of it having been devoured by the English department a few days earlier, all that's left of "Thank You, Clarinda" is a *T.* And two corners.

"Leslie, amore mio," it calls. I close my office door.

Qu'est-ce que c'est Cake?

All manner of sweet stuff arose concurrent with the invention of baking powder in the mid-nineteenth century. Fruitcakes, pound cakes, all that Victorian-era prim and proper goodness notwithstanding, how far back must one go for the history of cake? Does the history of man begin with an ape or a bang or a deity? Or does it begin with the first civilization? Is a cake the glimmer in a husk of wheat? Or is it cake the moment the flour, sugar, eggs, and butter are mixed to a perfect richness?

If we were to bake a cake to celebrate the birth of cake, it's hard to say how many candles would go on top. You can trace the *notion* of it, at least the desire for something sweet and doughy, back as far as you can trace agriculture, some 13,000 years. Syrian farmers grew wheat and rye, so cake back then meant flat bread with honey, the same kind made by ancient Greeks and Romans. Egyptians were the first culture to bake breads, and these breads were unleavened, resembling a "cake" of matzo, which the Jews eat on Passover to remind themselves of the time when, in their hasty departure to escape their enslavement in Egypt, they could not wait for their bread to rise.

Unleavened bread and humility are kindred, while leavened bread is prideful. (Never mind how puffed up my Grammy Ruth's Jewish sponge cake got with all those eggs—and how puffed up my Peepop Marcus got when you refused a slice!)

John Ayto says, in his *A–Z of Food and Drink*—a small book with tiny type that is full of goodies about food—"The original dividing line between cake and bread was fairly thin." Romans added eggs and butter to puff up their honey-sweetened cakes, while the English distinguished cakes by their shapes. Ayto gives a 1398 definition from John de Trevisa, "Some brede is bake and tornyd and wende [turned] at fyre and is called . . . a cake."

Some say the birthday cake tradition began by example, Caesar Augustus enjoying birthdays so much that he celebrated his own life once every month. Others believe the tradition began after the custom of placing a round cake with candles, symbolic of a glowing moon, in the temple of Artemis to celebrate her birthday. And still others say the first cake was a Germanic custom in the Middle Ages. Cakes of sweet bread dough were shaped like the swaddled baby Jesus (baby Jesus cake pans being hard to come by, perhaps the swaddling helped to create an amorphous shape). The *Kinderfest* grew out of this, and candles—added not to the cake itself but to a plate, encircling the cake—burned until dinner. *Geburtstagorten,* a cake closer to our modern celebratory kind, was sweeter than other cakes and baked in layers.

Cake is an Old Norse word, used first around 1230, when it meant "something round, lump of something"; it became a loaf of bread in 1420.

In the middle of the 1600s, those round lumps were constrained with wood or metal cake hoops and baked on a pan set upon a hearthstone. Without the refined flour, though, they were still pretty much lumps of "something," rather than cake. The boiled sugar-and-egg-white concoction poured over the top glazed and sweetened it a little further, but it still wasn't cake. It was more like a sugary biscuit.

Eventually, the word evolved to mean small bread, but, according to Alice Ross, an upstate New York food historian who gives classes on historical baking, what was called *cake* was made with much better ingredients. The more dough you had, the more cake you were likely to eat.

So cake is not cake because the word was used thousands of years ago to describe something we know now as bread. Cake is not bread, risen or unleavened—definitely not matzo!—any more than a bar or cake of soap is. Cake is not crumpets or muffins or scones like the kind you'd find at high tea; it's not any other hard, dry, breaded thing with, perhaps, a few sprinklings of raisins or alternate dried fruit (druit, I like to call it, because once it's wrinkled and baked in a bread, it seems so medieval). Cake is not a bun or a pastry, but it's pretty darn close to a doughnut, despite the deep-frying.

Let Them Eat It

Who said, "Let them eat cake"? Was it:

A. Marie Antoinette, who married Louis XVI in 1770;
B. a Spanish princess named Marie-Thérèse d'Autriche, who married Louis XIV in 1660;
C. Madame Victoire, Louis XV's fourth daughter;
D. Victoire's younger sister, Sophie;
E. Madame de Pompadour, their father's mistress; or
F. an unnamed Tuscan duchess?

The French connection seems to be the only sure bet, though there's plenty of evidence that Marie Antoinette would not—and could not—have said such a thing. "It was a callous and ignorant statement," said Antoinette's biographer, Antonia Fraser, at Edinburgh's book fair in 2002, "and she was neither."

Proof of the queen's sympathy with the plight of the poor can be found in *Memoirs of Louis XV. [sic] and XVI,* which has the breathless subtitle and byline, *Being Secret Memoirs of Madame du*

Hausset, Lady's Maid to Madame de Pompadour, and of an Unknown English Girl and the Princess Lamballe. The London Magazine called these memoirs "the only perfectly sincere ones amongst all those we know."

> Even at the moment of the abominable masquerade, in which Her Majesty's agents were made to appear the enemies who were starving the French people, out of revenge for the checks imposed by them on the royal authority, it was well known to all the Court that both Her Majesty and the King were grieved to the soul at their piteous want, and distributed immense sums for the relief of the poor sufferers . . .

Forget the character witnesses; we hear every day how perfectly lovely people can do monstrous things. Definitive proof that the headless queen could not have uttered those words is found in Book VI of Jean-Jacques Rousseau's autobiography, *Confessions*. It is a captivating piece of work that chronicles Rousseau's reading, drinking, and cake searching, among other things. In the evidentiary scene, he has just confessed to having stolen some bottles of wine—white Arbois—which he "took . . . into [his] head to covet," and now laments his predicament: The French philosopher cannot drink without having something to eat.

> . . . [T]he difficulty lay, therefore, in procuring bread. It was impossible to make a reserve of this article, and to have it brought by the footman was discovering myself, and insulting the master of the house; I could not bear to purchase it myself; how could a fine gentleman, with a sword by his side, enter a baker's shop to buy a small loaf of bread? it [*sic*] was utterly impossible. At length I recollected the thoughtless saying of a great princess, who,

> on being informed that the country people had no bread,
> replied, "Then let them eat pastry!"

The book was published in 1770, when the fifteen-year-old king and his fourteen-year-old bride were only just getting hitched.

Who actually said of bread-starved peasants that they should eat, well, fancy bread? Jean-Baptiste Alphonse Karr, an acerbic French critic and novelist born in 1808, attributed the comment to some unnamed duchess of Tuscany. Other writers blamed Madame de Pompadour, mistress of both Louis XV and the memoir writer with the endless byline. Antonia Fraser says Madame Sophie, a royal aunt, could have said it "in 1751, when reacting to the news that her brother, the Dauphin Louis Ferdinand, had been pestered with cries of 'Bread, bread' on a visit to Paris." She also indicted Madame Victoire, another aunt. "But the most convincing proof of Marie Antoinette's innocence" (and someone else's guilt), Fraser continues,

> came from the memoirs of the Comte de Provence [later
> Louis XVIII], published in 1823. No gallant guardian of
> his sister-in-law's reputation, he remarked that eating *pâté*
> *en croûte* always reminded him of the saying of his own
> ancestress, Queen Maria Thérèse.

He thought of her, he says in *Relation d'un voyage à Bruxelles et à Coblentz,* when he left France in 1791 and stopped for a drink of Bordeaux and a bite of *pâté en croûte*. The meal made him think of Marie-Thérèse's comment, upon learning that some peasants didn't have any bread: *"Mais, mon Dieu, que ne mangent-ils de la croûte de pâté?"* (Good God, why can't they just eat the crust from a meat pie?) Some say this was a sign of Marie's "naïveté and her good heart."

Why, then, has it been so easy to believe the legend? For one thing, Marie Antoinette's beheaded-ness is often seen as a sign of guilt. For another, she was unpopular, which some attribute to her having taken so long to put some of her own buns in the oven (this was the result of her husband's medical condition, not her frigidity). But the fast answer lies in the timing. In 1775 France, peasants were, indeed, rioting in the streets because they had no bread, a condition that could have been blamed on economist Jacques Turgot, whose slogan was, "No bankruptcy. No new taxes. No loans." (Sound familiar?) Turgot "lifted the controls on the internal trade of grain" at a time when crops were already failing. The result was rioting in the streets and the aforementioned cries for bread, a time dubbed the Flour Wars, which precipitated the French Revolution. A phrase, an appropriate era, an unpopular queen—the perfect ingredients for a wicked historical myth.

Now even the word *cake* is under scrutiny. In the 1700s, the phrase would have been *"Qu'ils mangent de la brioche,"* let them eat *brioche,* not *gâteau.* (And was the dauphin hearing cries of *"Brioche, brioche"*?) Was it the crust of pâté? Was it Rousseau's pastry?

And then there is the *brioche* debate. We know the bread as a fancy round bun with a silly little topknot—something not altogether different from white bread. But some believe the word, which seems to have been making the rounds since 1404, came from the early practice of kneading it with Brie cheese. Others believe the bread simply *originated* in Brie, France. And still others insist that the word comes from a German verb meaning *to knead,* and those who subscribe to this view have the bread originating in Normandy. The most farfetched of the *brioche* etymologies suggests that the word referred to a paste inside the ovens of bakers and that Marie Antoinette's— or whoever's—words were not so much callous as they were good advice: beggars should eat the oven scrapings if they couldn't afford bread.

So one of the few bits of cakelore we Americans have (though it belongs to the French) has been debunked, rebunked, redebunked, and finally rewritten completely. The person who said it didn't, the saying wasn't ever said, and none of the words mean what they meant. But the crummiest thing about it is that it has nothing at all to do with cake. And so we leave eighteenth-century France and its unlikely hero, Jean-Jacques Rousseau, the only man who has his priorities in order—at least for my purposes.

I sometimes went out alone for this very purpose, running over the whole city, and passing thirty pastry [cooks'] shops without daring to enter any one of them. In the first place, it was necessary there should be only one person in the shop, and that person's physiognomy must be so encouraging as to give me confidence to pass the threshold; but when once the dear little cake was procured, and I shut up in my chamber with that and a bottle of wine, taken cautiously from the bottom of a cupboard, how much did I enjoy drinking my wine, and reading a few pages of a novel; for when I have no company I always wish to read while eating; it seems a substitute for society, and I dispatch alternately a page and a morsel; 'tis indeed as if my book dined with me.

True Cake

One of the earliest wedding cakes in literature comes from Jane Austen, in her 1815 book, *Emma*. Linda Wolfe, in *The Literary Gourmet,* writes: "Nowadays hardly anyone makes wedding cakes at home, begging off because the procedure is so laborious. But it was in Jane Austen's time too. 'Beat in your sugar a quarter of an hour,' says the nonelectrically equipped author of this recipe, and 'beat your yolks half an hour at least.'" The recipe that follows, from *The Young Woman's Companion,* in 1813, calls for four pounds each of butter, flour, and currants, two pounds of "loaf" sugar (the kind you have to scrape into granules), thirty-two eggs, some brandy, and a pound each of candied fruits. The cake is baked in a hoop inside a moderate oven for three hours. It was customary, then, for unmarried wedding guests to put their slices under their pillows that night, so they might dream of their future spouses.

With brandy and currants, it's not the wedding cake of our dreams. But fruitcake is probably where the story of cake begins. Linda Stradley, a cookbook author and culinary historian who has operated the What's Cooking America Web site since 1997, says that ancient Romans made a concoction of pomegranate seeds, nuts, and barley mash. The heavy food helped hunters and crusaders stave off hunger. When England imported dried fruit from the Mediterranean in the 1400s, the British began adding it to their breads. In Europe in the 1700s, fruitcakes were a major part of the harvest ceremony. Nuts were baked into a cake that was saved for the following year, when it was eaten as good luck, to kick off a successful harvest.

The fruitcake has seen more than its fair share of derision and controversy. The very qualities that make it nutritious and satisfying contribute to legends of its use as a doorstop and more, as Marjorie Dorfman, a food writer with a site called Eat, Drink and Really Be Merry, writes in "Et Tu, Fruitcake!":

> One theory presented by an historian who couldn't quite locate his credentials dates back to the days of the American Revolutionary War. Commander-in-Chief George Washington asked Benjamin Franklin to come up with an easy to use barricade material to guard against incoming British cannon fire. Benjamin Franklin thought about it, went to bed early and rose early, healthy, wealthy and wise enough to tell the waiting general about his mother-in-law's fruitloaf. Her attempt at some kind of bread had been so hard that his uncle had broken a tooth while biting into it at the previous year's holiday dinner!

Some believe it was outlawed in Europe in the early 1700s; others say its consumption was made illegal at times other than Christmas. Its connection to that holiday is also fuzzy, but there was an English tradition of unloading fruitcakes on poor (in the financial way) carolers, as thanks for spreading their harmony door-to-door. There's also a popular story about Queen Victoria being presented with a fruitcake for her birthday, and, because it was the right thing to do not to make a glutton of oneself, she didn't touch it for an entire year. (After which time, she probably devoured it at once, hunched over a trash can and making grunting noises.)

At least two cakes were named for the queen, the first of them being the Victoria Sponge, which, before her reign, was made with lots of eggs (as many as ten in one cake) and no butter. The Victoria Sponge, which includes butter, is similar to a *génoise,* a French sponge cake. According to Patricia Bunning Stevens, author of *Rare Bits: Unusual Origins of Popular Recipes,* Victoria was so popular that "more places on the face of the earth than for any other single person" were named for her, "and this even included cakes." The Victoria Cake, a fruitcake, replaces raisins with cherries, her favorite fruit.

The Puritans, who once banned Christmas and birthday celebrations and were blamed, at least by one chocolatier, for calling chocolate "the devil's food," were never enamored of the fruitcake,* and even Cotton Mather, as noted by *Harper's* writer Lewis Lapham, led a charge to ban public commencement ceremonies at Yale on the grounds that they necessitated the "consumption of plum cake, which was 'very expensive and an occasion for much sin.' "

How does something so sinfully delicious through the nineteenth century become the object of ridicule in the twentieth? With butter, sugar, flour, nuts, fruit, and liquor, few things *sound* more delicious. Perhaps it's the long baking time, the color, the heft of the ring or loaf, or the bad jokes that keep people from enjoying—or admitting to enjoying—a fruitcake.

---

* They didn't mind a roll in the hay, though. In fact, though it may have looked to outsiders that they were cold and joyless, they actually believed that God's gifts were meant to be enjoyed—just not too much. "While Puritans were indeed conscious of the depravity of the world and the ubiquity of temptation, they took this, he says, as a spur to moral activity rather than an excuse to retreat from social life. Indeed, since God had made the world, it was incumbent upon the good Puritan to enjoy its many delights as well as to guard against excessive pleasure." So maybe a fun-size Snickers for them.

The fruitcake catapult is a main event at Santacon, an ironic con-
demnation of the commercialization of Christmas begun in 1994 and
held annually around the country in December. Manitou Springs,
Colorado, held its twelfth annual Great Fruitcake Toss on January
20, 2007. Comedian Jim Gaffigan jokes that the stuff is made with
Skittles and everything *except* fruit. He rates the ingredients: "Fruit?
Good. Cake? Great! Fruitcake? Nasty crap!" In 2003, Canada Transport banned fruitcakes from flights because their X-rays arouse suspi-
cion. ("What the hell is *that*?" is often asked after tasting it, too.) And
let's not forget about that fruitcake that went to the moon.

LAYER FIVE

Eatymology

Some etymologists believe the term *cakewalk* (and *piece of cake* and *takes the cake*) came about when contest winners in rural areas of the United States were given cakes as prizes, for just about any competition. The winners would strut around the room holding the cake, much as Miss America takes her famous walk.

But most attribute the cakewalk to American blacks. One source finds that it emerged in Florida in the late 1850s as the Chalk Line Walk, a dignified style of walking in pairs, similar to that practiced by the Seminole Indians; the most graceful pair, the one that cut a perfect figure, was rewarded with a prize.

The most likely origin, however, is the satirical strut done by slaves to lampoon the stiff ballroom dance steps of white plantation owners. At the behest of their owners, slaves often competed against each other in Sunday contests, embellishing their walk with some traditional African dance steps, the winners receiving slices of cake.

Eventually, the cakewalk became a jazz dance step, a kind of diagonal strut, and contests were held in jazz clubs. In 1906, Claude

Debussy composed "Golliwogg's Cakewalk," an early European introduction to American jazz.

When you do something really well, you take the cake—that is, you win the prize. It's most often used ironically. For example, my thirty-fifth birthday takes the cake for worst birthday (with the thirty-fourth running a close second). Some would say it takes the biscuit (it appeared at the beginning of the twentieth century). Or maybe the brioche.

If I Knew You Were Locked Up, I'd Have Baked a Cake

In the summer of 2007, in honor of Paris Hilton's incarceration, Los Angeles's City Bakery concocted the Paris Hilton Visitor Cake, spice cupcakes—cinnamon and ginger—baked with an emery board inside each. That's right, the ol' cake with a file in it, albeit a *nail* file. Owner Maury Rubin sold up to seventy-five a day during Hilton's stint in stir at five bucks a pop. Clever as it is, you couldn't pay me to eat a spice cake—especially this one, which was not even frosted!

We've all heard of the prisoner who escaped from jail using a file smuggled inside a birthday cake, but few know the story's origin. To my surprise, this is no urban legend, nor is it, as I had suspected, from an episode of *The Andy Griffith Show*.[*]

---

[*] Only one of these episodes combined cake and prison. Otis, the town drunk, was rounded up and stuck in the hoosegow by Barney Fife, when Fife learned they were being inspected. But when "Ange" came to work with a cake for the prisoner's birthday, the inspector was aghast and led a charge for Andy's impeachment. (That is, until the sheriff demonstrated his bravery in the arrest of a serious criminal.)

According to *Harry Boland's Irish Revolution,* by David Fitzpatrick, cake was instrumental in the prison break of Sean Milroy, Sean
McGarry, and Éamon (or Éamonn) de Valera. De Valera—or Dev, as
he was called—was considered the principal author of the Constitution of Ireland and was Ireland's president from 1959 to 1973. But in
his rebellious youth, he was imprisoned in London's Lincoln Jail for
his leadership of the failed 1916 Easter Uprising.

As luck—mine and the prisoners'—would have it, Dev was in
charge of the rebels based at Boland's Flour Mill.

Since he served mass in the jail, Dev had access to plenty of candles, enough that he could steal a few, melt them, and make an impression of the chaplain's master key. Dubliner Gerard Boland, who
owned the flour mill, was the recipient of one of those impressions.
He made a key and hid it in a Christmas cake, which was delivered
to the prisoners. It didn't work, nor did a second key, hidden in a
second cake.

Fellow inmate Peter De Loughry was not only the mayor of
Kilkenny, he was also a locksmith. Through coded messages in
Christmas cards, he suggested blanks and files, so he could make the
key himself.

Gerard's brother, Harry (played by Aidan Quinn in the movie
Michael Collins; Collins is, in fact, credited as the mastermind behind
this prison break), delivered the third cake himself, but the baked-
in blank had a slot in the center and was unusable. Fitzpatrick says,
"The Irish reputation for a sweet tooth was confirmed in the arrival
of a fourth cake, laced with files and a slot-less blank." Peter De
Loughry cut a usable key on the last day of January 1920, and the
group escaped a few days later.

More recently in Denmark, cake was used as a weapon against
four prison guards. At Nyborg State Prison, a few of the most
hardened inmates—members of vicious motorcycle gangs—added
something a little worse than polysorbate 60 to a cake they baked
themselves. The "unnamed narcotic" made two male and two female

jailers sick, and a new prison rule was enacted: "Guards are now banned from accepting cakes, sweets or other prisoner-made treats."

As nuts as I am for cake, I'm not sure I'd eat anything baked by members of a gang called the Black Cobras. Call me silly, but I'm not sure a Bloods bake sale would go over big, especially with the Crips selling their cakes on another corner. But in Denmark, it's fairly common for prisoners and guards to share both affections and confections. According to Danish prison spokesman Lars Erik Siegumfeldt, "Normally the guards and the inmates are very close in the Danish system. . . . Inmates bake cakes every day."

Birthdays from Hell

Just before my thirty-fifth birthday, even though there was no sugar in my urine, I was made to go for the five-hour gestational diabetes test. My doctor had good reason: I'd gained forty pounds in the first six months of my pregnancy.

Carrying my daughter gave me some pretty intense cravings. They weren't for weird foods like pickles and ice cream or chocolate-covered salami, but they were specific and severe. In the first trimester, I ate a ham, egg, and cheese biscuit for breakfast

every day for weeks. I had to drive across town to get to the nearest Hardee's until the McDonald's around the corner started making them my way. Then, beginning in my fourth month, almost every day at lunchtime, I drove myself across town again, to the Giant, our closest grocery store with a bakery, where I would buy a single square of white cake with white icing. I'd sift through the plastic boxes, tossing them willy-nilly in my search for the corner slice. If there was none, I'd hold the other pieces up to be sure I had the biggest with the most frosting. I'd buy one slice. I knew that eventually I'd get tired of driving five miles for a single slice of cake, but I promised myself I would never buy two. That second slice would not see the next day because I'd wander the house with a fork, trying to stay out of the kitchen but failing, returning to the countertop to open the plastic box, take a bite, close the lid, leave. I know. Because, at some point, I *did* buy two slices, and it went like that until the second piece was half gone. Then I put both elbows on the kitchen counter and ate the rest standing, mad at myself, cursing a belly that I knew was only half baby. I told anyone who asked that my daughter would be named Serena *Cake* Miller, a tribute to what she made me do every day.

So I spent Wednesday, October 8, my thirty-fifth birthday, in the blood lab, having my veins drained, one test tube at a time, every half hour. I had a book with me but couldn't focus and instead glanced up at what everyone else was watching: an episode of *Springer*, a few of the wrong (not my channel) soap operas. After drinking the bottle of orange pop, filled with as many calories as in a Thanksgiving dinner but all of them pure sugar, I squirmed and fidgeted on the hard chair, wanting nothing more than to nap. I fretted, too, hoping that my inability to sit still, coupled with my overwhelming and conflicting urge to sleep, was the normal reaction to the test. I was worried about the consequences—not of having gestational diabetes, which I thought, wrongly, would go away once the baby was born—but about whether I would be able to enjoy my birthday cake, planned for Friday-night consumption, whether I'd ever be able to eat cake again, whether I should just stock up on the experience and eat as much of it as possible.

I looked down at my sore arm and remembered how far I'd come in just a year. I was the skinniest I'd ever been at the same time the previous year, with the help of phentermine and running. And while I didn't eat much then, I could always down a Peppermint Pattie or a slice of cake. On my birthday, my husband, Marty, loaded up the Vanagon with me, my two best girlfriends, and my sister, Beth, and drove us out to Crownsville, Maryland, home of the annual Renaissance Festival. I'd been begging him to join us for years, but he was convinced it was little more than a "Period Mall." I wanted him to see what a great time it was, so I talked up the draws: the museum of torture; the live jousting; the Shakespearean theater; the comic routines like Danger Dan and Johnny Fox, Sword Swallower; the singing; the street theater; the women running around with their boobs pushed up to their own lips, nipples peeking out above the elastic of their period dresses—all of it held in a shady forest. And, oh, the food! My birthday cake would be Cheesecake on a Stake or perhaps Chocolate Suicide Cake or Thy Queen's Carrot Cake. Maybe I'd have all three. I could, at 132 toned pounds. I think the promise of cake is what eventually got my husband to agree to take us. (He still asks for a slice of each when I make my annual birthday trek.)

But the line on the Beltway just to get to the parking lot of the fairgrounds was backed up, and it took an hour to go less than six miles. By the time we'd arrived, the parking lot was full. So we turned around and drove the forty minutes back to our house while I cried.

I was disconsolate. One girlfriend whipped me up a blender drink with Ben & Jerry's Cherry Garcia ice cream and whatever she could find in the kitchen. The other went home. But Beth said, "We'll be right back," and left with Marty in a cloud of mystery. When she returned, it was with a perfectly inscribed cake. The handwriting wasn't the neatest, but that's because the store's cake decorator wouldn't write my sister's wishes. "Why don't you come behind the counter, hon," she told Beth, who did.

In the picture hanging on my refrigerator, I am nearly crying with melancholic delight, my hair pulled back to reveal my smeared tears and my widow's peak. The white cake, adorned with a sloppy shell border in peony pink, with painted-on flowers, says, "Happy Fucking Birthday Les." I shared that cake with everyone but ate most of the rest by myself the next day.

In the blood lab one year later, I was terrified that cake and I would soon be parted. The phlebotomist took pity on me for having to spend my birthday with her and put a RUSH on my test, so that I'd have the results by Friday. If I couldn't have cake, no one else could either. No sense in ordering something.

The verdict hangs on my refrigerator just below the previous year's photograph. I am hugely fat in a large black shirt that I seem to be wearing as a dress. *What was I thinking?* My hair is pulled back, and my smile shows relief, as I hold the cake out for display. It's similar to my last cake, a fancy orange border and a nest of orange and yellow flowers. The inscription reads: "Happy *Mother*fucking Birthday!"

Many Happy Returns of the Day, Cake!

We know about the births of nations. Our records never fail us when treaties are signed or bills become laws. And we can check the patents on the cotton gin and the spinning jenny. But food is a little trickier. We can find the first mention of a lollipop in 1784, but, just as cake didn't mean two-layer, sweet, flour concoction with filling and fluffy frosting, lollipop didn't mean hard sugar ball on a white stick. Foods, with ingredients, evolve.

Even if we talk about the introduction of leavening agents (baking soda and powder) in the mid-1800s, we've still not quite arrived at the most modern of cake's incarnations. It wasn't until the end of that era that the middle-class kitchen was equipped with a cast-iron stove that had an oven.

In the early 1900s, the standard cake looked similar to what we have now, filled and frosted with sweet, white fluff. When we speak of "the icing on the cake," it's to say that we're adding something even sweeter to an already sweet deal. But some of us think that it's not quite a celebration without a thick smear of buttercream on top. Frosting began as a cooked, sweetened egg white glaze in England

35

in the 1700s, and it was called icing because it was supposed to look like ice. Or was it called frosting because it looked like frost? There's a bit of a chicken-egg debate on which came first, but *The Encyclopedia of American Food and Drink,* by John F. Mariani, says frosting preceded icing in print (1670 to 1710). Which word you say was once considered a regional thing—like using *bubbler* for *water fountain*—but the terms are interchangeable, with *frosting* being a more American term. (It's also what my mom called what she used to do to her hair.)

So is 1908 the magic year for birthday cake because the earliest recipe for buttercream (though it's not even called buttercream) was published then, in a recipe book from Rumford, the baking powder company?

Or is it determined by the inscription? When writing on cakes first appeared, according to the Food Timeline, it was done by "professional bakers and caterers, who were proliferating in growing cities" in the late 1800s. Cakes were inscribed with "Many Happy Returns of the Day" and the name of the birthday boy or girl. That is, until the melody of "Good Morning to You," a classroom song written by Patty and Mildred J. Hill, was paired with alternate lyrics, probably in the 1920s, and became the world's most popular song, according to *The Guinness Book of World Records*.

And what of those candles, that tradition evolving out of the worship of the moon? Once a German superstition meant to ward off evil spirits (children were thought to be extra susceptible to them), candles were believed to work double magic. The fire would keep evil away, and the smoke from a snuffed candle would send a wish to God. (The lighting of incense is one of those ancient religious customs. Even the early Chinese, who didn't celebrate birthdays with cakes *or* candles, believed fire would forestall evil, while fragrant smoke sent prayers to heaven.)

It wasn't until the late 1800s that American cookbooks and style guides suggested that parents use a number of candles around the cake's perimeter to represent the child's age. So, while many of our birthday customs have evolved from ancient traditions, most modern practices are just about a century old. And that's a lot of candles.

●   ●   ●   ●   ●

BUTTERCREAM FROSTING

*The best frosting I've ever had, anywhere, is actually a **meringue** buttercream, which means it is made with lots of egg whites. And it's cooked. I stumbled on it by accident while messing up a recipe by America's Test Kitchen and mixing it with a recipe by Martha Stewart. The mistake came from not recognizing a yucky meringue frosting in the first place and having to add butter to it afterward in order to make it taste like frosting is supposed to taste.*

4 large egg whites
1 cup sugar
$\frac{1}{8}$ teaspoon salt
¾ pound unsalted butter, softened
2 teaspoons vanilla extract

Whisk the egg whites, sugar, and salt continuously in the heatproof bowl of an electric mixer set over a pan of simmering water (double boiler) for about 3 minutes to 160°F, until the sugar is dissolved.

With the whisk attachment, beat the mixture on medium-high until it's cool, about 10 minutes. Reduce the mixer speed to medium, and using the paddle attachment, add the butter a little at a time. Beat until it's pale and fluffy. Very fluffy. Mix for a long time. Longer. The frosting will be cool. Add the vanilla, and mix for a few seconds more.

Buttercream can be refrigerated in an airtight container for up to 3 days, but it will harden like the butter it once was. Let it come to room temperature and beat well before using. Frosting can sometimes break. Whip it a little longer, and it'll eventually come back.

Beefcake

Though you can find hundreds of Internet references to dressing like Marilyn Monroe and emerging from a cake for someone's birthday, not one suggests that Marilyn herself had ever, in movies or in public, jumped, climbed, or popped out of a cake. She did, however, have her portrait shot for a cheesecake promotion for which she wore a one-piece bathing suit, a baker's toque, and very high heels, in which she stood and attempted to cut the cake with a sword. This pose should make you want cheesecake very, very much, in the same way you want a Ferrari when there's a bikini-clad bimbo stretched across its hood. (Okay, maybe you'd want a Ferrari anyway, like I'd want a piece of that cheesecake anyway.)

Roland Winbeckler took the cheesecake-beefcake icon to ironic proportions. A cake sculptor from Redmond, Washington, Winbeckler won two gold medals and a crystal goblet in the World Culinary Olympics for feats less impressive than his life-size Marilyn, in her famous *Seven-Year Itch* pose, carved out of pound cake and frosted with buttercream icing. It was 125,000 calories and served 500 people.

The sculptures are created with baked pound cake, which is carved and glued together with frosting. It's not a freestanding tower of flour; everything is on an armature or a base, which is constructed out of whatever materials will work best for individual projects. Nearly all of Winbeckler's structures use buttercream glue, but for a life-size Christopher Columbus, when he knew the cake wasn't going to be served, he used royal icing, which "hardens like concrete!" (Another of his sculptures using royal icing is one of George Washington, currently preserved in the Ripley's Believe It or Not Museum in Hollywood, California.) Otherwise, cakes must be assembled onsite; delivery of gigantic finished cake statues is impossible. A life-size Winbeckler sells for somewhere near $7,000, including lodging and transportation.

I am thinking, of course, about having a cake fashioned into my own likeness—a nice little gift to myself upon garnering a cake book contract. Imagine all the photo opportunities—the cover photo, even—when I eat myself. I'd nibble first at my too-thick ankles and give my right breast a slight reduction to even out the set. I'd save my hair for last because I like it. It's my head's personal frosting.

Expensive Cakes

A *Seinfeld* episode called "The Frogger" makes astute observations about society's fascination with cake. The show opens in Elaine's office; everyone is gathered around a cake singing "Happy Birthday," while Elaine laments the fact that it's a special day for someone at this office of two hundred *every* day. In fact, she becomes so sick of her coworkers trying to socialize with cake parties that she takes a sick day. It backfires: when she returns to the office, four people walk in with a cake and begin singing a little "Get Well" ditty.

Elaine screams at them. A male worker says he thinks it's nice.

"What is nice? Trying to fill the void in your life with flour and sugar and egg and vanilla? I mean, we are all unhappy. Do we have to be fat, too?"

Later, Elaine enters the office of her boss, Mr. Peterman, visibly shaking, jonesing for some cake (but too ashamed to admit it after what she did to her coworkers), and she finds a slice in his mini-fridge and has some. So Peterman won't notice, she replaces it with something from Entenmann's. Turns out the thing was his "latest

41

acquisition. A slice of cake from the wedding of King Edward VIII to Wallis Simpson, circa 1937, price—$29,000."

But even the art of Seinfeld doesn't come close to gross reality. One of the most expensive cakes ever was a bejeweled fruitcake created for a diamond exhibition. The 223 diamonds earned the red Christmas cake, made in Tokyo, a price tag of $1.65 million in December of 2005.

Another Tokyo cake the following year, created for Mozart's 250th birthday, was covered with gold coins and priced at $2.16 million.

America will not be outdone, especially not by Japan. In October 2006, the most expensive birthday cake in the world, made by Nahid La Patisserie Artistique and covered with diamonds from Mimi So Jewelers, was brought into a Beverly Hills bridal show by security guards. More like a marshmallow display case for some large glittery brooches, the $20 million cake was never eaten.

But these are really just cakes for show. They are centerpieces, decorations, props. For an overpriced birthday cake, you'll want to check your own phone book. While a fancy half sheet from the grocery store might run about $30—double that for a slightly fancier cake from a small grocer in an upscale neighborhood—you can't get a novelty cake for under $200. Some places even have a $500 *minimum*! And judging by their flavor, these are for show, too.

But that didn't stop some New York socialite from shelling out $1,500 to Elisa Strauss's Confetti Cakes for a pink cake shaped like a Coach bag and stuffed with a dog, sandals, and a *People* magazine, beside a sculpted pink iPod mini. For her daughter's *tenth birthday*! Okay, my daughter had a blue iPod mini when she was nine, but— hello, you could give every kid on the guest list a *real* iPod to take home for the cost of that cake. Wouldn't *that* be something?

May As Well Face It:
You're Addicted to Cake

Comedian Jim Gaffigan loves cake so much that he devotes a stand-up routine to it. He calls it the "true symbol of gluttony" and offers an analogy: "If you eat a whole pizza, people are like, 'Wow, you were hungry,' but if you eat a whole cake, people are like, 'You've got a problem! Addicted to cake!'" Enough friends have regaled us with tales of drinking derring-do, so we recognize the truth of this. But, as Gaffigan rightly observes, "You never hear someone brag, 'Yeah, last night I had four pieces of cake!'" His tiny alter-ego voice asks, "Why are you telling us?" His manly voice answers, "Just want you to know I *partied*."

Cake addiction is surely a notion that elicits snickers. You can't help but chuckle at the idea that someone would sit down, with a fork, to a 9-inch-by-9-inch sheet of frosted cake and consume this 4,000-calorie meal solo. A person who does so is not likely to brag about it; on the contrary, she is probably sitting in the dark with the blinds drawn. I say "she" because more women than men are affected with binge disorder. (Some say adolescent and young women make up 90 percent of those suffering from eating disorders.)

The irony of that image is sad. Cake is for celebrations! We share it with our friends and family to honor a birthday or a retirement. We don't present one to a woman who's just had a miscarriage or a child whose dog has died. A person gorging himself on grocery store cake, absent the company of others—in fact, *hiding* it from others out of shame and embarrassment—isn't too funny. Unless Jim Gaffigan is talking about it.

I could say that I have never gone to such an extreme, that my love of cake is pure and unfettered, my forays into cakedom devoid of guilt and self-loathing. But this would be a lie. My adoration is edacious, idolatrous.

I have loved a lot of cakes. And I have loved some of them in shameful ways.

My most insane childhood food memory, the one that probably stoked my addiction (my grandmother's cakes fueled it), involves a spoon and a can. My mother, my sister, and I, each armed with our teaspoons, would share—albeit on a rare occasion—a whole can of Duncan Hines chocolate or cream cheese frosting for dessert. My mother doesn't recall, but Beth and I do. And what neither of them knew was that, at other times of other days, I would often walk from room to room with my spoon, trying to prolong the moments between dips, refusing to admit my gluttony by embracing that can as my meal, but instead attempting to overcome it by playing Lulu's "To Sir with Love" umpteen times and singing into the dirty spoon.

I have blamed my mother for introducing me to canned frosting (the spoon itself would come in handy for other things). I have blamed the baby in my stomach for her sugary subliminal suggestions. I have blamed Marty, who brings the stray slice home from his work at a Catholic school, where someone celebrates his or her birth—or half birthday, for those summer babies—nearly every day. He leaves the foil-wrapped wedge seductively posed on top of the bread box so that there's no mistaking its profile. I have blamed his aunt Margaret, who always knows he is coming and bakes a chocolate sheet cake—and a batch of peanut butter fudge—to send home with him in her nonstick pan, which he can, when he returns, trade for the next cake, as if this were a chocolate relay race she needed his help to win. I have blamed friends for leaving visible, when I visit, the residue of last night's birthday celebration.

But as Michael Pollan says, it's the flower's fault—or, in this case, the flour's. That is, something about the cake holds sway over me, some spell binds me, as if that final teaspoon of vanilla changes the chemistry and sends a plume of sparks in the air, breathes life into frosting, and imbues it with a potent "Eat me" potion. Only I don't get small.

I often make my husband leave in his truck whatever cake he brings home; this way, I won't hear it calling my name. My closest friends know how true this is. Long after the kids at a party have visited the cake table, the remains of their choices *still* on the paper party plates because the frosting's too cloying for them, I stand alone with a knife, cutting a sliver, then another, then another. I finish the cake on plates abandoned by strange eight-year-old boys. Across the room, parents watch me, smile, and shake their heads, as if I were some child with an endearing new trick: Oh, look at Leslie. Isn't that sweet.

One week, an Aunt Margaret pan of dark, gooey moistness had been crouching amid camping accessories, old files, and guitar amplifiers in the basement. That I had not found it was less a testament to willpower than to its good hiding place—and to the fact that my husband and daughter had made its presence in our home, at my command, a complete secret, sharing squares between the two of them when I was elsewhere. I walked into the kitchen one afternoon and saw them, their mouths clamping shut and eyes bugging out, brown crumbs glued to my daughter's lips with vanilla ice cream. "Now, Mom, don't get any ideas," she said.

* * *

Dr. Bruce Semon is a psychiatrist who focuses on nutrition as a path to healing a variety of medical complaints. His Web site explains how something as simple as food cravings can be detrimental to physical and mental health. "Food cravings are extremely strong desires for certain foods, so strong that one focuses on the craving above everything else."

I've had that.

"Addiction results," says Semon, "when one has lost control and given oneself over to these strong desires regardless of the consequences."

I've had that, too.

But cake is *fun*. It should be all *joy* (my daughter's middle name, by the way, is not Cake but Joy). What's all this talk of *addiction*? Such a serious word for a happy dessert.

The insidious chocolate ribbon cake from Gourmet Bakery in Pikesville is my stalker. A family friend, Sam Goldberg, works at the bakery and considers it his duty to insinuate the cake—more like a loaf of fudge—on us at every food event, from bris to the shivah. (At Passover, he sends the cardboard box.) When I walk into my parents' home for dinner, a camera pans to it for the close-up, and Bernard Herrmann's creepy "Knife" music starts up again. Everywhere I turn, this cake is behind me (and, consequently, part of my behind). It's not the deep green, pink, blue, and yellow layers that beckon me. It's the chocolate: thick, fudge-y, frosting enrobing the cake, with some extra whipped fluff piped along the edge where the cake abuts the Styrofoam plate. I run to it, suggest an embrace, then run my finger along that border. My mother and I are each *entitled* to a heel. Sometimes there's chocolate syrup between the layers; other times, it's jelly; in that case, I eat only the frosting from the top.

For my fortieth birthday party, I'd made some killer sugar-free cheesecakes (which are really pie) to keep me from succumbing to the flour-and-sugar buzz that keeps me awake nights. This is why my love for cake is sometimes detrimental. But the ribbon cake waltzed in with my parents. I decided I'd savor it, ration it, with the help of the freezer. But I was still eating it several times a day, so I decided to toss it. The garbage disposal would have been a great idea, but something—a half inch of chocolate, perhaps—prevented me from thinking rationally. I took a sharp knife and sliced the frosted top, back, and sides and threw away those colorful ribbons. I ate the remaining chocolate while hovering over the trash can. I devoured it like a dog.

I don't remember how it tasted.

Perhaps that's part of the problem with chocolate ribbon cake from Gourmet. Some things you never have to taste again to remember. I'll never forget the flavor of a frozen mudslide. I'll never lose the taste of a hard-boiled egg or broccoli or cottage cheese with strawberries—all of which I love. It's the decadent stuff you forget. I forget the taste of chocolate ribbon cake—oh, let's be honest, here: *most* cakes. One refresher bite leads to another. And then another. And before you know it, I'm in the dark by the back door. I might as well be sitting in a corner with a makeshift tourniquet and my works in a pile at my hip.

There's a great old diet trick I learned from one of the twelve times I was a Weight Watchers member over the past two and a half decades. Always ask that the fries or chips be left in the kitchen, but if you forget, or if they come despite your request, make them inedible the moment the plate lands on the table. Some people use an excess of salt or sugar or pepper. I use Sweet'N Low. Nothing works better. A French fry covered with sugar is, as Gaffigan observes, a funnel cake. A chip covered with salt is still a chip. Sweet'N Low is the taste obliterator.

My sister did her version of the trick after her son's birthday party. It was probably a week later when I visited Beth and was surprised to find the gigantic box from a local bakery still lurking in the kitchen, more surprised to find my nephew Graham's white-frosted, 3-D dump truck cake inside. It had been sitting out on the countertop for so long that both cake and frosting had a slight crunch. As I made my way toward the box, a monster voice in my head saying, "Cake. Eat," my sister warned me that it was full of party trash. But when I lifted the lid, I saw some crumpled napkins, a couple of red plastic cups, and some dirty plates on one side, unobscured cake on the other. I sliced off a piece with one of the plastic knives in the box. It looked clean enough. And the cake was just as cake is. Beth joined me at the stove, and the two of us stood there a few moments and polished off the important parts.

Even if cake *is* an addiction, even if I have to go out of my way to avoid cake, even if I have to make a dessert I detest every January in order to keep myself from devouring my daughter's birthday cake each year, it's still a relatively harmless and somewhat hilarious addiction. After all, I'm not stealing from my friends (unless you count the slice of cake I took from the foil-covered pan while my girlfriend wasn't looking) or eating it alone in the dark, except for that one time. And I'm not a stripper losing revenue.

Still, I do think of cake often, enough that I spent nearly $30,000 (of my parents' money) on an MFA, for which my thesis was a book about cake.

Perhaps it could be my final resting place, a casket without the *s* and *t,* the epitaph embossed in faux frosting: Here lies Leslie. She's done. Stick a fork in her.

Here lies Leslie. She had a cake jones.

You know you're getting old when you get that one candle on the cake. It's like, "See if you can blow this out."
—Jerry Seinfeld, comedian

Cake Love
SECOND TIER

LAYER TWELVE

The Soul of a Jewish Grandmother

In a twenty-six-year-old Ektachrome slide, my grandmother holds what I remember as a Thanksgiving turkey on a serving tray, high on her shoulder and cocked toward the camera. It's a still, but she practically curtsies. She didn't have the right to be so proud of that bone-dry bird; in my memory, it is the reason I still don't like turkey. But this is an anomaly, since everything else my grandmother touched turned to ambrosia and nectar.

I found the slide recently during a frantic craving for nostalgia, and it's not exactly as I remembered it. The holiday was Hanukkah (I know this from the lab's date stamp), and the plate at her left shoulder appears to have potato latkes, while another dish, in her right hand at waist height, holds sweet potatoes. She is dressed up fancy (something she stopped doing in later years—maybe because we were always arriving in jeans), and she has every right to smile. Both dishes were family favorites and whatever remained went home with us. She always made far more than she needed, so we were assured the privileges of a heavy doggy bag.

I have other pictures of Grammy Ruth: side by side with my pee-

pop, Marcus, at my wedding, wearing her pocketbook like a body part; the pair of them on the cover of a brochure for the hospital where they volunteered; Grammy with her sisters and brother when she was in her early twenties. I see myself in her. We share a critical eye, our naturally unsmiling lips. We share the doer's hands.

In her youth, my grandmother was a classic beauty. Maybe I think everyone in 1930s sepia looks like a movie star, but proof of her beauty was in her downstairs closet. Zipped up in plastic sleeves were dresses of black lace and velvet, a blue and silver mohair shift with a white fur collar (which she wore at my uncle's wedding), a pink lace coatdress, a shimmery champagne cocktail gown covered with glittering rhinestones. No one could wear these clothes anymore. By the time I had discovered them, I was a teen with a swimmer's body—wide shoulders, thick arms and waist, strong back. My mother, a former size five when a size five was pencil thin, hadn't worn one since her early twenties. I had seen photographic evidence that these dresses had fit my grandmother once, but she began to shrink and sag and flop the moment I laid eyes on her, as if it were my duty, as first granddaughter, to accelerate the aging process. I don't know how her breasts got larger so late in life, but I couldn't imagine them contained in the bodices. I remember her standing over the king-size bed in her room, aiming her gigantic breasts, both at the same time, toward the size EE Playtex cups whose straps were looped, loose, around her arms. Grammy held out hope that one of the granddaughters would squeeze into one of her cinched-up, glamorous frocks. After a crash diet I managed to stuff myself into a black lace dress with a velvet button placket and hundreds of tiny, velvet-covered buttons down the center front. It hung in my closet until I had gained the weight back, and my college roommate borrowed it and ruined it by ripping the hem.

Even at sixteen I knew the real treasure in that closet, the hats with net and feathers, still in their original round Hutzler's boxes. My favorite was a black velvet cloche, a more practical hat than the powder blue or the wide-brimmed red one adorned with a giant ostrich feather. The true beauty of hats is that they always fit. No matter how much cake you eat, your head stays the same size.

When I think of my grandmother, which is often, she is walking up the stairs to her bedroom, hunched over, nearly crippled from spending the day in the kitchen with all of her arthritic parts in motion. The apron ties are dangling at her sides. She moves deliberately, resting a second on each tread. I always thought the stairs creaked, but I realize now it was my grandmother. Once, she moaned, "Ugh! I'm so tired I feel like I'm fifty!" My mom said to her, "You're seventy-nine, Ma."

Baking and cooking are hard work. I made my first-ever loaf of bread (something my grandmother had never, to my knowledge, done) on Rosh Hashanah, at the age of forty-three. It was a six-strand braided challah, sweet and yeasty yellow bread. Rolling the strands was so much work that I had to take a break after three of them. But Grammy made holiday dinners at sixty and seventy and eighty, standing all day, tending to mixers and grinders and pots. I don't think I recognized what a feat that was: to cook many-course meals for ten and then twelve and then sixteen as our families grew. If Elijah had ever shown up for Passover, at the front door we'd always left open for him as kids, I don't know where we'd have put him. But he'd have wanted some sponge cake.

• • • • •

GRAMMY RUTH'S PASSOVER SPONGE CAKE

The Passover sponge cake recipe is written in blue ink on a slip of paper with the old Blue Shield logo in the bottom left corner. At the top, printed in bold, is "Medical-Surgical Plan of New Jersey," with an address. It's old enough that the phone number has a name, "Market 4-2600." The recipe, exactly as she'd written it, follows.

9 eggs (only large)
1½ cups sugar
½ c oil
½ c potato starch
½ c cake flour
juice of 2 lemons
"   " ½ orange

Beat egg whites well, **adding sugar gradually**. Mix together sifted potato starch & cake flour. Springle over mixture & fold in. Bake at 350. 1 hr invert to cool.

• • • • •

The real story of cake begins where we do, with our ancestors and traditions. It begins, even if we're not of a distinct, food-based ethnicity, in the kitchens of our grandmothers, the oldest, wisest cake bakers we know. My history is less likely to be remarkable because it's mine; in fact, it's probably much like yours.

My grandmother's kitchen, a squarish pink and olive room, was cramped and uncomfortable even before we arrived to help set the table or stir the soup or wash the pots. My aunt, my mother, and I, and later my sister, Beth, and later still my cousin Stacey were all a part of the kitchen's bumper pool. The two doorways made it easier to navigate, much like a commercial kitchen, only we were less organized and often barreled into each other with hot food or dirty dishes. I *loved* that kitchen, with its butterfly mural hand painted by my mother, its telephone with giant push-button numbers, and its one sickly plant rooting on the windowsill. Stacey told me once, "It seemed like it was always just trying to get started but never graduated to a real pot. I remember it being one of those furry roundish-leaved ones like on the table between the thrones in the living room." Those living room "thrones" were tall-backed, green velvet chairs that nearly swallowed us as children. Between them was a table carpeted with the purple-, blue-, and pink-blooming African violets that my grandmother rooted regularly on the sill. I took home dozens of my own, only to kill them with inattention or bad lighting or poisoned water. Upon her death eight years ago, I inherited all of her established plants, and now they are consistently plush with purple velvet blooms; my husband credits his care, but I think my grandmother's persuasive spirit is coaxing them along.

Because my grandmother's pot holders were all burned at the edges—black, charred, and frayed—I always wondered about her fingertips, calluses on top of burns on top of calluses, like the fingers of every professional chef I've ever known, from the cooking and the knitting and the crocheting. She crocheted right up to her death, despite the pain in her fingers, the knuckle knots. The last time I saw her before the hospital swallowed her, she sat in a chair in my living room, staring at her first great-granddaughter, balls of white transforming into a baby blanket before my eyes. My mother added the fringe to it and handed it down after Grammy died, almost secretly because it was quite a prize to have her last handicraft. I wrapped my daughter in it as if something about her life depended on it. Surely we could still find some comfort, despite my grandmother's absence from our lives.

Next to the sink was a pile of folded aluminum foil, stuff that covered leftovers and was washed and became a leftover itself, to be used and reused, covering and re-covering something else. The grandkids had no sense of economy then, and none of our perceptions were informed by history. We just took it for granted that this was our quirky grandmother, the one who always returned *something* at a restaurant and who carried a Baggie for whatever was left on the table, including packets of Sweet'N Low and bread. She always had half of a sandwich in her purse, and if you were out and hungry, she'd reach her hand in there and ask, "Want a chicken salad? I had it yesterday." I don't remember any of us contracting salmonella or botulism poisoning. But I don't remember any of us taking her up on the offer of the sandwich, either.

But Stacey thought the reusing of foil was gross. Anything even remotely unsanitary about food probably would have been repellent to her. My cousin's food issues began early; I don't know how much of that had to do with my aunt, Donna, a constant dieter, food worrier, and protector of her husband's and mother's health. At every Seder or Rosh Hashanah, she'd give them the look that said they'd had enough of whatever it was they were trying to sneak—more sweet potatoes or a second piece of sour cream cake. Their hands would reach across the table the moment my aunt left the room, and their mouths would clamp shut if she returned suddenly, crumbs hanging on their lips like bird feathers from a cat's mouth. Like everyone in my family at one time, Aunt Donna had lost and found and lost and found a significant amount of weight. Eventually, she became a Weight Watchers leader, a popular one, at that, for her brilliant sense of humor and her concern for everyone's health.

So Stacey began limiting the portions on her plate to a size not big enough for a bird when she was no more than ten, always

claiming she wasn't hungry. It worried us all, but more than that I think it amazed us. How could someone resist the sour cream cake? Whatever it was about food that tortured her, it seemed to end fairly suddenly. One day, years later, her plate had firsts and then seconds. I know she'd regret it today if she'd missed all that wonderful cooking.

For most of my life, my grandmother made everything from scratch, which meant Jewish holidays were likely to stink up the house. The scent of homemade gefilte fish permeated the air. Once, Grammy tried to pass the baton to my sister, who always showed up early to help. Beth doesn't remember any recipe card, but there were pots of boiling fish stock on the stove that she was required to taste, and the pair of them ran whitefish and pike through the KitchenAid grinder attachment—the same one that had just spit out onions, chicken livers, and hard-boiled eggs for the delicacy known as chopped liver. (Often, someone—my mother or my uncle—would turn the liver out in a mold and engrave it to look like a turkey or some other similarly incongruous creature.)

But it was a lot of work to make gefilte fish (from the German word for "full" or "stuffed," *gefuellt,* and so named because the mixture of matzo meal and onions and vegetables would be stuffed back into the fish skin), and with a generation of girls who would never take up bridge or mah-jongg, the shaping of this smelly, ground mixture into cakes or balls would die with her.

One day, though, the house ceased to smell like fish and promised only a near-future of brisket and cake. We knew Grammy had used the jars once before, and we were always suspicious, as if this constituted some sort of betrayal of her gefilte pact with the family. "Did you make this fish?" one of us would ask each time. She'd look at the floor and say "Yeah," but we started to connect the lack of fish aroma to the lack of eye contact and discovered she'd been buying the jars from the supermarket, arranging the fish on a baking pan with some sliced carrots and onions, then warming them in the oven. She was careful to get rid of the evidence so that all we'd see were warmed oblong loaves, delicious on our plates next to a dollop of *chrain,* or horseradish. It was almost always just as good.

My grandmother copied recipes for us (or sometimes, when her arthritis was acting up, had our grandfather do it) whenever we requested them, which was often. So much of the mystery of how I cook and bake is unlocked on these cards. Today's recipe writers are instructed, perhaps counterintuitively, to include precise amounts and baking times, but sometimes we do it by feel and intuition. How do you trust someone who says to bake at 350 degrees for exactly one hour, when we all have different ovens, we mix differently, we measure differently? On Grammy's kugel recipe card is a note to my mother: "Sharon," she wrote, "I don't know how long I bake it. Look at it in ½ hr. again at ¾ and see if it is browning—If you bake in glass, bake at 325. Use Comstock apples." I live for instructions like those. On a different card for the same recipe, she told us to "beat the eggs in the can" of Comstock apple pie filling; it wasn't only because she was frugal. The best part of the filling sticks to the inside of that can.

Though I don't have the original card anymore (one day, I decided to organize my recipes, which meant transferring all those lovely handwritten directions from their soiled cards to clean, typed ones), I do have Grammy's recipe for sour cream cake, the only cake without frosting that I ever adored. I made it for company recently, thinking that I could resist it. My husband and daughter had a piece every day until it was so stale and dry that I needed to eat the rest—to preserve their memory of it and my fine baking.

* * * * *

GRAMMY RUTH'S SOUR CREAM CAKE

2½ C flour
3 t baking powder
1 t (scant) baking soda
¼ t salt
½ lb. butter
3 eggs
1 C sour cream
½ t vanilla
1 C sugar
Topping
¾ C sugar
3 T cinnamon.

Cream butter and sugar.

Add eggs and vanilla; beat until creamy.

Sift dry ingredients into a bowl.

Add to wet ingredients alternately with sour cream, mixing as little as possible on low speed.

Pour half the mixture into a greased tube pan.

Sprinkle half of the topping mixture on top.

Pour in remaining batter.

Sprinkle remaining topping mixture on top.

Bake at 350° for about one hour.

Note that there is no instruction to preheat the oven, and the "topping" for this cake is actually in the middle and on the bottom since the cake is inverted out of the pan. I have not altered the original recipe's instructions.

• • • • •

Grammy shared her moist and tender brisket, her chicken divan, her chocolate pudding pie, and her sponge cake. And she shared her plentiful mandel bread—mandel from heaven—which she kept in tins on top of the refrigerator, where even she couldn't reach. I can remember only a single time the tin was empty. She thought her visible hiding place was clever, all of us being so short, but we scarred her floor dragging those green vinyl chairs to the fridge at every opportunity. She taught us, as we got older, to make the special Jewish biscotti. She even allowed me to publish her recipe in a coffee magazine, making several of what were surely obscene modifications, like dipping the cinnamon-and-sugar-sprinkled cookies in chocolate or subbing cocoa for some of the flour, adding chocolate chips, using macadamias. Or maybe my grandmother didn't mind the innovations. Even though her recipe was probably fancy enough with its chopped walnuts and squirt of orange juice, she had quite a few of her own odd tricks.

Grammy Ruth made her spaghetti sauce with half ground beef, half ground hot dogs. We all loved that spaghetti sauce, which didn't taste at all like hot dogs, but you knew something extraordinary was in the mix. It was that innovative spirit of hers that led me to the phone at midnight so that she could fix whatever I'd screwed up—from a slipped stitch to a stew. If a food could be substituted, she knew about it. And her house was full of substitutions: the kitchen pantries were so deep they seemed to go back the length of the house, and the basement was stocked with so many rolls of foil, so many canned goods, so many sodas, so many Green Stamps prizes that each trip to her house was like an exotic shopping excursion.

My grandfather had mysteries, too. His corner of the basement had a red vise that fascinated me, though a reglued artifact was rarely pressed between its metal jaws. It wasn't just for show, this shop desk. He *fixed* things and often showed us how. I learned to use a hammer and a screwdriver at that desk, learned the difference between a flathead and a Phillips. (Still wound up, years later, hammerless in my rented room, banging a nail with the spiked heel of my shoe, and tightening screws with a dime or a mat knife blade.) A Hungarian immigrant who escaped early anti-Semitism in 1924, at twelve years old, Marcus Weitz (a distant cousin of the fashion mogul John Weitz and also the rabid, growling cop on *Hill Street Blues,* Bruce Weitz) was an engineer at Westinghouse, and his drafting table was full of things I associated with math and perfection at the same time: straightedges and erasers and what he called "onionskin"—the thinnest tracing paper, which felt as if it had been pressed from the innermost translucent layer of the smelly bulb. His erasers were like wads of gum. His handwriting was an ethnic version of draftsman's block.

Peepop was the king of Sudoku, and taught me to do those numbers puzzles in under a minute. He also made a mean Farina and Cream of Wheat—better than any, with his slow simmer and cold water and constant stirring. But most of all, he was the protector of the Kitchen Queen. He had honed his guilt-making skills, taking lessons from the best of the best, the Queen herself. If we didn't eat enough, he'd remind us of the hours Grammy had spent that week in the kitchen preparing the meal. He'd click his tongue at us, roll his eyes, shake his head. And he'd mumble under his breath, "Can't believe it. Does all that work. Not even hungry. I'll be. Well, I'll be damned."

In some sixteen adult years at that heavy dining room table, with the pads beneath a tablecloth that never seemed to hold the stain of Manischewitz wine, I never ate the matzo ball soup. Each year, my grandmother would ask, and each year I'd decline. And each year, Peepop would look up at me (I sat to his immediate left much of the time) and say, "No soup?" while everyone but me was eating it, and I'd remind him that I never have soup, and he'd say, "You don't?" or "Since when?" as if I were pulling his leg to get out of eating a course.

The men in our families traditionally provided the money. They sat at the heads of our tables and led the Passover Seders, the only ones of us besides my cousins who could speak Hebrew without reading the phonetics. But the women were the matriarchs; they ruled our castles with iron skillets and frayed oven mitts.

Passing the Wooden Spoon

My mother held her own as reigning queen of wherever we called home, though her cooking repertoire may not have been so elaborate. From a neighbor, Mary Pezzella, she learned to make a real Italian spaghetti sauce: no hot dogs, but a spoonful of sugar to take the acid out of the tomatoes. One day, she discovered that her homemade sauce, with cans of Hunts Tomatoes Sauce (yes, it says "Tomatoes Sauce" on the can) and Paste, tasted just like Prego, so she started buying the jars. To that, she'd add onions and ground beef even, it seems, when we were poor, our father a traveling salesman peddling costume jewelry to lesser department stores.

Mom baked lasagna with the same meat sauce but subbed cream cheese for ricotta, simply because she'd never liked ricotta and thought cream cheese would taste good. I know no one else who makes it that way, and it's still the best, richest lasagna I've ever had. She made tuna casseroles, salmon croquettes (almost as good as Grammy's), and an occasional steak, lots of frozen veggies, especially cauliflower, which I tried to bury in ketchup but eventually gave up and fed to the dog under the table. After I had learned how to make it from a downstairs neighbor, she made shepherd's pie. We regularly had meat loaf, in which Mom made a hollow that she stuffed with mozzarella cheese, which melted as it baked and oozed, deliciously, on our plates. But one of our favorite regular dishes was chicken livers, served with wide egg noodles in a sauce of ketchup.

She was one of the first mothers I knew who worked. She was an elementary school teacher for years in Baltimore. When we moved back to Randallstown from a brief stint in Indianapolis (I was nine), she was a secretary for a well-known architectural firm, and then she became the owner of one, with her partner, Dick Schaefer. (They designed the home of a wildly successful local restaurateur as well as that of Brooks Robinson, one of the country's best-loved baseball players.)

Sometimes she didn't have it in her to make a meal, and, like nearly every family I knew then, we had the occasional TV dinner. Salisbury steak was my favorite, though the mere mention of it now causes distress. Some nights, we had strawberries and sour cream for dinner. "That's not dinner," my sister used to whine. She hated it. "It's dinner tonight," our mom would say. With those exceptions, and the mashed potato flakes, most of our home-cooked meals were painstakingly assembled from a combination of convenient parts (like canned salmon or tuna and egg noodles), fresh produce and meat (celery and ground beef), and innovation (ketchup on the livers, cream cheese in the lasagna).

If my mother baked my birthday cake, I don't recall. Aside from the cans of Duncan Hines frosting, I can't conjure a single birthday-related oven task. But she made use of chocolate chips—aside from serving them from the bag—by baking them in my grandmother's black-bottom cupcakes, as well as meringue cookies and Hello Dollys, those bars of coconut, chocolate chips, and walnuts with graham crackers on the bottom.

The kitchen I remember most was a tiny room with mustard-colored wallpaper printed with black outlines of acorns and pheasants. I had always remembered it as chickens until I saw a picture. I never liked it, but it came from a fancy wallpaper book, and I knew from the awed sighs of friends and neighbors that it was beautiful and that my mother had impeccable taste. She was always helping them spruce up their surroundings, bringing them an array of unusual paint chips, taking them furniture shopping. No matter how poor we may have been, our dwellings were glamorous. We were the first, for instance, to have a black-painted wall lined with vertical, floor-to-ceiling beveled mirrors. The coffee table, an underappreciated (by my sister and me) faux tortoiseshell–dappled, hulking square of heaviness, sat in the center of the room, its sharp corners reaching out to nick our shins at every opportunity. Our dining room had a chrome and glass table with white vinyl and chrome chairs to match; it was the seventies, after all. But as soon as the modern look was out of favor in *Architectural Digest,* the Queen Anne chairs had arrived. Even then, they were antiques—almost the first thing my mother bought with her salary from the architectural firm.

But our kitchen was where everything got done. The four high-back metal chairs with fancy scrollwork, which my parents got for their first house, were the color of brown mustard, matching the wallpaper, and the table was dark wood veneer with a metal base to match the chairs. On the walls and not ample enough were standard-issue, dark-wood, apartment-style cabinets. A freestanding pantry, bought at a yard sale, was the item I coveted long into adulthood. It was mustard with black handles in this kitchen, the panels inlaid with a gross foil floral wallpaper like the kind you'd find in an ugly powder room of someone who thinks she is modern; it was white with blue knobs in the next kitchen, of Pennsylvania Dutch decor. The refrigerator was well stocked with Tab and leftovers, and I remember bagels and doughnuts often occupying the countertop next to it. And I can never forget the pots: the orange Descoware set—similar to Le Creuset but probably a better buy without the French cachet—that looks nearly as new today. I covet them.

My mother did other things in our kitchen, too. The table was often the place for her sewing machine, where she made me a glorious pair of orange tweedy gauchos, or elephant pants, all the rage when I was in sixth grade, even though no one seemed to wear them but me and the fashion models on magazine covers. And she made all kinds of dolls with painted faces, which she sometimes sold at crafts bazaars. I still have one in an elaborate flower dress with a perfect head of curly brown yarn. She painted at the kitchen table, too, in acrylics on canvas: a hooker sitting on a window ledge; a guy named Stan copping a feel from his girlfriend, Marge, at the movie theater.

Once, after teaching my sister about tampons on the day of her initiation into the club, my mother hung a red-marker-painted tampon from the door handle of the kitchen cabinet over the sink. When friends came over after school during the few weeks it remained novel for her, she'd hitch her pants up and buck her teeth out and say, regarding their wide-eyed glares at our ornament, "What'sa matter? Ain'tcha never hearda Christmas?"

That apartment kitchen and the L-shaped one in a house we rented in Mount Washington hold some of my favorite memories. There was the time my father was a traveling salesman working out of Pennsylvania, only coming home for weekends. On one of them, my sister set the table, putting the plates at each of our places: "One for me, one for Mommy, one for Leslie, and one for the guest." There was the time my high-school stalker called my house, and, from the kitchen phone, my mom called her business partner (my dad was out of town), who in turn called the boy who was harassing me and threatened to do something involving a car and a bomb (though I remember it as a penis and a knife). There were the dough crafts we made at the table—my mother's always a naked Adam and Eve, with lifelike penis and breasts, respectively, of course. And there was the time I had a dream that our house was being robbed and that my mother's pocketbook was being stolen from the kitchen table. In the morning, we found the basement window broken and the pocketbook missing. I remember the very moment my mother made her spaghetti sauce with crab legs instead of meat, and it went on regular rotation. I remember meals of langostinos with yellow rice, thinking them so gourmet, even though they came from a box in the frozen seafood section of the grocery store.

But I barely remember cake, not even the family chocolate cake— which my mother assures me *everyone* made from scratch. She thinks it was called the Chocolate Town Cake back then, the recipe printed on the side of the Hershey's Cocoa tin. Now, Hershey's calls it the Chocolatetown Special Cake, and their frosting is updated, with milk replacing the boiling water.

· · · · ·

CHOCOLATETOWN SPECIAL CAKE

½ cup Hershey's Cocoa or Hershey's Special Dark Cocoa
½ cup boiling water
⅔ cup shortening
1 ¾ cups sugar
1 teaspoon vanilla extract
2 eggs
2 ¼ cups all-purpose flour
1 ½ teaspoons baking soda
½ teaspoon salt
1 ⅓ cups buttermilk or sour milk*
One-Bowl Buttercream Frosting (recipe follows)

1. Heat oven to 350°F. Grease and flour two 9-inch round baking pans.

2. Stir together cocoa and water in small bowl until smooth. Beat shortening, sugar and vanilla in large bowl until fluffy. Add eggs; beat well. Stir together flour, baking soda and salt; add to shorten-

ing mixture alternately with buttermilk, beating until well blended. Add cocoa mixture; beat well. Pour batter into prepared pans.

3. Bake 30 to 35 minutes or until wooden pick inserted in center comes out clean. Cool 10 minutes; remove from pans to wire racks. Cool completely. Frost with One-Bowl Buttercream Frosting. 8 to 10 servings.

* To sour milk: Use 4 teaspoons white vinegar plus milk to equal 1⅓ cups.

Use Magi-Cake strips, available from most cake supply stores, and the cake will rise but remain flat. It won't sink when it's cool, either. If you use the professional pans (with straight, three-inch sides), you can put the tops together and have a perfectly smooth surface for decorating, rather than having to chop off the tops, like many bakers do.

I have made this cake wrong nearly every time, putting the shortening, sugar, and vanilla into the bowl with the cocoa, rather than adding the cocoa last. It's hard to mess up the recipe. It always tastes decadent. I use the Special Dark chocolate when baking this cake for sophisticated adults. Children may prefer the regular chocolate.

ONE-BOWL BUTTERCREAM FROSTING

6 tablespoons butter or margarine, softened
2 ⅔ cups powdered sugar
½ cup Hershey's Cocoa or Hershey's Dutch Processed Cocoa
⅓ cup milk
1 teaspoon vanilla extract

Beat butter in small bowl. Add powdered sugar and cocoa alternately with milk; beat to spreading consistency (additional milk may be needed). Stir in vanilla. About 2 cups frosting.

The recipe says it makes two cups of frosting, but I've found a double batch (at least a batch and a half) to be necessary if you're going to amply fill between the cakes and frost the top and sides. But I'm a sucker for the frosting.

Recipe courtesy of the Hershey Kitchens, and reprinted with permission of The Hershey Company. © The Hershey Company.

The Reigning Queen of Cake

I went through a lot of kitchens before I found the one where I could even attempt to re-create the wonders that came from my grand-mother's kitchen. It didn't start off as nice and well equipped as it is now, but it beats every other place I've ever tried to cook. Long before I'd baked my cheesecakes in water baths (indeed, before I bothered with the kind that had to be baked), prior to pan-searing pork chops, kneading homemade pizza dough, baking and decorating a triple-layer coconut cake, and inventing a low-carb sponge cake for Pass-over, I discovered what it was about the kitchen that made people congregate there. Mostly, it was other people.

I had taken some classes at the Jewish Community Center when I was eight, but unless there was raw batter involved, I didn't care to cook. The desire to see a meal through from start to finish didn't flicker until I moved out of my parents' place in my first year of college. I was nineteen and singing in a new wave band when I moved into the three-story mansion with eight bedrooms in a hip but tragically urban part of Baltimore, across from Druid Hill Park. Filmmaker John Waters—when he was wildly notorious rather than

famous—lived in the apartments next door, but a few blocks south was never the place to be at night.

I was the sole first-floor resident in a room with a fireplace (there were green marble fireplaces in both the living room and the dining room). Two second-floor bedrooms had fireplaces, also; between each pair of bedrooms on that floor was a master bath. Another full bath was on the back wall of the second- and third-floor landings. I first learned of the house—and the available room—when my band was looking for rehearsal space. My best friend's boyfriend lived there. My future husband, Marty, lived there, too, and shared one of the fireplace-blessed bedrooms with his girlfriend of four years, Nancy.

Lest anyone get the wrong impression from *mansion* and *green marble*—and the name of our house, the Jockey Club—I should mention that it was in various stages of array, from vile and disgusting to mildly comfortable, if you forgot about the fact that your bed was on the floor of a house overrun with roaches and varmints.

The toilet across the hall from my bedroom was perpetually stopped up with foul unmentionables and grew an assortment of wild mushrooms—nonhallucinogenic, inedible, poisonous fungi—from the perennial dampness of the floor.

The living room was decorated with dozens of broken televisions stacked atop one another, some with roller-skated mannequin legs hanging out of broken screens; others with designs painted on the glass. It was what was known in those days as an *art installation*. I appreciated it then, at nineteen, in a way that I would fail to appreciate it now, were it to occupy a significant portion of my home. One corner was sucked up by a sculpture entitled *The Pious Enigma Goes Shopping,* which featured an enthroned commercial hair dryer with colored, blinking, musical lights in the lid. Another area was dubbed "the Tacky Corner" and hosted a many-animal-patterned sofa and chair, a lamp of a lawn jockey with a green-sequined tube top stretched over the lampshade, and plastic plants collecting dust on the floor and the wall. From a hole in the twelve-foot ceiling dangled a giant airplane model, with colored Christmas bulbs lighting its trail; a spaceman in a parachute hung low enough to touch.

And let's not forget the roomies, most of whom were hippies, artists, and students of various means. Marty's girlfriend was gainfully employed as an interior designer with a major architectural firm. She eventually married a Jewish guy, and they opened a record store in Portland, Oregon. One woman was a prostitute for a short time; she is now a terrific mother and wonderful cook. One guy was a waiter at an exclusive country club; he has owned one of Baltimore's most successful restaurants for about twenty years. Another guy, who now works as a builder for the movies, made dental appliances—and a plaster cast of his penis, which sat on my husband's dresser for about ten years before I got tired of looking at it. (I'd seen the real thing up close a few times while living in that house.) Marty was a philosophy major, communist, and bum; his ambition, when I met him, was to "travel the world, impregnating a beautiful woman from every country and creating the International Family of Peace." He did not see his ambition through, thankfully, and now holds a master's degree in legal and ethical studies and teaches middle-school social studies and math. I was an English major at Towson and worked for a wallpaper store part-time. I grew up to eat cake. With the possible exception of the Jockey Club's mad decorator, N. Scott Taylor, who grew up to be perennial presidential candidate Vermin Fucking Supreme, most of us overcame our dangling and misspent college years.

But the kitchen in this house was where I took my first interest in cooking, almost as a challenge or out of a desire to compete for a title. Much went on in that kitchen, which was infested, more than any other room, with cockroaches, large and small, many of them dead and glued to the wall, some of them living in a luxury condo built by the artist in residence, others roaming free on wall and floor. Next to the glued dead ones were plastic army men in combat stance and words cut out of comic books, action sounds like "Blam!" and "Wham!" and "Kerplooey!"

In addition to a *real* refrigerator, there was a fake one filled with big, naked dolls of every ethnicity. A broken toaster was turned into a rotisserie, with a plastic Holstein cow model on a spit, the whole thing lit up with red bulbs to indicate heat.

This was an eighties-style commune. We each put in sixty dollars for rent and utilities, volunteered to work at the Belly, a wholesale food co-op (I wiggled out of that arrangement), attended house meetings, and contributed to the cooking. I had never cooked for anyone before. Nancy was the housemother (some called her Mom) and nurturer and the only one who could really cook, though she didn't make much more than homemade granola and chili with tofu—not because of the vegetarians in the house but because grocery funds were too limited for meat.

In a house with cockroaches as objets d'art, the cuisine could be unpredictable. Our artist friend Scott sabotaged many a dinner with his innovations, his specialty the dreaded "secret ingredient." We'd often find things like chopped apples or raisins in the spaghetti sauce. Most unforgettable, though, was the large dose of orange Tang he used to flavor the chili. Inedible as it was, most of us choked it down. It was all we had then.

A few of my roommates were less discerning than others. On *several* mornings, I caught one of them pouring ice-cold, from a bottle in the freezer, vodka into his cornflakes; he ate the whole bowl, with a spoon, his back to the kitchen door, with no apparent self-consciousness or sense that this was a deranged thing to do. He went on to work in theater in Washington, D.C.

Who would have thought I'd long for a gourmet, Mom-cooked meal, *normal* meat loaf made from the flesh of a real cow, tuna casserole without the grape jam that would likely accompany it in this house, spaghetti with meat sauce and no Tang. I made a big production out of my turn to cook, making a list of gourmet ingredients and putting in some extra cash. I was nervous. On that evening, to calm my nerves, I probably smoked some pot (no use hiding it; I did my fair share of drugs in the Jockey Club), chain-smoked cigarettes, and drank a Wiedemann's. (A six-pack was $1.37 at the place we called Cut-Throat Liquors—really Cut-*Rate*—on the corner; we often collected pennies from the floor to buy the *liquid bread*.) I crushed garlic with the bottom of the can of tomatoes; I sautéed the onions and the ground beef; I added basil, oregano, bay leaves, a pinch of cayenne, and a tablespoon of sugar. And then I stood in the kitchen for at least an hour while it simmered. I didn't take my eyes off the pot for a moment. When Scott Taylor asked me, wide-eyed and eager, "Whatcha makin'?" I threw him out of the room. Every time he poked his head around the corner, I yelled. I didn't make much more than spaghetti and my mother's lasagna while I lived there, but their reception, and how I enjoyed their enjoyment, told me that I would take after my grandmother, at least in the kitchen.

When the whole lot of us were kicked out of the Jockey Club, I took Marty with me to a Twenty-seventh Street row house, where we rented from a junkie landlord. Fed up, we moved down to Twenty-fifth Street. My first mortgage was paid on this home with a four-legged, cast-iron Oriole stove, which had to be lit with a match; the oven never worked, and we eventually bought a Montgomery Ward stove, which we still own, so that we could bake a turkey and a cake. The Oriole stove became art.

I had a few specialties by then, and baking became a way of procrastinating the work on my master's degree in design. I became an expert in banana and zucchini bread, as well as the *Silver Palate* carrot cake. It is, as even well-known bakers like Leslie Poyourow (of Washington, D.C.'s Fancy Cakes by Leslie) attest, the finest carrot cake known to mankind, with coconut, walnuts, crushed pineapple, and lots of carrot.

But I stank at making cake! The layers were always lopsided! The middles always sank! I took this cake to every event, every Thanksgiving, every neighborhood and family barbecue, every party. And with it went a sign, which I propped up in front of my sagging, lopsided, and poorly-frosted-but-luscious-tasting monstrosity; it said, "Ugly but Good." I *had* to tell them; my cake was so ugly that it looked inedible.

My kitchen now, in an area of Baltimore called Beverly Hills (not a lot of swimming pools or movie stars, but Martin O'Malley— once our city's mayor, now our state's governor, with aspirations to a higher office—used to live across the street), is far from glamorous, but it has made some stellar cakes, including a flourless chocolate torte for Passover.

When we got here, the kitchen was worse than ugly, with its sticky, wounded yellow cabinets and undersize refrigerator. The floor, a brown, fake brick vinyl, was ripped and missing in places, which only made it easier to remove. Everything was covered with a thick layer of grease. The previous owners had rented the house to a family who ran what they called a "fish fry" out of it. Each week, they'd fry fish and chicken for their church suppers and picnics. Our first order of business was to pull everything out and replace it. The only thing that followed us here was the Montgomery Ward range.

The kitchen is fairly large—about 14 by 15—with a black-and-white ceramic tile floor that a girlfriend and I laid ourselves. Behind the stove and sink and under the wall cabinets is my mosaic backsplash. The basement door has a hole cut out of the bottom for my cats, when we first moved in, and now I often return home to find my crazy dog, Chance, wedged in to the shoulders. He can get through from the kitchen but not back the other way. A bookcase holds the cookbooks I still use—about fifty-five of them—and has a tiny television on it (on which we watch the news and *Everybody Loves Raymond,* which nearly *always* has a cake in it, with dinner). There is a dishwasher that gets used mostly to drain what we wash in the sink, and a large, freestanding base cabinet that held my cash register, bags, tissue, receipts, and other items when I ran my low-carb food store, La Vida Low-Carb. Yes. I am a cake lover who probably should never eat flour or sugar. It's not irony; it's hell.

My low-carb food store boomed nearly the moment it opened; every major television station, every local paper, did a story about it. But no sooner did Atkins tip as a fad than it plummeted off the planet. Dieters are fickle. They lose their twenty pounds and go back to the doughnuts and fritters—and gain twenty-five pounds. So I lost customers. I didn't have extra cash to fritter away, so I closed up shop and brought the good furniture home. This particular piece holds all of my fancy mixing bowls and dessert plates, my dish towels, tools, glue, phone books. The chrome cash-register shelf, which sits just at window ledge height, holds my grandmother's African violets. My spices, on a wall shelf under the cabinets, are in alphabetical order. The only one I don't use regularly is cardamom.

The inside of my oven has seen better, cleaner days. On November 8, 2007, it turned twenty. I know, because the appliance man was here to fix it last month, so I located the manual (I might not be the neatest person, but if it cost more than $100 and can break, I have the receipt filed alphabetically by brand). The appliance man, who is trustworthy in addition to being amazing with a wrench, says I won't find a stove as well made as this one, which cost over $500 with tax in 1986. He likes the old-fashioned stoves and would go as far back as match lights to avoid anything with an electronic part; they're all doomed. So I shelled out the $180 for a new thingamajig switch.

Since that day, I have made a hundred cakes.

My oven has baked Passover sponge cakes and tortes, low-carb cakes with almond flour and wheat gluten (which, when you are dieting, you tell yourself are delicious anyway), cheesecakes, triple-layer cakes, and at least fifty *Silver Palate Cookbook* carrot cakes. It's the *only* carrot cake, as far as I'm concerned.

When I first started baking for stress release and weight gain, I knew nothing about cutting off the tops to level them. I didn't have deep commercial pans or frosting lessons that, once learned, would never leave. And I couldn't make a cake that looked like someone relatively competent made it in her kitchen. My husband requests the carrot cake several times a year. My daughter promised that she would wear her hair down for my next birthday (eleven months away) if I would make the carrot cake for her birthday next time. I will (but she'll forget about the hair deal). And I will vow, as I usually do, not to have a bite. Her birthday is, after all, just six days from The Resolution, which will, no doubt, have something to do with flour and sugar, as it does every year for me and for most of the women and some of the men in America.

* * * * *

LOW-CARB CHOCOLATE CAKE

1 ⅓ cups unsalted butter, plus extra for greasing pan
¼ cup heavy cream
1 tablespoon white vinegar
1 cup Dutch process cocoa
1 ½ cups almond flour

½ cup gluten flour

1 teaspoon baking soda

½ teaspoon salt

2 cups sweetener (I use equal parts xylitol and sucralose)

⅓ cup sugar-free chocolate syrup (the kind used for flavoring Italian
   sodas or coffee)

5 large eggs

1 tablespoon vanilla extract

1 recipe Sugar-Free Chocolate Buttercream Frosting (below)

Preheat the oven to 350°F. Grease the bottom of a 9 by 13-inch
baking pan.

Combine the cream and vinegar in a small bowl and set aside. Combine the dry ingredients in a large bowl.

Cream the butter and sweetener until light and fluffy. Add the
syrup. Beat in the eggs one at a time, mixing well after each addition. Add the flour mixture slowly, beating until well combined.
Fold in the cream. Add the vanilla.

Bake for about 30 minutes or until the center is set; a cake tester
should come out clean. (Watch carefully! Do not overbake!)

About 4 carbs per serving.

SUGAR-FREE CHOCOLATE
BUTTERCREAM FROSTING

6 tablespoons butter or margarine, softened

2½ cups sweetener (I use half xylitol and half sucralose), processed
   fine

½ cup cocoa or Dutch process cocoa

⅓ cup milk (or Hood Calorie Countdown Milk)

1 teaspoon vanilla extract

Beat the butter in a small bowl. Add the sweetener and cocoa alternately with the milk; beat to spreading consistency (additional milk may be needed). Stir in the vanilla.

As always, you may need more. And that has been my general philosophy about cake and life.

I wanted to buy a candleholder, but the store didn't have one. So I got a cake.

—Mitch Hedberg

The Moist White Underbelly
THIRD TIER

LAYER FIFTEEN

Cake Cottage

Cake Cottage doesn't look like the witch built it to lure Hansel and Gretel. It sits near one end of a strip shopping center on the corner of Belair and Silver Spring roads in Baltimore County; Goodwill Industries is at the other end, and a few ill-used stores in between come and go regularly. The only landscaping items are a trash can and a newspaper box. Hot pink signs announce BRIDAL ACCESSORIES, CANDY, AND FUDGE and CAKE DECORATING, CANDY MAKING, SUPPLIES & CLASSES. The store name sign, which I dare not call a logo, has a line of piped frosting on one side, a pastry bag continuing that line on the other. It looks like a blowup of a cheesy office-supply-store business card, the kind printed in tacky raised type.

Before I decided to tell the story of cake, I knew a little about it. I could tell you a cake is made with butter, sugar, eggs, and flour, baked in a 300-ish-degree oven, and smeared with more butter and sugar. I knew that some cakes taste so good they make the angels sing in five-part harmony. And I knew cake makes you fat. In fact, there's an old joke about cake: When you mix flour and water, you get glue. When you add eggs and sugar, you get cake. Where did the glue go? It's what makes the cake stick to your butt.

But when it came to tools and tips and tricks of the trade, the differences between a pound cake and a sponge cake, a white cake and a yellow, I was green. I could learn from books, but I prefer the hands-on approach, learning by doing, the opportunity to eat research and write off my groceries at tax time. So I went to mine the cake ore behind the doors of the Cake and Wedding Cottage, whose Web site claims this is "A Wonderful Place to Start."

The original store might have been a cottage in 1977, when Donna Parrish opened it to sell candy-making supplies. She wanted her own business and thought there'd be a market for it, but a lull after the winter holiday months forced her to come up with something to sell in candy's off-season. Once she added wedding cakes to her repertoire, customers found use for her wares year-round.

It's not a unique idea; there's a Cake Cottage just about everywhere: Cake Art (Atlanta), Cakery (Boston), Cakes Plus (Tampa Bay), New York Cake Supplies (Manhattan), Make-A-Cake (Houston), Cake and Candy Supply (Topeka), Lynelle's Cake Decorating and Supplies (Huntsville, Alabama), Gumdrop House (Juneau). Within an hour's drive of my house, there are ten cake decorating supply stores.

The first thing that hits you fresh off the hot asphalt parking lot is the smell of buttercream frosting left over from a decorating class the night before. Or maybe it's the combined scents of bagged cream and jelly fillings, tubbed frosting, tubed food paste, bottled flavor oils and extracts, molded sugar and royal icing decorations, and boxed candy samples at the register.

Cake stores aren't merely aromatic; they're colorful. Before now, I'd seen only baking *aisles*—like at Michael's—never a whole store full of decorating media and tools devoted to the craft.

One rack displays food dye in about fifty different colors—one's called Flesh Tone (yum!). To paint your cakes or decorate your icings, you can use nonpareils, sanding sugar, edible glitter, sequins, luster dust (for painting on cakes with a brush), food pens (for hard icing or cookies), colored pastes, little sugar shapes—pumpkins and spiders and clowns—for any occasion, and edible dragées, hard silver or gold beads or almonds. (Avoid a cake faux pas; these are pronounced dra-ZHAYZ, not DRAG-eez.)

My neighbor Ann Roesner took decorating classes here. She showed off her creations to me, and I spent a lot of time in her kitchen once I learned where she'd stashed her practice buttercream: in a jar in the cabinet next to the fridge. When only the teenage daughters were home, I went in with a spoon—my own, yes—and headed for the jar. But when I learned she made her frosting from Crisco, I confronted her with the evils of shortening, conflicted about my indiscriminate taste buds and my whole-foods brain. "I'm pretty sure it's the only way you can make pure white icing," she said without a trace of indignation.

The Cake Cottage ladies concur. Butter will yield butter-colored buttercream. White food paste will whiten it some, but it won't be a true white. "The professionals," Susan Staehling tells me, "use high-ratio shortening." She points to a big tub called Sweetex, which contains partially hydrogenated soybean and palm oils with mono- and diglycerides added. "It doesn't give you that ungh on the tongue that Crisco does."

But which professionals? Reality show bakers like Duff Goldman or the homemakers next door with the newly honed knack for the shell border? Both. You probably can't imagine someone who is making a fortune on wedding cake squeezing his fillings or spreading his icings from tubes and tubs. But volume and purpose seem to be the determinants. If you're baking a lot or you're focusing on appearance, you're more likely to take a quicker route to the finish line.

It's a busy little store for a Thursday morning in the fall. The four employees, all women, are engaged in everything from inventory to phone orders, while customers come in for an item or two, like gift bags or a single cake pan. The two employees I meet, Rebecca Cook and Susan, are bakers themselves. All four are large women. They're not *too* large—all are agile and can climb ladders to reach items stored near the ceiling—but they are fleshy, as one might expect of cake hobbyists. (Aren't you just a tad curious about the skinny chef? A baker who isn't enamored of her own creations is somehow suspect.) When I comment on calories, the ladies shrug. When I grit my teeth over trans fats, they blow it off with a flick of the hand. I point to a rack of tubular plastic bags marked "Strawberry" and "Bavarian Cream" and "Cream Cheese." These, I'm told, keep for a long time when refrigerated. Susan uses them for filling the layers between cakes. But there's no nutrition information on the bag; what's in them? "I don't know," Susan says, and she's all right with that. In fact, she offers advice on what to do with the leftovers: just spoon some atop waffles or into pastry shells with a dollop of whipped cream. I think: waffles? I might have had one waffle in the last ten years. This stuff would probably defeat the purpose of the all-natural, frozen blueberry waffles I buy for my daughter. (I'm willing to bet the first ingredient is high-fructose corn syrup!)

I ask Rebecca what's new in the decorating world, and the answer is not so new, actually: fondant. The consistency of Play-Doh but the flavor of marshmallow (a homemade version calls for marshmallows, sugar, water, and shortening), fondant can be molded, sculpted, rolled, and stamped. You can make braids and balls, cut it with cookie cutters, even, it would appear, put it through the Play-Doh Fun Factory so that it spills out edible strings or stars. (Of course, they'll want to sell you the tools designed specifically for fondant.) The fondant shapes are attached to the cake by a bit of glaze or even water. But Rebecca says the taste isn't so good. A recipe for a homemade version, which she finds in a Wilton's catalog (they are to baking what Simplicity is to sewing), might yield better flavor, but she thinks probably not, as consistency is a challenge here. Indeed, the professionals (almost all of them, eventually) order premade fondant from various companies and color it themselves.

Also trendy in the cake world is the cupcake wedding cake. A customer agrees; she says they're easy, you can take them with you, you don't have to slice anything. I wonder quietly about how the cake cutting ceremony is handled, but I muse aloud that cupcakes have no corners or layers; the frosting is only at the top. Neither woman shares my concern. The cupcake cake is the wedding cake of the future, they say. But on an episode of the short-lived series *The Apprentice: Martha Stewart,* Sylvia Weinstock (perhaps the top cake decorator in the world) pooh-poohed this trend. People dressed for weddings shouldn't eat with their hands. Here, on blue-collar Belair Road, that seems to be less of a concern.

Cake Cottage offers decorating classes—a six-week session for just $45. Students buy their materials at the store: a kit of pastry tips, bags, a candy mold, and a flower nail for nearly $27; complete baking novices would need a selection of cake pans as well. And you can forget those flimsy, nonstick aluminum pans you buy at the grocery store; if this is going to be a serious hobby, you'll need the two-inch-deep pans with the rolled edges, the kind cake goddesses like Martha Stewart use. They can run anywhere from $16 to $30 each. Still, it seems like a bargain, especially for someone who has kids. Just a few cakes made at home instead of bought at Safeway would pay for the decorating lessons and equipment, and those skills are sure to come in handy later, when your sister needs a glamorous cake for her fortieth birthday next year.

To re-create that fancy bakery sheet cake, complete with the knickknacks that always wind up in the bottom of your child's toy chest, still sticky from being embedded in red frosting too bitter to lick, visit your local Cake Cottage. The books with the laminated pages of birthday cakes, which you use to select a cake from the bakery of your local grocery, are here; below them on shelves are the novelties to stick on the top of your own bitter red frosting: trucks, cars, airplanes; replicas of TV and movie characters like Shrek, Dora the Explorer, Frodo, and Harry Potter; random assorted junk like palm trees, dancers, surfers, clown heads, and bears; gambling-themed picks; and miniature equipment from every sport. My favorite is a plastic guy (Caucasian or African-American) on a plastic couch with a remote control in his hand and the slogan "World's Greatest Sports Fan."

"Where's the *woman* sports fan?" I ask Rebecca. Stupid question. She's probably in the kitchen baking the cake.

Some of the cakes have medallions in the center—flat, colored designs that look as if they're painted on. These are Edible Images, and they're kept in a file behind the counter. If someone wants to put her own photograph in the center of a cake, Cake Cottage can print it on a special edible paper with a Bakery Craft laser printer. I remark that the paper is ten calories and three carbs, and both Rebecca and Susan are surprised; neither has ever noticed the nutrition information on the package. Naturally. I am thinking about taking a sheet home and trying this in my own printer—daydreaming, really, about how cool it would be to type essays about cake on edible paper, the words in many-flavored inks—when Rebecca reads my mind and warns me. *Her* machine uses edible ink. I am not to even *try* to replace my own ink with the edible kind, as it would damage my printer and poison my cake's eaters.

I am overwhelmed by the number of products. Here are cake pans of every shape and size (except, apparently, five-inch round; the search for one is on when I arrive), dough blenders and rollers, dough molds and scoops, tart tampers, Roto Whippers, and all manner of rack and support and tier. (One of them—a seven-tiered, white plastic tower—I am told, is particularly popular for the wedding cupcakes.) For bakers who dislike dough beneath their fingernails, packages of white cotton Kneading Gloves await; the store has sold a number of them. Cake Cottage even sells premade buttercream frosting in nondescript white tubs similar to those containing high-ratio

shortening. This frosting is made with sugar, partially hydrogenated oils, a couple of imitation extracts, butter, and a few stabilizers and thickeners—a lot of ingredients for something that's supposed to be just butter, sugar, and a bit of milk. This is a whole tub of the trans fats your surgeon general warned you about.

Why, I wonder, would people go to all this trouble to decorate cakes and neglect to make them with pure ingredients? Susan used to make her frostings from scratch, but she was baking so many cakes that the premade route became easier. Besides, it tastes great. Her mother, she confides, likes to eat it by the spoonful. Perhaps Susan and I are cousins.

I want to take pictures of the rows of plastic clowns and toys, the wedding cake toppers that look like elegant dancers and kewpie dolls and dwarfs—glamorous couples alongside the cartoonish ones— but I am told that photographs aren't allowed. So instead, I buy two packages of frightening clown heads, a box of Magi-Cake strips ("For perfectly level, moist, prize winning cakes . . . everytime [*sic*]," a box of chocolate rocks for my daughter (who, when no one's looking, drops them on the playground at school, then bets a kid she can eat a rock—and does), and some Superior brand "The Original" Imitation

Vanilla, Butter and Nut Flavor, voted "best by test." Susan says the stuff goes like hotcakes because it has a pound cake recipe on it that people swear is the best. Customers don't write down the recipe because the cakes require this extract; it's the magic ingredient. I decide to try it out on my husband, since this is a cake I can surely resist eating. After all, the icing is what attracts me.

Like 300 million other American women, I could stand to lose fifteen pounds. And, like those women, I am always on a diet, except to my exasperated husband, who never knows whether he's supposed to offer me a bite of Aunt Margaret's chocolate cake this week or hide it in the truck. It's best that I don't know it exists; cake ignorance is weight bliss.

Before I leave, I add my name to the list of those returning for next month's cake decorating classes.

Pound for Pound

At five o'clock, I have no idea what I am making for dinner, but I am about to put a pound cake in the oven. I'm a sloppy baker. I can break eggs with one hand (a skill that not only looks impressive but is useful, as my other hand is often busy cleaning up the things I've knocked over with the egg hand), but I always wind up with batter on my shoes. Today, I'm wearing a pair of black toeless slides, and the drop lands between my first and big toes.

The recipe on the bottle of flavoring calls for shortening and margarine; I've already altered it by using all butter. ("It'll be richer," Susan Staehling told me earlier, her tone almost a warning.) Everything else—the six eggs, the three cups each of flour and sugar, and the cup of sweet milk—is by the book. (Sweet milk is whole milk. Susan once called the Superior Company to check, and they told her the recipe was from a time when "women milked their own cows.") The flavoring is added last, to the milk. It smells like an alcoholic version of candy corn—delicious. I am starting to regret my decision to make this cake. Maybe it won't be as resistible as I expect from a cake without frosting.

The last thing I do is soak one of those Magi-Cake strips and pin it to the tube pan. (I actually had to look up pictures of tube pans on the Internet to make sure I was using the correct thing. I had always called them Bundt pans, not realizing Bundt is a brand name.) But I should be *more* embarrassed that I didn't know pound cakes are supposed to emerge from the oven a bit like molten lava, split down the middle.

According to a couple of authorities on the subject—Rose Levy Beranbaum, author of *The Cake Bible,* and Bruce Healy, coauthor of *The Art of the Cake*—I have made my pound cake all wrong. I said I had made this cake "by the book" with the exception of my bad habit of softening butter in the microwave. Beranbaum may not have a problem with that; her pound cakes, dubbed "perfect," call for softened butter. But she orders her ingredients differently and uses baking powder and only a tiny bit of milk. Healy would find neither recipe very French. His traditional *quatres quarts* (named four fourths because the original pound cake recipe called for equal parts flour, butter, sugar, and eggs) wants each ingredient at a specific temperature: the eggs, for instance, are at room temperature; the butter is sliced and then creamed while still cold (unless your kitchen is cool); the superfine sugar is chilled in the fridge. Healy and Beranbaum can't even agree on what to use as a cake tester: she suggests a wooden toothpick; he opts for a knife, a toothpick or cake tester being under-endowed with sufficient surface area to which wet batter can cling.

If nothing else, I am a person who can follow directions, so I use this skill to sponsor my own Pound Cake Bake-Off, much to the delight of family and my many neighbors, all of whom seem to exhibit oodles more self-control than I. Or they are simply less foolish than to attempt weight maintenance and cake experimentation simultaneously.

My daughter comes in from tree climbing and wants to know what she smells. She spies the mixer attachment on a plate, and goes directly to eat whatever batter is left. She assumes it is for her and doesn't ask if she can eat it. Her eyes roll back in her head, our household code for yummy.

When it's out of the oven, I peel off a piece where the cake has split (despite the Magi-Cake). I am too impatient for a complete cooldown, so I turn the cake over onto the lid of a plastic cake holder. But, oh! It's far too pretty for plastic. I fish out my glass cake plate with the sterling silver base and reposition the fluted pound cake atop it, and then I take its portrait: my first cake as a—a cake researcher. My first pound cake. I pose it with a slice removed. I shoot the slice on a plate. I later upload its portrait to Flickr, a photo-sharing service that has dozens of groups devoted to cake making and decorating; group members share photos, tips, and recipes. And I add the recipe to my blog, A Cake Life.

I can't wait to take a hunk to my neighbor Ann, the cake decorator, who looks at me, wide-eyed. "It's so *moist*!" She's tried dozens of recipes for pound cake and always winds up with cakes that are dry on the inside and crusty on the outside. I tell her about the vanilla-butternut extract from Cake Cottage, and she reaches behind some things in a cabinet to find her own bottle. "There it is!" she says, surprised. I complain that the cake tastes a little artificial. Is it because I know the extract is imitation? Would real walnut and pure vanilla have made a difference? "Tastes good to me," says Ann's husband, Jim.

Back at home, my own spouse declares the cake as moist and delicious as any other. But my daughter thinks it's more *desert* than *dessert* and begs for ice cream. I want to tell her that she's right, that cake without frosting might as well be bread. But I am too busy chewing a piece, nodding, my heart starting to beat just a little faster with cake lust.

The pound cake has been around since at least the 1700s. In 1796, Amelia Simmons (whose byline includes "an American Orphan," as if this were her major credential) published this country's first cookbook,* entitled *American Cookery, or The Art of Dressing Viands, Fish, Poultry, and Vegetables, and The Best Modes of Making Pastes, Puffs, Pies, Tarts, Puddings, Custards, and Preserves, and All Kinds of Cakes, from the Imperial Plum to Plain Cake: Adapted to This Country, and All Grades of Life*. In an edition published by William B. Eerdmans Publishing Company in 1965, some of the original grammar is cleaned up a bit, though the author of the foreword assures readers that "[e]nough errors remain to leave the proper flavor of the original." (Also note that the printer's long or medial *s* [*f*] symbol of the time was used where we now use the short *s*.) Her recipe for pound cake calls for:

> One pound sugar, one pound butter, one pound cake flour, one pound or ten eggs, rofe water one gill, spices to your taste; watch it well, it will bake in a slow oven in 15 minutes.

Another recipe, which she calls "Another (Called) Pound Cake," says:

> Work three quarters of a pound butter, one pound of good sugar, 'till very white, whip ten whites to a foam, add the yolks and beat together, add one spoon rosewater, 2 of brandy, and put the whole to one and a quarter of a pound flour, if yet too soft add flour and bake slowly.

In more than two hundred years, the recipe has not changed much. Though we don't measure in gills (about five ounces) or use rosewater or, alas, brandy, a pound cake is a pound cake.

---

* Earlier cookbooks, such as E. Smith's *The Compleat Housewife,* published in 1742, were mostly reprints from European cookbooks. But so was Simmons's work, much of which was lifted, verbatim, from Susannah Carter's *Frugal Housewife*. Simmons's book was the first to incorporate native ingredients such as cornmeal and pearl ash, however, making it more American.

Simmons, the editor notes, was probably illiterate and relied on the assistance of someone for transcription. But this unknown person may have had designs on destroying Simmons's book with improper measurements. For instance, her rice pudding called for a half pound of butter and eight eggs, not a whole pound and fourteen eggs. The same year *American Cookery* was published, a second edition emerged with an advertisement explaining how she was undermined and correcting many of the errors. The first seventeen pages of the original book were detailed instructions on how to choose and prepare meats and produce. And though this was actually *good* advice, Simmons claimed it was included without her knowledge, as she'd never insult her readers' intelligence by implying their ignorance of such matters.

Bruce Healy's *quatres quarts* is in the oven. The countertop has a light dusting of flour, egg drops have dried there, too, and everything near the stove is covered with a greasy film from a morning spent attempting to clarify my own butter. (You can buy a ten-ounce jar from some fancy cooking catalogs for about ten dollars.) Both *The Cake Bible* and *The Art of the Cake* recommend clarified butter for the greasing of the cake pan; otherwise, the cake is likely to stick to the milk solids in regular butter. In economic terms, this means turning two sticks into one. I boiled the butter, skimmed the foam from the top, and strained the solids—several times. Eventually, I wound up with a delightfully clear butter with which to coat the loaf pan (to keep the cake from sticking), but I never got to use it. My loaf pans have a nonstick surface too slick to hold melted butter; it runs down the sides and pools on the bottom. I put the clarified butter in the fridge and rubbed a cold stick on the pan, which I then floured, same way I've done it all my life without incident.

Healy's instructions are easy, and the book is written in a way that made me feel he was standing over my shoulder, guiding me. "Faster! Keep beating," I imagined him saying as I gingerly upped the speed of my mixer to halfway between the six and the seven. "Medium-*high*," I heard him tell me, and I settled the lever on the seven. The butter and sugar mix was nearly white after five minutes of creaming. When I finished adding all the ingredients, I realized something was missing—missing from the butter, too. Salt! A sweet recipe that doesn't call for salt is a terrible mistake.

And then I licked the whisk. The Hallelujah Chorus sang.

The last cake had a sweet batter, but the taste was artificial. This one tasted like the liquid version of my beloved grocery store cake.

Silky and perfect, the batter went gently into the pan, and I smoothed and resmoothed it, eating whatever extras were captured in the process, and the loaf went into the oven. Within ten minutes, the aroma filled the dining room, calling me.

Now, twenty minutes before the cake is to be checked (after about an hour and fifteen to twenty minutes), I decide to get started on *The Cake Bible* version. Rose Levy Beranbaum is a woman's baker. Throw the wet ingredients together, throw the dry ingredients together, toss the in-between ingredients in, add some of the wet, add some more of the wet, add the rest. Voilà! I don't have to count mixing minutes or worry about temperatures (except for the eggs, which she likes at room temperature). And while I work, I hear the voice of my Jewish grandmother guiding me, only she isn't saying, "Beat it faster." She says, "This is how you live?" She says, "You're only going to have a *taste* of these cakes, right? You really don't need it." This is baking *and* guilt. This is home, at least mine, when the matriarchs would thrust the food upon you, become bitter if you reject it, then look at you askance if you put on weight.

The batter isn't quite as silky as the French version, but it is close, as is the color. I want to say that the flavor is *nearly* as outstanding. (Do I detect the most subtle hint of baking powder?)

It's ten minutes early, but I open the oven door to put in the second cake and check on the first. It's ruined! The top has browned. The sides have blackened. I turn it over on a plate, and a brick plunks out. If this were a state fair, I would be out of the competition instantly, though the judges would still taste the cake. I have to know what might have been, too, and I slice an overbaked heel from the right end and put a less crusty portion in my mouth. Despite the burn, it tastes like a sugar cookie. The interior of the cake is tender and finely crumbed but not moist. The flavor is light and fresh but not nearly sweet enough after all. I toss the rest of the hard heel and the one from the other end in the sink, quick to run water over it so as not to be tempted to give it a second chance, or a third. I have that tendency—to be a human garbage disposal, as if it doesn't count when you're only taste-testing it.

I watch Beranbaum's cake like a hawk. Her instructions call for covering it with buttered foil after thirty minutes, which I do. Then, every five, I check it to see whether it's done. My Jewish grandmother tells me to keep checking it. None of us trusts my oven now, despite its decades of faithful service. Fifteen years ago, it was reliable enough to accompany us to our Beverly Hills home. It has turned out many a perfect lasagna, meat loaf, turkey, custard, and cake, despite the window's layers of grease and burn.

When *The Cake Bible*'s cake is done, I compare all three cakes to each other. I don't want to feel as though the Healy concoction has been given short shrift by the nasty brown crusts, but the French version does not compare. It *shouldn't,* after all, get a thick, hard crust around it, should it? The first cake had no hint of a crust, just a golden color. The Beranbaum version, slightly crusty, also tastes like a sugar cookie. It is fresh, dense, and lightly sweet, though I still find it lacking in moisture.

Of the three, the first—with the recipe from the bottle of imitation extract—made the best-looking, moistest cake. I take some of today's experiment to Ann and her husband. They are happy to oblige me but are not impressed with the results. Both liked the first cake best. Marty thinks the flavors of the two loaf cakes are nearly identical; Serena says they taste like pancakes without the syrup. Both agree that they aren't sweet enough to remain frosting-less.

When I next make a pound cake—though I need to lose at least three pounds first—it is version #1, with pure vanilla extract and superfine sugar. It is delicious. After taste-testing it over and over again, because one can never be too sure, I cut a small hunk and drop it at my girlfriend's house for her birthday. She has a bite and calls it "the best pound cake *ever*!"

"Better than Sara Lee?"

"Ew! Sara Lee is *terrible* pound cake."

I remember an old friend who was hooked on the stuff for breakfast and recall that she considered herself a connoisseur. I am officially flattered and decide that this is the cake I will enter in the Baltimore Book Fair's Tenth Birthday recipe contest. It doesn't make the final round, in which, of seven oddly misshapen and interestingly homemade-looking cakes, one is a pound cake—maple.

At least on the butter, Healy is the winner. My mom calls one day to tell me that Mark Scarbrough, from the Ultimate Cook, told radio listeners that butter should *not* be added to cake batter at room temperature. It won't hold any air unless it's cold. This way, the butter can provide a protective coating around the flour, and that will keep it from getting too wet, which would result in a chewy, breadlike cake. "The fat molecules must be fairly cold (68 degrees F or below) to build structure and trap air molecules when beaten. Otherwise, the fat molecules liquefy, which means they'll trap as much air as water when beaten—in other words, a very little, not a lot." If you're making brownies, though, "liquid-ish fat" is good.

Scarbrough says, when I ask him one day in February, that the information comes from the brilliant Harold McGee's *On Food and Cooking*. "I believe there's more of the same in Corriher's *Cookwise,* but I wouldn't swear to it on a sunny Saturday afternoon in rural New England where I could just be addled by the freakishly warm weather." Hands and old-time mixers are far less powerful than the hulking kitchen machines we have today, so the warm butter tip was probably out of a necessity that no longer exists. So why haven't cookbook authors stopped adding that instruction? "I'm not sure why more people don't pay attention to these sorts of things—except to say that cookbooks, as you well know, are sort of like Dante's *Inferno:* a strange business, as much lore as fact. They tend to exist in some red-state universe where re-creating the past is as important as creating the present." He even has to fight his own editors to keep them from warming the butter in his recipes.

Greg Patent, author of *Baking in America* and other fine explorations of cuisine, has similar experiences in his kitchen, especially when it comes to pound cake—particularly Eliza Leslie's "receipt" for a version with cornmeal. He says, "Baking the almost two-hundred-year-old recipe made me feel an unexpected kinship with Miss Leslie. It was as if she were with me in my kitchen. Past and present coexisted. What other treasures, I wondered, might I find by delving into old cookbooks? Would I be as successful at resurrecting them as I had been with the Indian Pound Cake?"

Following that 1829 recipe does not conjure the spirits of Miss Leslie or Mr. Patent or Indians or colonists. But it is the first cake my daughter makes, almost by herself, from start to finish. The day before her school closes for spring break, the fourth-grade class wraps up a history unit called Westward Ho (this time, the ho in question is someone else) with a party. The kids can dress like colonists and are invited to bring in treats such as beef jerky, corn muffins, and root beer. A sign-up sheet came home a few days earlier, and I chose the easiest and healthiest of the snacks, beef jerky. (Its diet friendliness had no influence on my choice; I swear.) Serena wasn't pleased; she is as gung ho for root beer as I am for cake. My husband voted for corn muffins and offered to supervise, so I am prepared with cornmeal, a cheap stone-ground version with an Indian on it, and an easy Internet recipe, one with more than the ¼ cup of sugar called for on the bag.

The KitchenAid mixer on the counter and most of the ingredients out, including brand-new muffin tins (this project was a good excuse to replace the ancient tins with the fork gouges from where cupcakes have stuck for the past eighteen years), Serena announces that two other students have also signed up for corn muffins. "What's the point of a sign-up sheet?" I wonder. It's supposed to ensure an equal mix of goodies, variety instead of three different versions of the corn muffin for twenty-four.

I have my aha! moment. I'm no history expert—that's my husband's area—but Westward Ho is mid-1800s colonist stuff. What could be more perfect than Miss Eliza Leslie's receipt? I wrangle the last seven eggs, round up two whole cups of sugar, cornmeal, and cake flour. It's perfect, and I'm excited that we're going to contribute some authentic historical food. But Marty and Serena are not convinced that a cake from Miss Eliza Leslie, herself a Westward ho, will be a welcome contribution, so we call Miss Novak. She's a tough cookie, but even I know the sign-up sheet was for the benefit of the snack illiterate. Otherwise, strawberry frosted toaster tarts and malted eggs would be on the menu.

Miss Novak's not home, but I get my family excited about a historically accurate cake, and there's no turning back. We have everything except rosewater—the recipe calls for two tablespoons—so I double up on brandy; we have some apricot Leroux (a whole case of it). I add a quarter cup to the batter and make Serena promise she won't tell anyone that there's liquor in the cake.

I should not have been such a fervent supporter of this idea, as I am officially "off cake" for a while. I am off cake off and on, like some people are off coffee or off beer or off their rockers.

I call out the instructions, and Serena follows them, sifting flour, measuring salt and spices, breaking eggs into separate bowls, and adding the eggs to creamed butter, one at a time, using my clever discovery: break all the eggs for a recipe into a bowl, even if they are to be added one at a time. As long as you don't pierce the yolks, you can simply tilt the bowl until one yolk goes into the batter. The right amount of white will follow it, as evidenced by the last remaining yolk, which is surrounded by the perfect amount of white.

My kitchen is a mess. Where are you, Miss Leslie? Why aren't your cleanliness and godliness here with me, in this room? But among the technological noises—background hum of TV sitcom, strum of guitar wafting from the basement, and whir of mixer on low—Eliza Leslie's spirit is exorcized.

Halfway through baking time, the kitchen fills with billowing smoke. Some batter has leaked from the tube pan onto the bottom of the oven, and it's burning. I scrape a thick, hard blop with a spatula and drop the steaming bubble into the sink, and all is well for the remaining thirty minutes. When the cake is done and has cooled for ten minutes, I lose my head and attempt to remove the ring of cake from the tube. It doesn't slide and instead breaks into three pieces, which is exactly what my daughter had hoped would happen. She waits next to my mixer for any kind of accident, like my dog, Chance, waits for pretzels to fall while I make lunches every morning.

Serena gets her bite. She says she can taste the brandy and worries that it will make her classmates drunk. We later discover it's the nutmeg imparting such an overpowering flavor. It's worth keeping for authenticity, but I'm not a fan. (If I liked pumpkin, and if I liked pie, I would still dislike pumpkin pie because of the nutmeg.)

On second taste (and third, and fourth), nutmeg notwithstanding, the cake is pretty delicious. It's probably a little too sophisticated for the twenty-four nine- and ten-year-old kids, the crumb not so fine, the spice strong, but my daughter has the verdict. I pick her up early for our third annual let's-avoid-the-stations-of-the-cross-school-mass luncheon. "Lauren and Deanna were the only ones who didn't like the cake, and Miss Novak wants the recipe. Everyone said, 'Wow, this is good.' " I could see the delight in her face.

Like anyone who cooks or bakes, I live for that. Now, so does my daughter.

Decorating Tips

I return to Cake Cottage sometime in November with my supplies list, which includes the aforementioned kit; a small, angled spatula (called *offset*); toothpicks; a practice board or cookie sheet; a damp dishcloth in a plastic bag; a paper and pencil; an empty sack for used equipment; an apron or smock; and, included with the kit, two couplers (used inside a pastry bag so that you can change tips without needing a new bag), two 10-inch pastry bags, and decorating tips, metal fittings with a large opening on one end and a narrow, odd-shaped opening on the other, through which frosting is squeezed out in various shapes. I pick up the required tips: 1, 2, 3, 4, 12, 13, 16, 18, 21, 35, 48, 104, 190, 349, and 352. Three hundred fifty-two? Could there really be more than three hundred tips among those designated for petals and leaves, closed and open stars, drop flowers, shells, basket weaves, ruffles, dots, and Hershey's Kiss–shaped blobs?

The Wilton Web site displays at least 151 tips in twelve different categories, each pictured beside a colored-frosting example of the pattern it makes. Southpaws can even purchase special left-handed drop flower and petal tip sets. Though the numbering system is baffling—

for instance, decorators can choose from among twenty-three drop flower tips, but the tips are not numbered sequentially; a few are in the 100s, some are in the 190s, and there's a 220. A seasoned decorator knows her #1 from her #2; however, beginners must rely upon the tiny numeral barely etched in one spot of the metal tip.

In addition to the tools and tips, I must bring a batch of butter-cream icing to the first lesson. The recipe—a special concoction of the instructor—calls for an assortment of unnatural ingredients, the flavor shortcomings of which are made up for with artificial extracts. The first ingredient is a famous brand of shortening whose label boasts "half the saturated fat of butter." (What it doesn't tout is its dangerous trans fats.) Though I am an opponent of faux foods like high-fructose corn syrup and hydrogenated oils, I still want to be one of the girls at the decorating class. Baker Leslie Poyourow, of Fancy Cakes by Leslie, advises me to go for the canned stuff; after all, she says, "You're not going to eat it; you're just going to decorate with it!" Ha! I go to the grocery store prepared to get the icky white lard when another option presents itself: icky *butter-flavored* lard! This would surely eliminate the need for the imitation butter, though I will be stuck with yellow-colored buttercream, which I won't mind. My choice has also negated the need for the clear vanilla extract (which comes only in artificial, since vanilla has a color). I also forgo the Van-O-Van, a powdered vanilla that our instructor says gives this frosting a natural aroma.

I am early so I can buy what I still need and save 10 percent with my paid class membership receipt. The class is held in the back of the store in a large room with three tables, a mock kitchen, and a mirrored ceiling over the instructor's work counter. Carole Eaves has been teaching this class for fifteen years, and her methods and techniques haven't changed much, though they do, now and again, accommodate this or that technological miracle. First, Carole wants us all to relax. "We're gonna have a lot of fun!" she says. The people in the room are nodding and smiling. This is, after all, cake decorating; it is not colonoscopy prep. She tells us it's okay if we're late; if we haven't eaten yet, she urges us to stop at Wendy's and bring dinner with us. "It's a relaxed atmosphere."

My buttercream is blended, my tips are lined up, and I am ready to learn. Beginner decorating lessons are not just for frumpy moms and old ladies; this is the way even top bakers begin. Like former *Sugar Rush* host Warren Brown, they discover that what they bake is delicious, but it doesn't look as pretty as it could. So they buy a book (in Brown's case, *The Art of the Cake*), or they take lessons (often Wilton lessons at Michael's or their local crafts store). Students decorate their kids' or friends' cakes for practice and fun, and soon those friends start to commission birthday cakes, rather than buy a baked-without-love sheet cake from the local grocery store bakery. A couple of years later, those same friends request wedding cakes. After a decade of baking, perhaps one could become another Leslie Poyourow, a contest-winning D.C. baker who started exactly this way and now bakes cakes for the likes of senators and celebrities, among them Annie Leibovitz.

I do not want to become a cake decorator. I am content to be a cake ogler, cake eater, cake lover. But it would be nice to display my delicious *Silver Palate* carrot cake without its hideousness misrepresenting its taste, so I am eager to learn these sugar secrets, like how the buttercream basket gets woven, how the perfect rose blooms from a #104 tip. Perhaps I will discover a new talent, learn that I am a natural who really can be called upon to make the cakes for whatever family celebration happens to be just around the corner. Corner. Best part of the cake. I want to work in square.

After a brief overview of the six lessons, Carole invites us to stand and hold hands with the people to our right and left. It's not some sort of get-to-know-your-neighbor, touchy-feely love fest; she wants us to identify whose hands are cold and whose are hot. To my right, a woman named Stacey has warm hands. The woman on my left is cold. My own usually frozen fingers are surprisingly warm; I have had both a hot flash and a beer in the last hour. This will be my weekly fate and failing. Those who have cold hands have the advantage in that the heat from warm hands will penetrate the pastry bag, rendering icing limp and pushing lazy shapes through the metal tips.

The room is full to capacity, with five people at each table. Most of us are women of about forty, though two are significantly younger. Four women and one man are black, and there is an older white man who has so much to say one might think he has done this before.

Our first lesson is on the ingredients. Carole extols the virtues of Crisco, explaining why all buttercream frosting should be made with it; she does not mention hydrogenization or trans fatness. I ask if I can use butter, and, though she's not averse to it, she thinks it best that I use Crisco for the class; this way, she can be sure it will set up properly. After telling us that icing keeps, unrefrigerated, four to six weeks, that any longer and it won't taste fresh, she introduces us to yet another artificial flavor called Cream Bouquet, which, she says, makes the frosting taste fresh. Each ingredient in her recipe has a purpose: the artificial butter extract to make people think the frosting is made with butter, the clear vanilla extract to keep the frosting white, the Van-O-Van because it "makes it smell good," the salt because it cuts the sweetness of all that "confectionary" sugar. It seems lots of faux freshness is needed when the ingredients themselves aren't real or fresh. Someone asks why she adds marshmallow fluff. "Oh, it just tastes good."

While Carole talks, she frosts a cake that we will be eating later. This is now the focus of my night. (Ever try to teach a dog a new trick while you're dangling a steak?) She shows the class how to use cardboard and a lazy Susan, how to use icing as glue to hold the cake still. She discusses the crumb coat (the thin layer of frosting applied over the bare cake to keep the crumbs contained) while demonstrating the process. And while she talks and frosts, she gives us more hints about baking and gadgets: for instance, a previously frozen cake tastes better and more moist than a fresh one (perhaps because the moisture freezes, then melts); fondant smoothers can be used to spread icing; jelly filling bleeds through the cake. For a moment, I feel like I am in the audience of an infomercial. In just thirty minutes, our instructor has pitched must-have tools like cake towels (to smooth icing without leaving a pattern), Wilton cake keepers, lazy Susans, and six food items not sold in other stores. She tempts us, in a hushed voice, with her back alley prices: "They sell 'em in the store for $2.99, but I have some back here for $1" (we all line up for those fondant smoothers after class). In weeks to come, she will have a gigantic cardboard box full of metal tips for a quarter apiece (they're regularly a dollar), containers of white plastic baskets used as wedding favors, trunks full of children's cake toppers that didn't sell well, and some single items to the lucky first-comer.

We all marvel at the flatness of Carole's cakes, which gives her the opportunity to plug the Magi-Cake strips, which kept my husband's annual carrot cake from sinking in the middle. The reason these work is that the oven tends to cook the outside of the cake—the part next to the metal—first; the strips keep the edges cool so that the middle of the cake can finish baking at the same time. Still, our teacher has had to cut about an inch off the top of each layer because her recipe makes the cake a little crusty. She puts the two cake layers together by turning the top one upside down. Next, she hefts an unwieldy tubular bag of red glurp, the same nutrition label–less stuff that Cake Cottage staffer Susan Staehling says is great on waffles. Carole likes this filling because it doesn't bleed, and the leftovers taste great on toast. While she works, our instructor teases us; she will not share her cake recipe until the end, after we have tasted it. She is confident that we'll like it; she wants us to gasp with surprise and awe when she tells us how it's made: not from scratch but from two different mixes, the way many of the neighborhood baker ladies have learned. (My neighbor Val, a gourmet cook, recently confessed to cheating with a coconut cake. She doctors a mix with cream of coconut and sour cream.)

When the display cake has been frosted and smoothed with various devices, when the new top layer is no longer tacky, she begins the decorating process by placing a chocolate candy basket on the top and filling it with frosting flowers. She makes hyacinths and sweet peas in an instant. In between decorations, she has us cut and put couplers on our reusable pastry bags, add our tips, and fill the bags by folding the tops down over our hands. We make a handmade bag out of parchment triangles; the benefit of these is that they are disposable and only a penny—as opposed to the ready-made disposable plastic ones that cost a nickel apiece.

Students converge on the front of the room to watch more closely as Carole makes decorative stars and swags on the outside of the cake using a pink plastic garland marker ("just $2.99 in the store") to measure, and then we are sent back to our seats with instructions: create large stars on our practice board, then make our initials out of small stars. While we work, she comes around to test the consistency of our frostings and check on our progress. My stars are declared fine; my frosting, medium (medium-soft is desired).

When the first lesson is all over, while our mouths are stuffed with sample cake, and some of us are oohing and ahhing over its goodness (not me, by the way; I am prejudiced against boxed mixes and scratch frostings with artificial ingredients, and I suspect this cake uses both, not to mention that it was ruined with jelly between the layers), Carole tells the story of how her recipe won a contest and became Governor Mandel's cake. She was embarrassed when she had to tell them it was a combination of Duncan Hines and Washington Pound Cake mix.

After class, the store is open for about twenty minutes more, which gives Cake Cottage the perfect opportunity to sell all those interesting gadgets Carole pitched. I get in line for an offset spatula and some colored gels.

The following week, we return with six cupcakes, frosted; a batch each of yellow, green, and white frosting; and some clown heads.

Some of the students, like Jessica, have piped the icing on with a special tip; some have arrived with bare cupcakes, waiting to see what others have done; the talkative man has store-bought, emerald-green-iced chocolate cupcakes with colored Necco-wafer sprinkles; most of us, however, have our white cupcakes smeared with a big swash of white (or, in my case, pale yellow), not unlike the sloppily frosted gourmet cupcakes sold in Warren Brown's CakeLove on U Street in Washington, D.C. My cupcakes, made from scratch from an Internet recipe, have a slight mound at the top, and their consistency is dense and muffinlike, a problem that Carole thinks might have been caused by too much flour.

We don't do the clowns right away. Instead, we gather at the front to learn a few new moves: rosettes, rosettes with stars, rosebuds, leaves, stems, sepals with the #1 tip, sepals with the small leaf tip, and the shell border, probably the most oft-piped design in the whole cake-decorating repertoire. Carole's hands are large but graceful. With flicks of the wrist, she makes precise, controlled patterns. Then she shows us the ways we could screw up this motion: by not touching the tip to the board, by leaning it too far forward or backward, by holding it too far away or too close. "Don't do this," she says, erring gracefully. "And don't do this," she says, another mistake made with a subtle change of motion. And then she makes several more perfect shells. Between each lesson, we're sent back to our seats to practice on our boards, green and yellow icing in our pastry bags. But it's a lot to remember, so we go back up with our boards and bags, at her urging, to watch her do it again or have her guide our hands.

I had decided, both because I am lazy and because it's okay to do, to use disposable plastic bags, but I suffer now with this decision. They don't open widely enough to fill, and they trap so much air that most of my practice moves have skips and squiggles from bag farts. Eventually, I get the hang of the rosettes and roses; my leaves are a little more realistic than the cookie-cutter jobs turned out by Carole and many of the students, but here, originality is undesirable. Stems and sepals are not much of a challenge, but I cannot master the shell, and I fear this has more to do with me than my pastry bag. Our last trick, the sweet pea, finds me hopeless. I am not a natural. I may never get that "Ugly" sign off my carrot cake.

What's the matter with me? I have created enormous mosaic sculptures, have cut glass in perfect quarter-inch squares; I have requested things like jigsaws and shop vacs for birthday presents. I have been on HGTV for my artistic prowess, for heaven's sake! How can squeezing shells and sweet peas from a bag with these fine, work-horse hands elude me?

For each new practice session, we wipe our boards clean with our spatulas; I mound my icing on a paper towel, which I plan to throw away at the end of the lesson, but most of it winds up in my mouth. I seem to be the only one with sticky fingers, and there's a white crust of sugar at the corners of my mouth. Each week I become more self-conscious about my eating the test patterns.

Now it's time to make our clowns. We're armed with bags of plastic clown heads, mine bought on my first visit for their creepy appeal, six frosted cupcakes, and our green and yellow pastry bags with the #21 and #16 star tips, respectively. Carole grabs a woman's cupcake and makes a sitting clown. First, she pipes a giant green shell for the torso. She plunges the clown head into it, then draws arms and legs. With the yellow, she makes his buttons, hands, and shoes. It's a perfect little character.

When it's our turn to make a seated clown on our own cupcakes, I get up a few times to eye the example, plan my squeezing strategy. I can barely manage the torso; the limbs come out wiggly, a combination of pastry-bag air and decorator's impatience. I attempt to hide my clown's flaws by adorning him with yellow stars in unusual places.

Carole demos a different clown at each table: one reclines on his side, an elbow propping his head up; one lies on his stomach, behind up in the air, hands holding on to the cupcake's side; still another lies on his back, belly up. I can make none of these, and to compensate for my lack of skill, I pipe sloppy stars around the rim of the cupcake, then pop them all into my containers before anyone can see the mess I made. The woman to my left—with the ice-cold hands from the first day—has clowns that look far worse than mine. She is a small wisp of a woman with a powder blue turban and flowing clothes. She has said nothing to anyone, just makes a silent mess and seems content with it, even proud. And someone at home loves her. She takes home to them her drunken clowns, like she takes everything else, and her kids are probably as grateful as mine is. They probably see her as a confectionery queen in a powder blue crown.

The following Wednesday is the evening before Thanksgiving, and I will be at my mother-in-law's house on Maryland's Eastern Shore and so will have to miss the class to which we will each bring our own prefrosted cake and prepare to transfer a design (turkeys, footballs, pumpkins, and pilgrim hats are the examples) and decorate it; students are encouraged to make something festive for Thanksgiving dinner.

Patterns are transferred by an easy process. Usually, decorators begin with a simple coloring-book-style picture. A piece of waxed paper is placed over the design, and black gel (available in tubes from any grocery store) is piped on the black outline. The waxed paper is then turned upside down atop a frosted cake, the black pressed into the cake to stain it with the sticky gel pattern. The next step requires black buttercream to be piped over the place-holding black gel, and then the colors of the pattern are filled in using various star tips.

To keep up with the class, I make a carrot cake at home and attempt the lesson without guidance. I slice off the tops, which are gobbled down greedily by my daughter and her friend, then sandwich cream cheese filling between the layers. On top, I use buttercream instead of cream cheese, which never firms up enough for a perfectly smooth surface. Just as I'd been taught, I give the naked cake a crumb coat, that thin layer of frosting designed to hold the crumbs that come loose in the icing process. The secret is that once your spatula touches the cake, it can't be reinserted into the batch of frosting; otherwise, you'll be spreading tiny ruinous crumbs around, and the surface will never be smooth. It is as easy as it looked that first night of class. Once the coat has set, I load my offset spatula with thick blobs of icing and smear it on the sides and top. Then, with the tool at an angle, I even out the mess. A longer spatula would be ideal, but I work with what I have, turning the cake as I smooth. I do the same with the top.

I remember a trick Carole taught us for smoothing out the cake, and I try it first with a paper towel. I fold it into a small square, press it against the set frosting, and smooth the towel with my fingers. Except for the tiny dots—goose bumps, really—left by the paper towel, it's smooth. In fact, it looks *almost* as professional as any cake I'd buy at the store.

I choose a clip-art oak leaf in orange and yellow for the top of the cake and trace it on waxed paper with a tube of black gel. It transfers perfectly to the cake top. Rather than using black buttercream to outline the leaf, I use brown (mixing the yellow and green I already have with some red food coloring). I pipe the leaf outline, the stem, and the veins with my #2 tip. With my smallest star tip, and with yellow and orange frosting, I fill the leaves. Though they are not sensational, I am feeling tickled, so I attempt a bottom-edge border, sort of a squished star pattern—a mistake turned into an invention, only it doesn't look so good. I repeat the pattern in a different color on top of the first, and the look doesn't improve; now it looks like an off-register, two-color print, the kind that looks blurry and messes with your eyes.

Mired in misguided "more is more" philosophy, I attempt to write "Gobble" in a large blank spot where butter-color space had already worked its magic. We will not learn cake writing until week five. Anyone who's ever tried to write on a cake would know how difficult it is, so it's no surprise to me that even something as simple as lettering has a trick. I have not learned yet that letters should be tall and skinny, the strokes made north/south, rather than east/west. Unhappy with the *G,* I attempt to remove it with a toothpick. But because my pastry bag was not completely dry when I filled it, my cake now has an unsightly smear of green on the bottom right. To hide it, I cover the cake with small green measles. I tsk and fret. But my daughter—who views cake with a lust similar to my own—declares it magnificent.

My attempt to save a few dollars by buying a cake carrier at Shoppers (made by Betty Crocker) instead of at Cake Cottage (made by Wilton) proves not only futile but foolish. The night before Thanksgiving, after the cake has survived a two-hour drive to the Eastern Shore and a night in the refrigerator, the frosting meets an untimely demise. As my brother-in-law carries it to the car, the handle of the Crocker cake carrier (which nowhere bears her name once the sticker is removed) becomes unhinged, and the lid, which doesn't seal shut, slides off as the cake hits the ground. Both layers of carrot cake are intact—nothing is crushed or lopsided—but the frosting is covered with black dirt and blue fuzz from the rug in the garage. I spend the next twenty minutes drinking snifters of brandy and scraping off three batches of buttercream and two hours of hard work. I feel like a soldier having come home from a brutal war only to get hit by a car. Okay, it's not that bad. It's just a cake, after all. But damn it!

Once we take turns inspecting it (some of us have poor vision; others have too much brandy) to be sure it is dirt- and fuzz-free, I frost it again, this time with cream cheese, butter, and confectioners' sugar. I make sloppy crisscross patterns in the icing with a fork and declare it done. Truth be told, it tastes—and looks—better this way. At the Thanksgiving dinner, guests will be told of the cake's former glory, of a masterpiece the likes of Rembrandt, of the glorious painted dessert that had arrived in good condition just yesterday. But no one will care. As usual, it will be one of the first of eight assorted pies and cakes (including various pecan and pumpkin) to be eaten. (The sugar-free chocolate ganache cheesecake, which I made, goes first; the hall is full of fat, dieting, and diabetic family members.)

One week later, after I've gotten the homework from my young classmate, Jessica—whose work is the envy of table one, if not the whole room—and sent it to Stacey, who also missed the Thanksgiving week class, I arrive early for cake class to have a heart-to-heart with the instructor. I tell her about the cake, about my feelings of inadequacy. "I know you said this is supposed to be stress-free and fun. But I suck!" I say. A pathetic, exasperated sigh follows my admission.

Carole's look is earnest. "Now, are you speaking as a beginner? Or are you comparing yourself to me?"

I look around the room for Jessica, the girl whose cake is two layers of perfection, crumb coated and iced smooth, an elegant, flat, perfect blank canvas. She is rummaging through a deep box full of assorted odd metal tips. I point: "Her."

Jessica smiles. I must have been blinded by her white frosting and forgotten that she had worked in a bakery a few years ago. Though she's enrolled in a beginner's class, she's technically a pro.

"See?" my cake teacher asks. She's not quite sure what's wrong with the way I frosted my cake this week. While it's clear I don't have icing towels, it's a fine start. Carole does, however, locate a problem: my cake plate, which is nothing but the plastic bottom of a cheap cake carrier. "This is flexible," she says. It has made my icing crack.

Once again, having the right equipment is essential. So I turn around and march into the Cake Cottage with my credit card, where I rack up a tidy sum on a Wilton cake holder (which I will use at least six times between now and summer), a large offset spatula, and some cookie cutters. I don't spend the additional twenty on a lazy Susan; later, I get a sturdy wooden one for five dollars at Ikea.

Tonight, the table usually piled high with stock is topped, instead, with various types of candy, leftovers from a candy-making class. Peppermint buttons and white-chocolate-covered pretzel sticks and turtles and brickle and more delicious handmades line the table, and students are encouraged (begged, even) to partake. I have arrived with new resolve (having, as we say in my family, "eaten like I had two assholes" over Thanksgiving) to avoid sugar at all costs. I bundle up a few of the red-and-green-sprinkled, white chocolate pretzels— for my daughter and husband—in a paper napkin and put them in my bag. The milky pink peppermints call to me, and I muffle their voices in another napkin.

This evening, we temper chocolate and pour it into our basket sugar molds; Carole pops these into the freezer, while we practice some patterns we learned the first night: the sweet pea and rose, the stem, sepals, and leaves. Though I rush the process, I learn that I don't suck. I am adept at a few of the patterns; I have wanted to call them "moves" or "stitches" or "dance steps" since this whole thing began. I practice my sweet pea about forty times before committing it to cake top. We squirt some frosting glue near the bottom of the cake and stick the chocolate basket to it. My rosettes and rosebuds are nearly perfect. My hyacinths—three columns of stars on a stem, long leaves on either side—are well formed. Though my leaves are inconsistent— some like natural beauties, others resembling penises—they will come. (The leaves, I mean.) I'm still not comfy with borders, but my garland around the side of the cake works.

When I return home with my finished Easter cake that night in November, I unveil it with pride to the ooohs and ahhhhs of my husband and child, who wait a day before having a slice. I can hardly stand to be sugar-free in a house with a cake. It takes four days for my resolve to crumble, and, to my surprise, the cake tastes awful. Made from a mix—Duncan Hines Moist Deluxe White Cake (one dollar per box)—it is so cloying that it seems to climb up the back of my throat and crawl into my nose. My own frosting is halfhearted, too; to keep from wanting to lick it, I made the stuff with pure white Crisco and no butter flavor or marshmallow fluff.

Despite the fact that I hate the flavor for all of those reasons, I eat it, much of it, until very little is left. I am able to convert my taste buds—or at least acclimate them—to this bad cake. Even a bad cake is attractive. Even the shortest orgasm is a good one. I attempt, one afternoon, to throw away the stale reminders, but at least as much as I discard winds up in my mouth before it hits the wet sink.

The following week, we practice our roses. "Roses are really more advanced, but I kept them in the beginner's class because people really wanted to learn them," Carole tells the group assembled at the front counter. She pipes a Hershey's Kiss–shaped blob on a rose nail (really a long, fat nail with a half-dollar-size flat head), then explains the motions involved. Using the large petal tip, #104, narrow end upward and tilted in, she builds the tight bud. She makes it look so easy that we are all eager to try. Next, with the narrow end straight up, she pipes three of the bud's petals. Then, with the narrow end tilted outward, she pipes a row of five petals under those and a row of seven around the bottom. She makes five of them in seconds and sends us back to try it.

Nervous giggles and frustrated sighs begin to fill the room. Carole announces her availability, and almost all of us allow her to guide our hands. My first few roses look like freaks of nature; the petals appear thick and waxy looking. I've had my tip upside down. Once I right it, I expect the roses to form perfectly, but nearly all of them sink as I attempt the tight center bud. The petals have cracked edges, as if the icing is too dry. (It's not; the rose Carole helps me form is perfect.) Our goal is twenty roses that look good enough to top a cake. We're to return the night of the last class with these and ten drop flowers, air dried, along with a batch of chocolate buttercream and a cake that has a mounded top (no Magi-Cake strips!).

Many of us are frustrated and exhausted, so Carole invites us up for a drop-flower lesson before sending us back to practice those on our boards. This one is a breeze; I don't have any problem making perfect little drop flowers. So I go back to the rose and wind up with a few keepers, which I place in a box. Jessica, having made her twenty

in the first few minutes, is helping a classmate. Carole calls attention
to Jessica's box of roses, and someone on the other side of the room
yells, "She's the teacher's pet." He was kidding, of course, but there
is a bit of friendly competition in this room. I can't help but notice
the work of the woman next to me, the frigid-handed turban lady.
She hasn't uttered more than a grunt (I think I asked to borrow her
scissors, and she nodded) in five weeks. Her cake is short and small.
It's lopsided, and the flowers look like the reflection in a fun house
mirror. They are warped and wobbly. Though I am sad for her, I am
secretly pleased that my cakes don't look half as bad.

In two hours, we have each, with a few exceptions, made and recycled at least fifty roses. It's time to go home, and many of us are still
trying to get it. Carole tells us the story of her first rose lesson while
we clean up. When she first learned to decorate, she couldn't get
the hang of these things. They looked just awful. One night, when
the kids were in bed, she took out her bag and tips and began to
practice. Something clicked that night, and she has been making perfect roses ever since. It will happen that way for us, too, she promises.
One day.

I feel much better about my skills now that I've seen some im-
provement. I'm still working on resisting the cake, but Carole says a
time will come when I will see buttercream as nothing more than a
sculpting medium. It's possible, at least with the Crisco version. After
you've spent any amount of time attempting to remove it from your
hands and decorating tools and trying to scrub the greasy film from
your pastry bags, it's hard to feel romantic. (I remember overhearing
a discussion on the first night about which dishwashing liquid works
best on this cleanup challenge and bought Dawn on my classmates'
recommendation; it works.)

I spend the week before the last class researching frostings, trying
to come up with one that yields a perfect consistency but doesn't coat
the tongue with a greasy film. I find something made with less Crisco
and more butter and make a batch, which I color the brightest, most

artificial blue. My last cake will be a chocolate buttercream basket, and I love the way blue looks with brown. I plan to make the drop flowers white. It will be breathtakingly beautiful and delicious tasting at the same time. I have psyched myself up to do this.

On the weekend, when my husband and daughter have gone out for a few hours, I plug in a rose petal tip and fill my pastry bags with blue, then make myself comfortable at the kitchen table, where I have plenty of room to work and a place to rest my twenty perfect roses. In one hour, I have nothing—not a single flower wrapped itself properly around the nail, not one rosebud sat, tight and perky, atop the wide nail head. I keep a cool head, though, and wait a few days before dumping two double batches of frosting down the garbage disposal. I am so crushed, even resentful, that I don't taste a lick of it. I punish it by withholding my affection.

Roseless and cakeless on the Wednesday before Christmas, I choose, instead, to finish the two scarves I am knitting. I ditch the last class.

I doubt the time will ever come that real, buttery, creamy buttercream frosting on a moist white foundation no longer floats my boat. But I also doubt that I will put my new decorating skills to use; they'll likely lie dormant until someone begs me to dust off the old #104 tip. And it's just as well. For me, the pleasure of a bite is that much more sublime when someone else is responsible for its perfection.

In the holiday edition of *PCD's Cooking Enthusiast,* a catalog for "passionate cooks," one can purchase, in addition to Polish pottery and professional torches: five pounds of fondant for $30; a "Professional Decorating Tube Set," which is a kit of 26 *tips,* not tubes (even *I* know *that*), a coupler, and two flower nails for $39.99; a revolving cake stand, with a "heavy cast iron base . . . [that] stays in place while the 12" diameter turntable manually revolves for creative cake decorating ease and perfection," for $69.99; polyurethane-coated cotton pastry bags, one each of three sizes for $24.99; and a "Three-Piece Offset Pastry Spatula Set," for $19.99, which "let you ice the center of a large cake while keeping your knuckles clear of the frosting."

I turn to page 58 frequently, longing for that elegant cake stand, reminding myself over and over that I am not and never will be a cake decorator. The little voice says: *Better tools make better cakes!* And the big voice says: *Leave it to the experts at the bakery!* And the little voice says: *Cake!*

LAYER EIGHTEEN

Cake Wins

My sister orders her *real* fortieth birthday cake from Patisserie Poupon, whose owner, Joseph Poupon, made the cakes for both of our weddings. But she wants me to whip up an extra something. I select Martha Stewart's Coconut Teatime Cake, a ridiculously high layer cake covered with a basket weave of coconut buttercream, which I watch Martha and a guest make on her show one afternoon. Although I was absent for the basket weave class, Martha makes this pattern look easy as pie.

My attempts at everything are usually fraught with the perils of impatience. I need to get my way, and get it quickly, in order to feel like I have any control over anything. It's been my method with dog training, child rearing, writing—anything I'm passionate about—so it's no different with baking. A friend visiting from Ohio feels my mounting frustration for two days as I first mix the wrong ingredient into the wrong half of the separated eggs, wasting a dozen whites. Next, I mix up a batch of coconut buttercream frosting, for which ten egg whites and sugar must be simmered over boiling water to a temperature of 160 degrees. Butter is then beaten in, but I make the first mistake of hurrying up the softening process by putting it in the microwave. The frosting is too runny to use. The second mistake is that, in my haste, I misread the directions and add only four sticks of butter, instead of four *pounds*. Four *pounds* of butter! Even after the addition of two solid, unmelted pounds, the frosting doesn't thicken, and I give up, worried that the final pound will make no difference. I toss it.

In my defense, Martha Stewart's recipes are notorious for their difficulty. These are tough creations for novice bakers already; add the injury of hard-to-follow instructions. Each step in the process requires not one but several verbs and bowls. Mix, stir, beat, simmer, fold—all are done in different containers around the room but found in the same numbered step.

My friend and I set out to locate two-inch-deep cake pans, and I do not, foolishly, visit Cake Cottage first, where I'm sure to get a better deal than the thirty dollars I eventually pay for *each pan* at Bed, Bath & Beyond. I find them in the Beyond department. I can't afford to buy three, one for each layer, so I get two and plan to bake the third layer when the others are finished. When I return home— with more butter and eggs, too—I start from scratch again. I remove the paper circles that count as packaging for cake pans and spy a ding, the kind of tiny dent that would make you insane if you found one in the hood of your shiny new sports car. Nah, I think. It won't affect the cake. If it does, it'll be on the bottom, anyway.

Wrong! The layer in the dinged pan is smooshed on one side, lopsided, wrinkled. The other is nearly perfect. And so I must bake a fourth layer, dividing the recipe into thirds to create enough extra batter for a fourth panful.

The layers baked and cooling, I make the frosting again, and put it in the refrigerator. The plan is to decorate the cake the following day, on the morning of my sister's party. But by morning, the frosting has solidified. It's like a bowl of butter. I put it in the mixer and whip it into shape as it comes to room temperature.

The rest of the cake—from crumb coating to decorating—goes like a dream. Each layer gets brushed with a syrup of Coco Lopez and sugar (Jamie Williams, owner of SugarBakers, tells me later that a sugar syrup is the best tip for keeping a cake's layers moist), then spread with a cup of coconut buttercream frosting, then sprinkled with sweetened, shredded coconut. The basket weave pattern is a cinch, and when I'm finished, this towering cake doesn't fit in any container—even the ones we can scrounge from local bakeries aren't tall enough. But at last, a box under my guest bed, which once housed a Levenger orange leather tote I tried to hide from my husband, does the trick.

At the party that night, my fluffy white creation shares a table with the eighty-five-dollar Patisserie cake, a large, flat, beige display with fancy brown writing and a few large, elegant white chocolate flowers. Inside is a delicate and creamy cake that's not overly flavorful, but it shows up most of the boutique cakes I've tasted, in both flavor and price. But long before the cakes are cut, almost all of the forty guests approach me to say they cannot wait to get a piece of the cake they've heard so much about. And when they finally do, I am a powerful cake goddess. Men kiss my hand. Women kneel at my feet. Some weep with delight; others sit alone, moaning with pleasure. (One woman later begs my sister to have me make the cake for *her* fortieth in a few weeks.) Moments later the party winds down, as every party does once the cake is cut and eaten, and the sugar buzz has dipped to a sleepy hum. And we all depart, slowly, the memory of Martha Stewart's Coconut Teatime Cake, as re-created by Leslie, the newly crowned cake queen, forever etched on our tongues, a benchmark for all cakes, past, present, and future.

Is this how Martha Stewart feels? Or is she so used to her greatness that she accepts accolades as she breathes air—as something so second nature that she doesn't think about it, yet, if it were gone, she would surely die?

I think instead that the cake queens among us—and the bakers and chefs, the painters, photographers, writers—make these things because it's our way of both giving and receiving love. To stand by a cake table and hear people you know and don't know saying "oh—my—God" after their first bite of your white chocolate–caramel cheesecake with milk chocolate ganache and almonds is to be loved, albeit in a kinky, lusty way. To watch every Thanksgiving as your offerings on the dessert table disappear first and quickly is to be embraced wholly, despite what you might have said to Aunt Betty at the last Thanksgiving. Artists—whether they practice in the studio or the kitchen—want nothing more than to swap tokens of affection.

Cake Cottage Revisited

When I first stepped into the Cake Cottage, I thought of their ilk as amazing toy stores for bakers, full of trade secrets that, once employed, would give the uninitiated an edge. Instead, I find them spectacularly lacking. These are not stores for *serious* bakers; they are for the cat-sweatshirt wearers, country crafters, people who are interested in getting the richest shade of pink and finding barely edible sprinkles with which to "dreck"-o-rate their chocolate-dipped pretzels, the chocolate itself being full of stuff you shouldn't eat.

If I was a snob when I first walked through those doors two years ago, I'm a bigger (in all ways) snob now. I don't deny that the Magi-Cake strip's benefits far exceed its stupid name and poor packaging (with spelling mistake); they are worth the $9/pair price tag. (At least they aren't called Magi-Kake; then I would keel over and die.) But what I need hasn't been invented or is just impossible to find: a twelve-inch plate that is flat for at least nine inches in the center, and a cake carrier that will hold my plate and the three-layer cake atop it; every carrier is just a smidgen too short for a cake of that height.

I visit again for something tall in which to transport another cake for yet another event (this time, my sister's baby shower), but I leave disappointed in the excessive amount of junk, while there's still so much missing. For instance, why not sell the very best cake flour in bulk or some superfine sugar? Why not peddle elegance in the place of schlock? Who needs half a dozen creepy clown heads, which even children find nightmarish? Who needs hundreds of tacky cake toppers—not one of them designed for the interracial or homosexual couple?

When I leave bakeries and cake supply aisles and shops these days, it's with thoughts of what I'd do to make them better. I'd pretty up Warren Brown's famous CakeLove cupcakes—make them *look* as inviting as they taste by doing nothing more than smearing the frosting in a way that looks like I care about that, too. I'd sacrifice a few cents more for some butter instead of margarine at Gourmet Bakery, where they make my chocolate ribbon cake. I'd require nutrition information on every bag of fruity glurp I carry (because, face it, I'd go out of business if I didn't sell Sweetex frosting and bags of fruity glurp, which can be smeared on my customers' waffles the next morning).

It doesn't matter, of course, because I don't have the personality for retail. You can tell, because I began my rant by insulting people who wear sweatshirts with cats on them, and they probably compose the biggest portion of home cake decorators in the country.

You can't, as I once did, tell your customers how wrong they are about their diets and their health and insist that they put eggs and shellfish back into their diet and ditch the but-they're-fat-free! pretzels.

So my dreams of pretty from-scratch cupcakes and luxurious ceramic cake plates that fit inside a cake carrier remain where they belong: in my head.

A great empire, like a great cake, is most easily diminished at the edges.

—Benjamin Franklin

Tiers

FOURTH TIER

The Hierarchy of Cakes

I think of bakeries in hierarchical terms; that is, they are organized in my mind a little like tiers of a wedding cake, their position based on quality and quantity, which are inversely proportional. The more cakes you bake, the less care you are able to commit to each. I was all ready to be a snob about this fact on principle. My cupboards are empty of trans fats and high-fructose corn syrup (except for, of all things, Worcestershire sauce, which doesn't seem to come any other way). But when it comes to cake, I am willing to forgive a multitude of culinary sins, the worst of them hydrogenated frosting. Sometimes—mostly in private—I embrace them.

But one should make no demands of snack cakes that come wrapped in cellophane with a slip of waxed cardboard beneath them. They are made to look and taste exactly the same as the last one you had and be identical to the one being sold 5,000 miles from where you bought it. So quality control at the bottom rung of the cake ladder, the snack cake factory (Tastykake, Hostess, Little Debbie, Capitol Cakes), is not about appealing to the gourmand. It's about your eye catching the wrapper's glint as you pay for your 7-Eleven coffee. It's about making your kid grab the underside of your sleeve and tug, whining, "Mom, *please* can we get a Yodel, just this once? Bobby always has a Yodel in *his* lunch." When it comes to little snack cakes, the well-look-at-Bobby refusal is no more effective than the Bobby-jumping-off-a-bridge analogy. You beg for them when you're seven, and then you blame them for your eating disorder when you're forty-seven.

Hostess? No-stess

My theory about anything political, even business, is that the opposite ends of a spectrum are so much alike that you could join those ends for a practically seamless circle. Communism may be far in philosophy from fascism, but a cursory look shows similar limits on freedom, which is why you find Democrats and Republicans smack dab in the middle; there's hardly a difference. Red and indigo both fade off into invisible waves. And Hostess, at the bottom, is more like Charm City Cakes, at the top, than it is like your neighborhood bakery.

Whether you are feeding millions of people a cheap product or a small number of people a costly one, your secrets must be closely guarded. Trying to get into the plant of one of those snack factories these health-conscious and litigious days—even without a camera or a digital recorder—is like trying to interview George Clooney. You need to be well connected.

Forget the warmth and love that usually go into baking. Machines do most of the work here, squirting batter into pans and spitting out perfect Krimpet-shaped Krimpets, while a hairnetted, plastic-gloved lunch lady or gentleman nearby attends to the precision of the squiggle maker, ensuring the machine doesn't hit a snag and produce a squaggle instead. It's no wonder that these places don't want us around anymore. God forbid we should find out how the Ding Dong is assembled. We already know what is in it.[*] Many people, my next-door neighbor among them, remember taking tours of the Hostess or Tastykake plant on a junior high school field trip. Crista looks surprised when I tell her; she went to the St. Louis Hostess factory more than once as a child. But when I call, "insurance reasons" are cited. Entenmann's (Frank Sinatra's snack of choice),[†] Tastykake, Little Debbie, Hostess, and even the local Capitol Cakes (who would let me come talk with execs but won't let me look around) cite "insurance reasons" when they reject my requests for a plant tour. The more they tell me no, the more I want to know what they are hiding. Is this *Fast Food Nation*? Are people losing appendages in the Tandy Takes? Bleeding into the Devil Cremes?

Perhaps I would, in my zeal for chocolate frosting, have my sneaky index finger sliced off by the electronic filling squirter. Maybe Anna Ayala (of Wendy's chili–finger fame) will finally catch her big break and walk into a San Jose convenience store and come out with a finger-filled Ho Ho. Or maybe I would see cake's more miserable side—underpaid, bored factory employees all dying of some heretofore unheard of hazard on the scale of fake butter spray in the pop-

---

[*] Sugar, partially hydrogenated vegetable and/or animal shortening (may contain one or more of: soybean oil, cottonseed oil, palm oil, beef fat, lard), enriched flour (niacin, iron, thiamine mononitrate, riboflavin), water, cocoa, skim milk, corn syrup, eggs, mono- and diglycerides, starch, whey, leavening (baking soda, sodium acid pyrophosphate, monocalcium phosphate), salt, sodium caseinate, lecithin, cellulose gum, polysorbate 60, artificial color, artificial and natural flavors, sorbic acid.

[†] According to Entenmann's Web site, "In the early '50s, Frank Sinatra used to call the Bay Shore bakery to place weekly orders for Entenmann's crumb coffee cake."

corn factory, their offspring born with physical deformities: Twinkie pinkie, Ding Dong dong, or Sno balls.

But I'm no Barbara Ehrenreich; applying for a job at the plant, where I'd have to cover up the only part of me that I like most days— my hair—is simply not an option. I just want somebody to let me do what children all over the country used to be able to do. I want some souvenirs! Steve Almond, author of *Candyfreak*, advised me to "cast a wide net and find the operations that say yes" but warns "the big companies can be extraordinarily paranoid."

Once I decide that Interstate Bakeries Corporation (IBC) is my true choice, I call at least six people, leaving messages for everyone who seems important enough to be able to make the decision. Its allure for me is the wedding cakes made with Twinkies and Ding Dongs, a phenomenon so odd you can't tell if it's kitschy or just tacky (unlike the traditional wedding cake, it would probably *taste* good!).

Snacks probably don't get much bigger than the Twinkie. According to the Hostess Cakes Web site, this Depression-era invention designed to satisfy sweets eaters on the cheap is baked with "8 million pounds of sugar, 7 million pounds of flour and 1 million eggs" each year. What isn't disclosed is the quantity of high-fructose corn syrup, fifth on the nutrition label (does anyone find "nutrition label" ironic on snacks like these?); nor is Hostess bragging about how much dextrose, hydrogenated oil, and polysorbate 60 go toward making those 500 million Twinkies each year. But 1 percent of sodium stearoyl lactylate[*] is still 60,000 pounds.

Calls and e-mails go unanswered until I issue my veiled threat—that I would just let corporate know I'd hit a dead end. It is then that Casey DePalma, a PR person with Linden Alschuler & Kaplan Public Relations, offers to mail me a videocassette of

---

[*] Of the eighteen ingredients listed under the "less than two percent of the following" heading, sodium stearoyl lactylate is fifth from the bottom.

Hostess products being made. It comes a week later via Federal Express. Only the tape is in the envelope, like a spy's assignment or blackmail.

I wait until I have a chunk of time to view the video undisturbed and sit down one Monday morning to watch. I am shocked by what I see. The action begins without warning—no music or graphics, no title—and it continues for about twenty-three seconds. From the fuzz of a blank tape comes a silent machine squirting squiggles of batter into Twinkie-shaped tins for about five seconds; for two seconds, they silently emerge half-baked (I guess); for a few more seconds, a machine silently squirts some more glurp into the Twinkies; they emerge golden brown, silently, for another couple of seconds; an automated wrapper drops logo cellophane on the treats without so much as a crinkle; finally, the wrapped, finished Twinkies fall in an orderly, silent way onto a conveyor belt covered with white fabric or paper towel material, like an antimacassar. Then the tape goes to fuzz again. There is no narration. There is no music. The tape is over. I fast-forward it, but the rest is blank. I take it to another videocassette player, where it plays exactly as it did in my kitchen.

For twenty-three seconds.

I e-mail Ms. DePalma at 8:15 a.m. that I must have gotten a defective tape, and she—a woman who had failed to respond to my first two e-mails a week apart—replies at 8:19 a.m. that she is sorry, but all they have is this tape used mainly for media purposes. If Hostess does something newsworthy, all the networks and their affiliates get the same footage, over which anchors or reporters dub their individually spun stories.

The video is no fun without context. I invent some and play it again: "In other news, Hostess announcing—" (newscasters rarely use verbs these days) "—an effort to appeal to vegetarians. Their press release stating they will no longer use *beef fat* in their most popular snack item, the Twinkie." Pause. Cut to anchors. "Wow, Stan, beef fat? I didn't know Twinkies had beef fat!" "Me either, Denise! And speaking of beef fat, let's check in with Norm for news on that thunderstorm situation."

Twinkies are probably no worse for you than local news, which isn't saying much. But they're probably not as bad as many items in the snack aisle of the supermarket, which is also not saying much. They are certainly equal to all the other treats laden with preservatives and HFCS and trans fats and things you can't pronounce. Aren't they? That they explode in the microwave—like many other food items—has no bearing on anything. Neither does the other experiment that has budding scientists submerging Twinkies in water for fifteen minutes. One Web site calls the result "the Gremlin Factor," indicated by the altered appearance of your treat: "Your innocent Twinkie should have transformed into some kind of primeval goo from which several new species could evolve." Now, I'm no scientist. I even protested the dissection of frogs and cows' eyeballs in high-school science class (only advanced science students got cats). But even I know that stomachs have digestive juices—enzymes, I'll bet they're called—that break the Twinkie down. So the Twinkie, despite its infinite shelf life, is not as sinister as all that.

Even though it is. In his book *Twinkie, Deconstructed,* Steve Ettlinger digs up the sources for many of the preservatives and vitamins and miscellaneous ingredients in our foods, items we can't buy in, say, the spice aisle of the grocery store. They come from gypsum and phosphate mines and oil fields. Rocks. The ABC News *Nightline* story asked IBC what they thought of Ettlinger's identification of some of the Twinkie's thirty-nine ingredients as glue and petroleum and plaster, along with some unregulated vitamins from China: "The core ingredients in Twinkies have been the same for decades: flour, sugar, and water. Deconstructing the Twinkie is like trying to deconstruct the universe. Some people look at the sky and think it's beautiful; others try to count the stars . . ." In other words, ". . . Twinkies just taste great."

Despite his findings, Ettlinger thinks Twinkies are fine to eat. "I mean, my gosh, they're not gonna kill you! They are a treat."*

This is a good thing. Because less than an hour after I found this out about the Twinkie, my daughter announced to me that her classmate Jai-Ivy had just given Serena her very first Twinkie.

I tell Ettlinger that these crappy ingredients are in everything. Nearly every food item in a box, except raisins, has something you won't find in the spice aisle at the supermarket. Aren't we getting too much of this from other sources to make Twinkies "safe"? He says, " 'Too much' is subjective. If you're concerned, eat whole and local, sustainably raised foods as much as you can. I do."

I wonder whether the origins of all these ingredients really matter. After all, if margarine is a molecule away from plastic, then it's not plastic in the least. "No, not really," he says: Often the same stuff is used in nonfood things, which is simply fun and interesting to contemplate. Sugar helps concrete settle. Salt is used to melt ice on roads. And polysorbate 60 emulsifies shampoo. And cellulose gum helps gel rocket fuel. I like that kind of stuff. I think it is hilarious that we make light and fluffy cakes with five different kinds of rocks. In fact, three rocks are used to make baking powder, which is there only to make them light and airy. Wild, when you think about it. Love it.

---

* Not even if you're San Francisco mayor George Moscone or supervisor Harvey Milk. Their murderer, Dan White, was described as having been depressed; he had recently begun eating junk food, a tiny blip in a trial that satirist Paul Krassner blew up into what he coined "the Twinkie Defense," a diminished-capacity defense. " 'I don't think Twinkies were ever mentioned in testimony,' said chief defense attorney Douglas Schmidt, who recalls, 'Ho Hos and Ding Dongs,' but no Twinkies."

The Bakeries' Bakery

One step up the confectionary ladder is the bakery that feeds the bakeries and restaurants, all those jewel cases filled with triple-layer cakes topped with toasted coconut or dark chocolate and cherries, the upright refrigerators, desserts inside rotating like a fashion show. Though the items are often not made from scratch, many bakeries still make these up by hand. My experience with kitchen machines being limited to old KitchenAid stand mixers and new ones, and all my requests for plant tours denied, I am eager to get behind the scenes at a bakery making mass quantities of sweet things. My wish is granted at Gourmet Bakery, in Pikesville, Maryland. It's an especially relevant place for me to be. This is the home of my sweet stalker, the Chocolate Ribbon Cake. Now who's stalking *whom*?

Sammy Goldberg, my "in" at Gourmet, is, in addition to being a close family friend, our pusher. He seems to tote ribbon cakes and rugelach wherever he goes. I'll bet he has a fresh loaf of emergency challah in his trunk. "Pssst," I picture him saying to the members of his Jewish men's club and their wives. "Yo, Goldstein, I got the chocolate tops." The bakery, where he works in the office manning the phones and preparing production sheets, is well known for its everything—chocolate tops, ribbon cakes, apple betty, rugelach, hamantaschen, and mousse cake—depending on which baker you ask.

I am introduced first to "the Lawrence," Lawrence Crawford, one of the production bakers. When I ask what he does, specifically, he tells me, "I'm the *lover* of the company."

When Sammy introduces me to the group, he tells them I'm writing a book about cake. "Honeychild," Pearl Floyd tells me, "I can tell you what to put in it." Pearl has seventeen years of her life invested in this place. And except for her dislike of chocolate, she is not unusual. Nearly everyone at Gourmet has worked here for at least a decade; two bakers have spent *three* decades at this job. I tell Pearl that she is, no doubt, nicer than my great-aunt Pearl, who sent me a check for my wedding. When I thanked her for helping make our honeymoon trip to Europe wonderful, she wrote back telling me the money she sent was for my future, and how dare I spend it on something so frivolous! Pearl agreed that she is nicer than my aunt. Most of the time I was visiting Gourmet, Pearl was rolling dough through the dough roller, stamping out circles, dotting them with a thick, perfect circle of apple filling, and folding them into hamantaschen. I once stole some hamantaschen for me and my daughter as we escaped the musical portion of a Purim service, so they are a good memory for me. Also lovely was that Pearl thought I was in my thirties. I told her I was forty-five, and she said, "Are you *sure?*" Now, when I think of Pearl, I can replace the image of my crotchety great-aunt (who, ironically, died while dancing!) with the smiling, warm picture of Pearl Floyd folding the Haman's hat cookies.

Closed in the cookie room—no doubt to keep the cold in and the riffraff out—is Velma Haywood. She wears a dark jacket, a pastel green sweater, and a man's fedora. She is black, as is everyone else here, except for two Russian sisters. Her hair is shoulder-length, and her voice is so deep that I can hardly hear her over the tiny TV (*Tyra* is on) and the electronic buzz of fluorescent lights that bounces off stainless steel walls and six-foot-high rolling carts. A table holds a heated tub of melted white chocolate (every time I say "white chocolate," my mother has to tell me it's not really chocolate; duh, Mom!) and some random things, including a photograph of a fire truck with a Dalmatian, printed from a photography Web site, Flickr, which she used for reference on a cake. Shelves to Velma's right hold everything from her purse and office supplies to food coloring and pictures of her grandson, who wants to be a baker. The cluttered room is not clean, but it's not dirty, either. Let's put it this way: after spending a few hours there, I still adore the cake. My mom's business partner, architect Richard C. Schaefer,* was once a fan of Berger's cookies, but a dismal visit to the plant ended that. It was his idea to visit this place, thinking it might have the same effect on me, and I'd be free. Nuh-uh.

Velma looks bored as she tackles, by rote, one of the rolling carts stacked to the top with giant pans of colored cake. These have already been assembled—pink layer atop yellow atop green atop blue atop orange, a thin smear of chocolate frosting between them. Velma is at the cutting and leveling stage. Armed with a knife almost fifteen inches long, she cuts the five-layer, 18-by-26-inch sheets of cake into eight 12-inch-by-4-inch (by 4½-inch-high) cakes, setting them on foam trays and placing them back on the rolling cart. When this batch of cakes is cut, she'll roll the cart into the frosting room, where she will ladle on a generous portion of outrageously delicious chocolate, smooth it with a spatula, and decorate with a middle squiggle and a border on the top and around the bottom. (No squiggle machines at Gourmet; these really *are* crafted by hand.) That bottom

---

* This formality is appropriate. After nearly thirty-five years of working with my mother, he still begins every phone call to her with, "Dick Schaefer here." Likewise when he called his mother: "Hi, Mom, it's Dick." He has no brothers.

border is where I usually slide my finger before dinner, before anyone has even noticed that a ribbon cake will be dessert.

I've been calling this cake a ribbon cake because it appears to be made of ribbons of color; others may know it as a rainbow cake. Velma tells me, "You know how they have the gay commitment services? This would be the ideal cake for them. . . . It's their logo, their sign and everything. And I would love to do this for that purpose. . . . Something special just for them, not something everyone else has." I have the perfect topper, too—a pair of ceramic brides stuck to a wine cork, which I picked up for twenty bucks one summer in Rehoboth Beach, Delaware, a popular vacation spot for families *and* homosexuals.

(Later, however, in the chocolate room, when I ask Nella Mednikova and Velma whether it's technically called a *ribbon* or a *rainbow* cake, they each choose a different answer, Velma, who'd just told me the rainbow was the gay logo, choosing *ribbon*. On Gourmet's Web site, www.chocolatetops.com, it's called a rainbow cake, so that's that.)

Measuring—to cut the individual cakes—is the part that could mess up Velma's whole operation, and it's why she still does it, day after day, despite her desire to move on. She's trained dozens of people in a variety of methods, but she can't trust a single one of them to do it right. I don't get the problem. I can, by eyeing it, find the middle points to make these cuts. She teaches with a ruler because an imprecise measurement can render an entire pan of eight cakes useless, except as petits fours (which they do sell, and they're especially popular in shivah trays).

I come up with the idea to make a cardboard comb. It's the width of the cake and has a tooth every three inches. Mark it, and make your cuts. Her solution seems almost as easy. Velma folds the layer of parchment that covers the top of the cake in half, then cuts the cake. She folds it in half again and makes another cut. Finally, she folds it again to cut the last cake, leaving about an inch on the edge, so she can trim the edges smooth. That folded parchment is now the size of a slice, and she can move that to the other side of the cake, like a template.

Still, she says, it's not enough. She pulls out a big contraption, a steel accordion-folding instrument with rollers on the ends, the thing I'd just invented in my head and called a comb. These can be stretched to even widths. She stretches it so that each segment is three inches and holds the wheels to the cake. A no-brainer. But no one else seems to have the touch.

I watch Velma Haywood trim the edges off the stacked cake and slide the ribbons into a trash can brimming with bright, delicious scraps. I can hardly keep from reaching in and almost have to, if I want a taste. Velma's removal of the trimmings from her worktable is swift. How can she just brush them off like that? How can she not eat them? Even once?

She can't bear the thought. "What used to be good suddenly becomes bad. . . . If you've got a serious addiction for something, go work it," she tells me. "You'll eat lots of it when you first start, but after a month, it's all over." Dare I? "It's the cure for everybody."

My husband once thought he could cure smoking by putting the smoker in a glass room with no windows. He'd be both humiliated and choked. I'm not sure I could survive for a month of daily doses of chocolate ribbon cake, total immersion. I would most certainly become as big as most of the people in this place! (Only a few of the men seem to have been unaffected by their product.)

Velma's been with Gourmet for twenty years. Before that, she worked for Ms. Desserts, Harbor City, Safeway, and Giant. "I dare anybody to buy me a birthday cake. I will beat the life out of them. It's enough to look at it every day." Them's fightin' words, and she is just getting warmed up.

Though she has no formal culinary training, she believes she can hold her own against anyone, regardless of his status in the industry. Take Duff Goldman. "I would match my skills against a culinary student because I don't think they've got anything on me. I've often thought of putting myself on the food channel network."

"She can do zis," says Nella, pointing out that Duff Goldman may be her personal hero, but Velma is a "cake diva." Unfortunately, she'll have to pick a different stage name, Cakediva having been taken by Charmaine Jones, also a Food Network competitor.

But in order to be a star on that channel, Velma would have to know her way around fondant. "To me, I believe fondant is a lazy baker's way out, and it's because you don't have the skills to work with buttercream. Because I have ultimately worked with people that had no finesse and no skills when it comes to buttercream. They have no technique; they can't smooth it." But, yeah, she can work with fondant and offers it to her customers, who, she says, usually decline once she tells them it doesn't have a taste. "I can practically create the same cake in buttercream that you can create in fondant and it will look just as good and taste way better."

Fondant became all the rage, she says, because you get only about fifteen hours of cake lessons in culinary school. That doesn't give you much time to learn how to work with frosting. Besides, she says, "I got an imagination that's off the charts. What makes me be able to match my skills against a culinary student is because I can visualize."

I spend about four hours at Gourmet Bakery, mostly enjoying the banter and soaking up scents and flavors. I wander around the bakery poking my nose into ten-gallon mixers full of batter and frosting and shortening. I help myself to a smidgen of Cleveland Milton's delicious almond *mandelbrot* dough, which tastes nothing like my grandmother's, made with walnuts and orange juice, then rolled in cinnamon sugar, but it's baked twice, like hers, and it's all just Jewish biscotti. Cleveland was trained in culinary school in Jamaica. He is the only person in the bakery wearing a traditional chef's hat. All but one head, a bald one, is covered. "The Lawrence" wears a backward red baseball cap; Sugg (pronounced like the first

syllable of *sugar,* naturally) Eddings, the éclair man with long braids, has a black bandana, or do-rag; the women wear what look to be clear shower caps, except for Velma, who wears her fedora. But there's something besides the all-white uniform that draws me to Cleveland. He reminds me—for reasons inexplicable at the time— of family, my grandfather in particular. It isn't until later, when I look at my photos of the day, that I realize Cleveland Milton is the spitting image of the man on the Cream of Wheat box (except that the baker has silvery-white facial hair), hence the connection to my grandfather.

During Cleveland's lunch break, I join a conversation about avocados; he eats one nearly every day and is peeling today's, discussing its use as a fruit in Jamaican cuisine. I share my recipe for a smoothie and for avocado ice cream, to which Cleveland's coworker reacts with a look of disbelief. After his break, Cleveland fills one of those enormous mixers with a mound of fluorescent yellow substance, which, he tells me in a faux French accent, is *mar-ghar-EEN*. It takes me a minute, and, responding to my look of surprise, he says behind his hand, "It's cheaper."

No matter where I wander, Terry Perkins finds me. He seems to be under the impression that my photographs, which I take as obsessively as I eat cake (partly because I can't trust my handwriting), will appear in the book and wants me to chronicle all of the steps in his making of the apple betty, a confection so delectable that Gourmet can't keep any in the freezer. Terry's head is smooth and hairless; he's the hatless one. He is large and round, with thick fingers and strong hands—a necessity in this business, despite the number of machines. In the first stage, Terry uses a dough-rolling machine to flatten the dough. While it rests, he mixes mass quantities of apple pie filling with *cake,* buckets and buckets of cake scraps, which become the binder, absorbing all that syrup and gluing the apples together. After the dough's rested, Terry stretches it some more, then cuts it into strips about five feet long by eight inches wide. It takes a while to accomplish each step in bulk; the two tables he works will have four rolls each. I leave to visit other stations, and when I return, Terry is piling a generous portion of filling in the center of each dough strip. Then he rolls them closed, pushes them together, cuts them into individual servings about the width of his large hand, and slashes each pastry with three vertical strips. He loads twelve apple bettys per aluminum tray and puts them in the freezer. The process is over, and I am disappointed. "When do they get baked?" I ask, like a dog that has spent an hour watching his family dine only to be denied a table scrap. But these are shipped frozen to bakeries, which make them to order. And so I saunter off, tail between my legs, dejected, and rescue a chocolate top, one of Baltimore's most famous cookies, from a rolling cart before it, too, disappears into some refrigerated room.

CakeLove Love

Warren Brown is adorable. There's no question. He has tightly braided hair that curls at the ends with a cheerful *boing*! Even when he is gesticulating madly and defending his products and raging against impure ingredients, he's just plain cute. So he's going on about "those terrible, unhealthy, gross, disgusting ingredients that give you intestinal distress," and, in my head, I'm going, "Oh, baby, yeah, shake that springy hair, and smile your sparkly smile."

It took me more than two years to land a face-to-cute-face meeting with the CakeLove owner and former *Sugar Rush* host. His overprotective agent, while failing to shelter him from Oprah and writers from local papers like *The Sun* and national magazines like *GQ,* refused my requests, afraid that a book with Brown in it might reveal secrets for which he'd already been contracted by a publisher. We exchanged a few unpleasant e-mails, the agent telling me, essentially, to get a life (hey, dog, this *is* my life). And I dropped the bone for a long while—that is, until Brown opened his Baltimore location in February 2008.

Now I'm eagerly waiting. This week, I'm off cake, as I've just begun an eight-week challenge to shed what I've gained gorging on cake these past months—sneaking scraps off the worktable at Gour-met Bakery, baking fancy cakes for houseguests and all the birthday and baby-shower celebrants in my life. But it's easy here, in the little retail shop on Boston Street in Canton, across from a spectacular view of Baltimore's Inner Harbor. It is aromaless! It appears—with its whirring KitchenAid mixers in every color—to be a bakery, but there's no oven. (So it's a *fakery*?) Each morning, a shipment of pre-baked, naked cakes comes in from Silver Spring, and the employees assemble, fill, and frost the layer cakes and smear flavored butter-creams atop the cupcakes.

Before Warren gets here and tries to give me something free (that always seems to influence the taste buds), I order a single vanilla cup-cake and a single chocolate cupcake from Kimi, one of the counter girls. I reconsider and ask which of the cakes is Warren's own favor-ite. Courtney chimes in, and Kimi wraps up a slice of New German Chocolate Cake. I'm not usually a vanilla or chocolate person, but I want to focus on taste rather than the surprise of an unusual flavor, which can make something seem delightful even if it's average. I get a T-shirt, too, because CakeLove is what I am all about.

Brown's fifteen minutes late, and I am out of questions with which to pester the girls. The employees are not exactly bakers; they are more like hobbyists. Both enjoy baking at home, and both find themselves still in love with cake. If you ask, they will give you the recipe for frosting or tell you the backstory of Courtney's Conun-drum, a cake assemblage of her own combination of flavors. I move my goodies to a brown leather sofa for two with square white cush-ions in this wide-open room scattered with ottomans that look like pastel cupcakes. I size up the front display case, which has a relatively small collection of sweets, and I scrutinize the cupcakes, which are frosted sloppily with lime, peanut butter, strawberry, lemon, and other assorted flavors. Now and again, I get up to see if I read one of the names right—Neil's Hat Trick, a cake is called. (My husband and I have made a game out of our failing vision. Sometimes, while driving, we'll compete to see who can be the first to read a distant road sign.)

Owning a bakery doesn't sound the least bit desirable to me, yet I find myself daydreaming later about all the things I'd do differently, among them train Courtney and Kimi to frost the cupcakes *nicely*! I'm not saying that the case should be full of many-dozen identical, frilly treats. But they ought not to detract from the delicious flavor. My reverie breaks when I see Warren bounding toward the shop from the Safeway parking lot, his hair bouncing.

He sits close to me on the little sofa—CakeLoveseat, I want to call it, but we've only just met. Warren Brown made headlines years ago because he gave up his careers in law (he specialized in health care insurance fraud) and teaching reproductive health to follow his bliss as a baker. But now his bliss is whatever he's doing that *isn't* in the CakeLove kitchen, as he does not consider a production shift a good use of time for a business owner. I'm surprised that he no longer bakes—except at home in his own kitchen, where he makes a lot of scones (blech—*stones* is more like it) to keep himself current in his understanding of the relationships between flour, sugar, butter, and eggs. "I like food; I'm into the food," he tells me, whether it's "evaluating the appearance, what we're doing, devising recipes, thinking of it as I go for a run. . . . I like the whole process." He teaches a few classes at his Silver Spring store, and he oversees his shops, the new one in Baltimore daily for its first month of business.

Before we get very far, I address a touchy subject. On food forums and blogs, CakeLove is often subject to criticism because they refrigerate everything. "We're the only ones that do use a refrigerated display case, that I know of, that have products that are 'potentially hazardous' foods as defined by the health department.*

---

* According to the FDA's Web site, potentially hazardous foods are "any food of such type or in such condition as may spoil." In a bakery, it's anything made with milk or milk products and anything made with eggs.

"It's a very long issue that we should talk about," Brown says, and we do. Posted on the refrigerated case are yellow stickers. A pictogram—here, the universal symbol for a person, often seen at crosswalks and on restroom doors—shows a woman holding a gigantic cake with three candles on it next to a thermometer pointing to 72° F. A numbered list asks the following:

1. Why serve cake @ room temp? Because it tastes better!
2. Why refrigerate the cake? The health department requires that we store perishable goods at a cool 41° Fahrenheit.
3. How long will it take to hit room temp? 10–25 minutes for cupcakes, pastries & slices. 1–3 hours for a cake. Bigger cakes take more time.
4. In a rush and can't wait? We don't recommend it but . . . you can microwave items for *no more than 10 seconds*.

The bottom of the sticker has the bold, trademarked admonition: "Serve cake @ room temp™."

Posted elsewhere are requests that customers wait fifteen to twenty minutes before consuming their desserts. Forty-one degrees is not the optimal temperature at which to sink one's teeth into a cake. Often, though, when a cupcake is a little messed up, the employees will cut it into bite-size pieces for samples and put it right out, cold, and customers can get the wrong idea if they should grab a cold piece.

But who wants to wait? This is America! We get what we want, when we want it! So if CakeLove sometimes gets a bad rap—some say the cake is dry or the frosting tastes too much like butter—it is, in part, due to the impatience of consumers.

Why don't we have to wait at a diner? A few reasons, among them: hydrogenated shortenings and other unnatural ingredients that don't require refrigeration; confectioners' sugar, used in American buttercream, which forms a crust on the outside, making frosting less likely to melt and more likely to stick; and simple failure to follow health codes, which, for some sensitive stomachs—like Brown's—can result in gastrointestinal distress. He is empathetic and doesn't ever want to be the cause of someone's stomach troubles.

"It's an easy rule to follow," he says. And it's a sacrifice he thinks is worth it for Italian buttercream. While American buttercream, made of confectioners' sugar, holds up better, meringue deflates and makes a sloppy mess. "Refrigeration, while a pain for people to wait through, makes it possible for us to actually handle the product."

Brown returns to a criticism of American buttercream (the recipe found on the side of the Domino's box—a pound of powdered sugar, a stick of softened butter, one to three tablespoons of milk, and a teaspoon of vanilla) time and again, as if it's somehow a bad baking practice rather than a flavor preference. It's sweeter, yes, and volume from this type of frosting comes from the amount of sugar rather than the air whipped into egg whites. But is it a matter of health?

Brown and others hold a mistaken belief that the powdered stuff reaches the bloodstream and the brain faster than the big crystals. He says confectioners' sugar is "what gives you the sugar rush because it passes through your mucous membranes, and it gives you a headache."

But that's not true. "Your body won't differentiate between the sources of sugar," says Joanne Larsen, MS, RD, LD, of Ask the Dietitian.com. She doesn't believe particle size has any bearing on the absorption of sugar, which dissolves as rapidly in saliva as it does in water. She adds that its effects are more the result of quantity and says you should feel them in about fifteen minutes. So it hardly matters whether it's superfine 10X powdered sugar, granulated, or liquid—unless you're shooting the sugar directly into a vein. (In that case, you'll want liquid. Trust me.)

So is it a matter of sophistication, then? A fellow baker and former classmate, my friend Barbara tells me that she thinks that as she gets older ("or perhaps more sophisticated?"), she's less attracted to sweeter things, and I chastise her for being pretentious. That one enjoys a Hostess cupcake (albeit alone, in the dark, in one's car, in one bite) doesn't mean one can't also enjoy a grilled lettuce salad or sautéed fiddlehead ferns. But if your palate is less exposed to sugar, a small amount is likely to taste sweeter to you than it does to, say, a five-year-old kid. Or to me. But lots of us, including some CakeLove critics, find that the taste of butter overpowers the taste of sugar in traditional Swiss and Italian buttercreams, and we'd rather be sweet-talked than buttered up (though in the end the results are the same).

It boils down to sugar snobbery. Brown thinks that American buttercream is the stuff that children love but parents don't. I'm not sure it's true. That obesity is linked to the soda rather than the super-size fries seems pretty clear to me. Besides, I've had the sugar jones from birth, when I must have suckled at the *tsitskehs* of Mrs. Mani-schewitz, which spoiled me for Merlot, to which I must always add a tablespoon of Splenda or a partial packet of Sweet'N Low in secret shame.

"Manischewitz is really sweet?" Brown asks. "I've never had it."

"It's Ripple. It's Mad Dog," I tell him. I should've guessed that if he's not had the one, which at least has its sacramental value, he's not likely to have had the others.

I talk about some other bakeries I've seen and find myself jus-tifying their methods. For instance, Gourmet Bakery's use of those fifty-pound bags of Pillsbury cake mix, which are filled with what Brown calls "dough conditioners" (things added to the flour so as not to gunk up commercial machines). After all, the same lady, Velma Haywood, is baking and assembling two hundred of the same cake in just a couple of hours each and every day. I can even make excuses for margarine.

"The problem I have with that is that shit will give you diarrhea—I mean, excuse my French, but that's exactly what will happen. That's what would happen with me, and that's gross." Maybe it is a little, but how many people get to cozy up to Warren Brown while he talks about having the runs? I am a lucky, lucky girl, and I just nod and let him go on. "I bet you most of the people out there—that's what would happen. Because you can't handle that kind of oil. . . . It's too heavy on the body. There's oil in the frosting, there's oil in the cake, there's oil in the filling. You take the cake off the platter, [and] it's got a wet mark like it's someone's underarm. It's disgusting! It's nasty!"

When you put it that way, sure. Maybe that's why Gourmet sets its ribbon cakes on a foam tray. I've never seen anything but the delicious (cooked from scratch by Sugg Eddings, by the way) frosting waiting for my finger to swoop it away.

Oil is clearly Brown's pet peeve. He often hears people claiming that cakes are "moist"— cakes like Duncan Hines and Betty Crocker. (He's even heard them referred to as scratch-made cakes because they are often altered.) "What I would proffer is what you're tasting that creates the sensation of moisture is not a water molecule; it's oil, and that oil is . . . just sliding over your tongue—that's the wool being pulled over the eyes of these Americans out there," many of whom are satisfied with Krispy Kreme doughnuts and Tastykake, despite their chemical contents.

With all Brown's health consciousness, what does he think of his own nutritional contribution? "There's butter in the stuff, there's sugar in the stuff, that's something kids should eat in moderation, but I don't feel that I'm poisoning them with plastic. I don't feel that I'm poisoning them with something that I myself wouldn't be able to handle." And that's why, he says, a Safeway cake ought to be off-limits for kids.

Even if I argue, as I do, that a Safeway cake is really *okay* once a year, because it's once a year, after all, he doesn't agree that it's ever appropriate. I try to entice him with a seductive description of a hot dog nestled in a soft, squishy potato roll and doused with a healthy squirt of French's yellow mustard, but he's not buying it. His hair bounds sideways in protest. "C'mon," I say, incredulous, "isn't there *something* you find a guilty pleasure? Something you can't resist?" He can't think of anything, so I make a list of popular items: Snickers bars, M&M's, Peppermint Patties.

"None of it," he tells me, and I don't believe him. He gets still and quiet and comes up with "Goat cheese."

"Come on! Goat cheese? That's the best you can do?"

"Goat cheese."

Answers like this make me wish I were paid to be a food spy or a member of the paparazzi, tailing Brown in search of his secret stash of Hershey's Kisses or seeing him post-jog, hood pulled up to cover the trademark braids, paying the corner hot dog vendor, his head darting nervously to make sure the coast is clear. I'm not above looking through his trash, either.

The child of a customer points to the display case, repeating "pie, pie, pie, pie" a dozen times. Does Brown ever bake pie? Will he ever offer it to customers? He shakes his head. "Interferes with cake sales," he says. We laugh at the truth of it, and it leads me to the question I ask all the bakers: cake or pie? "I was gonna say I prefer pie, but I prefer cobbler," he admits, and a cakey cobbler at that. I tell him

about the apple betty from Gourmet, mixed up by Terry Perkins, who added buckets of scrap cake to canned apple pie filling. Brown interrupted, as if he might somehow get some of this stuff on him. "This is all disgusting! It really is. I think it's disgusting."

"Unfortunately," I say, "it tastes really good!"

"It tastes like sugar! It's all it is, just sugar and goop. . . . That's just as lazy baking as it is lazy cooking when you go to some restaurant, high class or not, and they just slather the whole thing in butter or oil so they don't burn it, because the chef that's there doesn't have any skills, doesn't know how to actually test for when it's done, doesn't know what to look for. . . . I don't think it's acceptable. . . . If you're gonna be that sloppy, you might as well just say two plus two equals five."

Sentiments like these, full of articulate gesticulation, are exactly why I'm here. Early in our conversation, Brown wants to know whom else I've interviewed. Did I talk to *Cake Bible* author Rose Levy Beranbaum yet? Did I talk to Bruce Healy, his mentor and author of *The Art of the Cake*? I explain that I'm here because Brown is sort of a—a *freak*, and I mean that in the nicest way, that his passion for cake led him to ditch a legal career. And here, in his passion for purity, Brown lets his freak shine.

After a deep breath, he adds, "I know I sound a little bit of a zealot for it, but, please!"

Duff Goldman's cake freak shines pretty brightly, too; it might be a prerequisite for the job. Though he will claim his product is equal parts style and substance, he makes fondant-covered cakes. I just figure he has to work a little harder in the taste department, as wedding cakes are notoriously foul tasting. Walk by any wedding table post–cake service, and you'll find plates of fondant and half-eaten slices. Shouldn't those cakes be delicious naked? "I think it would matter *less*; it follows what the practice is," Brown says.

"If the wedding's on a Saturday, they probably have that thing fondant-covered by a Tuesday, sometimes even well before that—like a week and a half before. That cake ain't gonna be butter made, because it will be dried out as all hell by then. . . . And if they're making that decision, then they have sacrificed beyond what's reasonable their concern for making it taste really good." Something, he says, has to take priority. "Anyone can tell you their cake's gonna be awesome."

And Brown's cake? What do you get for seven dollars a slice or three dollars a cupcake? "I think that our cake is good; I'm not gonna claim it's better than any place's, but I'll say that our method of production and our ingredients can guarantee a taste that's going to be distinct from other bakeries', and I think that taste will equate to quality and mouth feel."

His customers seem pretty satisfied. It's a busy store at 6:00 on a Tuesday evening, bustling with families, executives in pumps picking up sixty-cupcake orders, moms ordering birthday cakes. He is recognized by quite a few women who are smiling like groupies—shameless! They see my pad and pen, guess this is business, and reach across us to shake his hand, eager to sit here and bask in the glow of Warren Brown's smile.

To paraphrase Claire from *Six Feet Under,* cake light is the best light of all; "we should just live in cake light."

The Acing on the Cake

The ruling chefs of cakedom—Colette Peters, Mike McCarey, Duff Goldman—find themselves on their thrones primarily because they are able to make a cake that looks like one. They can turn batter into a pitcher—hell, an entire baseball field. They can carve cake to look like a Thanksgiving turkey dinner. If you can think it, they can make a cake to look like it. And they can charge what is known in technical terms as "up the wazoo."

The most expensive cake of my life, not counting my wedding cake (I never saw the price tag, so that's a guess), comes from *Ace of Cakes* host Duff Goldman, of Baltimore's Charm City Cakes. I thought it would be a fun experiment to watch my own cake being made, in person, and then have company over to devour it and several others, in a cake-off.

When I arrive on the Friday before my Forty-third Eating of the Cake, I am ambivalent. While I am eager to watch the decoration of my very own cake (I've been looking forward to this for more than a month), the downside is the missing gasp of awe: that moment the flap on the cake box is lifted, and you see the creation before you and are dazzled. Those moments are almost as special as the eating moments (Okay, *moment;* I tend to inhale food).

The back of Charm City Cakes is littered with research and possibilities: black-and-white photocopies of toilets, camel heads, logos, motorcycles, Prada shoes, and a scooter. A table near the front of the workshop holds power tools and sawdust. Lining the walls are several sets of commercial metal shelving, used to store everything from finished cakes to foam dummies. Egg cartons hold newly pressed fondant flowers, and empty plastic cups once filled with glitter paint add even more color to the saturated room. A bottle of vodka sits beside a drying gum-paste horse, which is propped between wooden dowels sunk into a foam base. I am drawn to all that glitters and find myself gazing into a container of tiny silver balls—dragées. My future, they say, is sweet.

Jeff, the model maker, is engaged in what Duff dubs "Cake of the Week," a motor scooter, to scale and beautifully constructed. Every so often, the rest of the crew—including two women on staff and an intern Duff believes is destined for oblivion—gather around Jeff's work to offer him their awe. It is spectacular that cake can be carved in this manner and buttercream can become the glue that holds cake to itself.

It's time to work on my own, an eight-inch round of white-fondant-covered white cake. What was I thinking? *White* cake? This is Charm City, home of the pumpkin and chocolate chip, cardamom and pistachio, pear spice, butterscotch-walnut, banana-caramel, and peanut butter and jelly cakes. The shop offers more flavors than Baskin-Robbins—forty-six at last count. I'm no vanilla! I'm mint chocolate chip! Alas, it's too late to reconsider.

The contract I signed on September 28 calls for a "1-tier mosaic cake w/ sproing elements coming off." I believe *sproing* is a word of my own invention and not the lingua franca of decorators. The flavor is "white cake w/ vanilla buttercream," and I realize my mistake was not knowing that Duff decorated exclusively with fondant—or that there wouldn't be sufficient buttercream beneath the decorations, which, I recall, Duff said could simply be peeled off and the cake eaten nude. I was hoping to be able to match this extravagant—at $190, which is supposed to include delivery—gourmet creation to a $19 sheet cake from Safeway.

The cake looks too tall to be just a single layer. Duff says it's made of two—maybe even three—short cakes. To cut down the baking times, he uses smaller pans. Rather than baking a tall cake for forty minutes, he can bake two shorter ones for twenty-five. He wastes more cake—bakers slice off the cake tops to make them level—but saves valuable time.

I had originally suggested a mosaic cake because I'd seen one on his site, and I am a mosaicist. It began as a hobby in 1994 when I returned from my European honeymoon with a plan to make a funky kitchen backsplash. I wrapped tiles in towels, bashed them with a hammer, and glued them to my wall, then grouted everything. Since then, I have encrusted two enormous public art projects for Baltimore city, a fish and a crab, which sold at auction for $7,500 and $10,000, respectively; I have built a few chess tables and backsplashes for clients; I have made stained glass dog portraits; and I have created a magnificent buffet countertop for my sister's house. For that one, we both appeared on an episode of HGTV's *Look What I Did!*

So I want Duff Goldman's cake to represent one of my interests. That's the way it is with birthdays. Your kid gets a cake with Harry Potter or the Teletubbies; your husband gets a cake shaped like a guitar; your marathon-running neighbor has a running shoe cake. I need more than a cake-shaped cake. Duff asks me which of the sample cakes out front I like the best; we'll work from that. I choose the bottom layer of a three-tiered novelty cake, which has a harlequin pattern—diamonds and balls. I pick green and orange, my two favorite colors at the moment. I resent, a little, that I am getting a knock-off, that more original thought isn't going into this. Perhaps, I ask in my tiniest voice, some mosaic can be incorporated?

Mary Yeskey, the shop manager, talks to Duff about a client who wants SpongeBob SquarePants riding a Ducati on her groom's cake. For this, Duff figures a charge of five hundred dollars. Gulp.

Sitting at an unoccupied—and mostly clean—table, Duff fills his airbrush with a bright yellow paint and coats my cake. I once lived in a row house on this very street; it was nearly impossible to keep clean. I look up at the ceiling and around at the electrical cords, checking for the grease and dust that inhabited my house. Everything's spotless.

Duff, who doesn't look at all like an artist, works in a tan UMBC Ice Hockey cap, a long-sleeve white RICTA T-shirt, and loose-fitting navy athletic shorts with a triple white stripe down the sides and thick reflective trim on the bottom.

The chef obliges my airbrush curiosity with a lesson, guiding my hand as I spray. I wonder aloud about what we're inhaling, about whether some toxic particles are being dispersed into the air and heading to our lungs, like that killer butter sprayed on popcorn. He switches on a giant, screaming motor, which drowns out all the errant voices. I assure him I'm not worried for my own health at this moment, and he switches it off. He uses it mainly when they're working with metallic paints. My cake gets a second coat of brighter orange before Duff whips out the vodka and some glittery paint.

"It's like ninety bucks a bottle" (the paint, not the vodka), which lasts the shop a couple of months. "I'm notorious for putting sparklies on stuff. Actually, everybody ganged up on me last time and wouldn't let me sparkle any of those things that you saw going out there, and that's all I wanted to do," he said, referring to the cakes shaped like a Prada shoe and bag leaving for a party that afternoon.

"I would've sparkled the shoe," I give him.

"Not even the shoe, not even the shoe," he laments, as he mixes some vodka and gold paint in a plastic cup. He uses alcohol instead of water because it evaporates more quickly. We have a mesmerizing, intimate moment, Duff and I, as we stare into the liquid, watching it swirl around. I'm reminded of my husband, who, every morning for the past fifteen years, has watched the pattern made in his coffee by the Coffee-Mate. Duff's voice gets low and hypnotic, like a stoner. "It'll do that for hours," he tells me. "Actually, as the concentration changes, as it becomes more and more saturated, the patterns change." At the moment, they look like coffee beans.

"You just found a way to trip without drugs," I tell him.

"Yeah, pretty much. Now, this settles really really fast, so . . . every time you use it, you have to shake it." The airbrush motor hums, and my cake is transformed like magic, with a little of what Duff calls "pixie dust." I inspect a little further than the cursory glance at the ceiling and cords and discover that the whole place seems to be covered in a thin film of glitter—the counters, the chairs, anything in airbrush range. It's hard to look dirty when you sparkle.

It's time for the fondant, which is mixed with green food paste and kneaded to achieve a uniform color before it's rolled flat.

"So this mosaic thing you're talking about," he finally says, "um, you basically want to do like an indentation, right? Now are they going to be squares, or they going to be all different shapes?" I choose irregular, though I want to leave it up to Duff. He decides it would be best to indent the designs in the green diamonds once they've been applied to the cake.

"Why don't we put you here, Leslie?"

"I don't want to be in the way," I say.

"That way, as Ana's going and spinning, you can be drawing."

"As she's doing what?" As *I'm* doing what? I can bake fairly well, but cake decorating—let's just say that every cake I've ever made for someone else needed my sign.

"As she's putting the actual triangles on."

Oh. Uh.

"Are you sure?" Some coherent words have formed.

"I'm sure," he says, and gives me instructions. "I'd do it on the green."

While I stab at a green triangle with an X-Acto knife, Duff takes pictures of me with my own camera. I will scrutinize these shots later: that's my favorite pink shirt; why is my hair in such a high ponytail?; my shoulders are hunched like my grandmother's; I look positively Jewish from that angle.

In a few short minutes, I give up. I'm pretty good with a knife—despite the time I chopped off the tip of my thumb cutting a piece of drywall—but my contribution looks like crap. Ana and Duff agree, politely, but neither makes a motion to help me out and do a better job. And so the mosaic idea is scrapped, so to speak, and I move out of the way.

Duff has his hand in a few other projects while my cake is getting patterned. He also attempts to manage, giving the intern something to do. "I don't know how to do that," she tells him at once, her hands behind her back. I notice her comment is *not* followed with, "But I could learn, if you wanted to show me," and my skin prickles with disappointment. But Duff doesn't make a big deal of it. Instead, he makes a couple of daisies in an open egg carton. I think I'd like a couple of them on my cake, and that's Duff's idea, too. I am asked to make another executive decision regarding a choice between silver dragées or white balls at the diamond points, and I select dragées.

After cutting some lengths of wire, Duff goes to the back wall for a Styrofoam cake, which he carries back toward me. He sinks the wires in foam and rolls a few orange balls out of fondant, attaching them to the ends. The wires arc with the weight. Instant sproing!

Duff remembers that his *Roker on the Road* episode airs tonight and makes an announcement to the staff. No one moves.

"They look excited," I joke.

"Yeah."

"They didn't hear you."

"No, they did."

Someone pipes up. "Duff, are you gonna tape the show?"

"I don't have a VCR," he says, showing his technological innocence, as no one has called them VCRs in aeons, and Mary offers to
tape it.

We decide on white fondant balls around the cake bottom, so
Ana rolls and applies them in no time. I admire some festive, fall-
colored gum-paste leaves on toothpicks, so Duff pokes them in some
perfect places. While he and Ana adorn, I stand back and take in
the peaceful atmosphere. No one is stressed. People mold and sculpt
cake toppers, press out flowers and leaves, put materials back in
their places. Everyone steps back every so often to admire his own
or another's work. A few cakes are eager to get to their celebrations,
but the sole driver hasn't returned from his morning delivery. Duff
will probably drive the cakes himself.

This is not my first time at Duff's place, but today's visit is more
comfortable, warmer. He has a soothing voice, a serene, almost Zen
demeanor. I can see that this little shop of sweets is a happy place
to work. This, Duff assures me, is as crazy as it gets at Charm City
Cakes. It's kind of eerie, too, because if I knew I had no one to drive
cakes to Columbia and the Eastern Shore by this afternoon and other
cakes to finish up by the weekend, I wouldn't be poking around,
slowly making daisies. No, I'd be stressing out everyone in the room
with my negativity and impatience.

Duff puts the finishing touch on my cake by writing, as per my
request, on the silver-foiled cake board: "Happy Freakin' Birthday."
Almost a decade has passed since the first f-word cake; I'm a mom
now with a daughter who can read. He puts together a topless cardboard box, covers it with plastic wrap, and sends me on my way, thus
saving himself the effort of having to deliver it by 4:00 tomorrow, but
keeping the extra fifteen- or twenty-dollar charge. I'll eat that. That's
my fee for helping.

It's been raining, and I am sent, alone, to the car, balancing the
two-hundred-dollar cake (when I think of the price, it is always

spelled out in my head) on my left arm as I unlock the car door with my right. Little drops of rain sit on the plastic, wiggling as we ride the lumpy streets north and east to my house.

You Paid *How Much*?

Before I bring the cake inside, I cover it with my jacket to keep the rain from getting the plastic too wet, and I remove it from the box within minutes, clearing off a space on my table for the photographs. I shoot it from above, while standing on a chair. I shoot it from the side, with natural light, with flash, on a different table. And then I decide on a shot and send it out to a handful of folks in order to tempt them into attending my birthday party and helping me assess the edibility of this beauty.

My husband comes home from work and can't help but notice that he is interrupting some deviant cake fantasy. He smiles when he sees it—*her,* I want to say now, as if she were some sort of tricked-out ride. "How much did *that* cost you?"

"Oh, please don't ask me that." But he is going to, so I make a deal. "How about this: What does it *look* like it cost?"

"Two hundred dollars."

I think we're cool.

But the moment of truth comes the following evening. On my dining room table are four cakes: a white chocolate cheesecake (cream cheese pie, really, as it's crust and filling) I made using a ten-year-old *Bon Appétit* recipe, which calls for nearly a pound of white chocolate (which my mother says . . .)—half used as *ganache*—raspberry jam, and sliced almonds; a marshmallow cake covered with toasted coconut; another coconut cake so delicious that it has already been devastated by the just-one-more-little-piece thieves prior to cake cutting; and the ceremonial cake, star of my show.

I cut it while someone snaps a picture that will, later, make me swear off carbs for life (though another cake event—and there are many—will force me back far too early). I give everyone a slice, and we all taste it together. No one wants to say anything. It's good, but good isn't what you say of a two-hundred-dollar cake. You say, "WOW! Holy shit! Boffo!" Or you say nothing and keep chewing and moaning.

This is a moist cake, but it's almost candylike with the fondant. And without it—well, I might as well eat a muffin, right? There's barely any icing left beneath the marshmallow fondant, and what's there has melted under the heat of this polyester-ish top. The white cake is a little more crumbly than other cakes I've eaten. But there's nothing to distinguish it from a box mix, really.

It's my fault. I could've chosen mint chocolate chip. Next time. And to be fair, there should be a next time, shouldn't there? Even though frosting is my passion?

But if there is a next time, won't I worry that Duff would be pointing to *my* cake and telling some visitor to his shop, "Yeah, but I hate the person that cake is for. Freakin' bitch"? I will have to pretend to be someone else.

While we continue to nosh and nibble and drink more beer, my friend Kim removes a few of the cake's decorations and applies them to places on her body. I slice another piece of cheesecake.

Within a couple of days, I do what I've not done with a cake in forty-three years, and I am somewhat ashamed: I toss it, "frosting" and all. I guess my taste buds, at least where birthday cake is concerned, have arrested development.

I long for a Safeway cake. I want to eat all four corners. In private.

The Center of the Cake Universe

Those extremes of cheap snack and expensive boutique cake are all about excess. In the end, it's the guys down the road—the old German baker and his wife who own an old-fashioned bakery or the French patisserie in the heart of town or even CakeLove (the one with the oven)—who will give you the closest thing to your grandmother's baked love. Most of them are using things you have in your own kitchen, and a lot of them are not using box mixes (some of them are, and so did some of your grandmothers). You're bound to find, as I have, that theirs are the best-tasting and most satisfying desserts. They may be a little too expensive to give to your son's class on his birthday, and they are usually decorated to look like cake, but as far as I'm concerned, they're perfect. I can trust them not to kill me, however slowly, with their chemicals, and it's a safe bet I won't be breaking any teeth on a gum-paste frill. And to Fenwick Bakery, where my husband, the Immanuel Kant of doughnut eaters,* buys ten cinnamon Bismarcks every single Saturday morning, I'm just Mrs. Miller, who sometimes breaks her diet for a chocolate doughnut, rather than someone the baker finds loathsome.

Yeah, there's something to be said for the middle. That's where the filling is.

---

* It was said that Immanuel Kant's walks around Königsberg were so regular that the philosopher's neighbors could set their clocks by his passing by their homes. It is apparent the ladies at Fenwick feel the same about my husband. An overheard Saturday phone call went like this: "Good morning! . . . Just ten today, thank you!" The part I missed went like this: "Good morning, Fenwick Bakery . . . Oh, Mr. Miller! How many today—ten or twelve?"

It's very easy to confuse Sean Connery with James Bond. Sometimes in the entertainment industry, people believe the cake is more real than the baker.

—Judd Nelson, actor

Competitions
FIFTH TIER

Gentlemen,
Start Your Mixers!

I know guys who are hot for the perpetual left turn, others who paint their faces in team colors to watch the Super Bowl in their own *living* rooms. Some get a thrill from wrestling or (snore) tennis or golf. But give me a heat of toque-clad, white-coated, spatula-wielding bakers on the starting line, and my heart will race to the finish. Ooohh, bake 'em!

Food fights are nothing new. While the Grammys are only half a century old, and the Oscars are just over three-quarters, the food industry has been staging national contests for well over a century. In 1880, Cadwallader C. Washburn (a name like that is destined for fame) paraded his company's flour before a panel of judges, and Superlative Flour cakewalked away with the grand prize. Its name was changed immediately to the brand you know as Gold Medal. Its package is so bright that you've probably passed up all other brands for this winner. True bakers know the difference (there's a Gold Medal on Wondra Cake Flour for a reason; it's dreamy).

I'm something of a cynic when it comes to cake competitions.

Sure, they're fun to watch, but what do they prove? We can see a clear winner when the Colts assault the Ravens or when Serena Williams clobbers her opponents. But unless a cake topples over, for a clear loss (as it's done a few times on the Food Network), how does a cake contestant win? How does pumpkin chocolate chip trump yellow cake with raspberry filling? How can white square boxes show up round pink and brown ones? When all the batter's beaten, and a baker declares victory, is his or her cake really the *best,* or is it just what the judge was in the mood for that day? Perhaps it was simply that 137,082 voters preferred one look and imagined they'd like one flavor over another. Two people, Sarah Raley and Mark Dale, were hoping that America's favorite cake would be theirs, too.

In 2000, the *Today* show began giving one lucky couple an all-expenses-paid wedding. The only catch is that every important detail—from the bridesmaids dresses to the honeymoon destination—is left to a national audience's fickle, and often questionable, tastes. Fortunately, viewers are limited to the respectable choices of the segment's producers. Someone in East Lansing, Michigan, for example, can't write in a vote for a honeymoon in Motor City, nor can a viewer in Lynchburg, Virginia, request a sheet cake from the Piggly Wiggly (not that I would mind the latter).

Raley and Dale, a Maryland couple, are the sixth recipients of the Hometown Wedding. They are tan and attractive and wholesome, exactly the type of people you'd expect to win a free wedding from *Today*. It is, after all, a popularity contest. To get this far, they had to sell themselves—and solicit enough e-mail votes from friends and relatives of friends of friends. Raley is the director of sales at a hotel, and her husband owns the gym where he was once a customer—and Raley an employee before they began dating.

The couple's input went as far as these three questions:

1. How adventurous are you?
2. Did you ever have a dream gown in mind when you were a kid?
3. Is there a cake flavor you don't like?

Beyond volunteering that they both hated mocha, they were not involved in any of the choices for their wedding. When you think about it, it's better that no one can blame *you* for tacky brides-maids dresses and a smarmy wedding singer, and you don't have to get into a fight with your mom over the centerpieces. The producers searched online for wedding venues and vendors, including baker-ies in the Baltimore area, and wound up with four able candidates for chef: Duff Goldman, of Charm City Cakes; Leslie Poyourow, of Fancy Cakes by Leslie; Jamie Williams, of SugarBakers; and New Jersey's Cakediva, Charmaine Johnson.

Leslie Poyourow got a call out of the blue from *Today*'s producers and was invited to submit pictures and drawings of cakes that would look glamorous on television. She wasn't aware that their annual wedding competition had begun; she'd been too busy with her grow-ing D.C. clientele and their end-of-summer to-dos.

Today had parameters, of course. One might expect a show like this to test its contestants' mettle—or at least their cakes—but it was nothing so extreme. From each of the contestants, *Today* wanted sketches of four cakes: a square cake, a cake with flowers, a cake that had an embroidered look, and a cake that featured candy.

For Duff Goldman, the question of whether to compete had an obvious answer. Of *course;* it's good—and free—publicity. Duff, a frequent Food Network contributor and star of his own series, *Ace of Cakes,* is a publicity hound. Someone recently paid homage to Duff for making Baltimore famous for something other than homicides, teen pregnancies, and TV shows about homicides and teen pregnancies. Duff vigorously pursues what he wants. Instead of four sketches, he sent eight.

SugarBakers was among the chosen four because Darcy Miller, editorial director of Martha Stewart *Weddings,* one of the producers of this contest, knows Jamie's work. She's the most traditional baker of the group and probably already had one of every cake *Today* wanted. She was able to submit photographs instead of drawings.

The last contestant, New Jersey's Cakediva, was chosen primarily because she has a reputation for unusual creations. One of the country's few high-profile black bakers, the Diva is often seen on the Food Network in glittery frocks and a blond wig. Still, with her bakery in New Jersey, several hours away from Baltimore, she seemed the odd girl out.

It's the Cakes, Dummy

Once all the sketches and photos were in, the show's producers decided which cake they wanted each baker to produce for the competition. Contestants were then asked to make a dummy cake (fondant-covered Styrofoam replicas) that they'd schlep to New York along with some slices of real cake for the on-screen judges—Natalie Morales (the segment host), Darcy Miller, and the couple—to taste.

The team at Charm City created the Swarovski Crystal Cake. MSNBC's Web site description doesn't do it justice: "This spectacular four-tiered pumpkin chocolate chip cake has ivory fondant and buttercream icing. Sarah's wedding gown was the inspiration for this creation. In order to illustrate the sparkly and shiny feeling of her dress, Duff and company suspended a variety of Swarovski crystals on several layers of the cake. And to compliment [*sic*] the bridesmaid dresses, three of the layers are adorned with black magic roses."*

---

* The cake for the wedding of Carmen Electra to Dave Navarro was nearly identical. Who had the idea first? Well, they were married November 22, 2003, almost two years before Charm City's cake was created. Now, everybody on the planet is doing it, including Planet Cake, from Australia, which makes what it calls the Carmen Electra Couture Cake. Not incidentally, Carmen and Dave had split by the end of July 2006.

I can't do much better with my description. When I visit Duff Goldman's too-small Remington cake shop just after the contest has ended, no dummy is propped on a pedestal, and no giant photographs of it are offered. I'm assured, though, that it was a spectacle to behold, with its glittering glass drops and mounds of red roses between layers. When he and his sculptor, Jeff, watched the unveiling of the cakes in New York, they had their chests puffed out in anticipation of the gold medal. "Ours was by far the best. By far." I squirm a little. He looks at me a bit too long, as if to discern which cake I rooted for. It's almost an accusatory glance. But in seconds, he doesn't care.

Sarah, the bride, confides to me a year later that she had thought Duff's cake elegant, but that look—the red flowers with white—was not her taste. The producers could tell it wasn't her favorite and tried to get her to look at the bright side. If the American audience were to choose it for her cake, she could use the hundreds of dollars' worth of Swarovski crystals on it in one of her crafts projects.

The edible-looking mock-up of Leslie's cake sits near the entrance of her Gaithersburg shop, and it's even more beautiful in reality. The bottom tier is a brown square box with vertical pink stripes. Above it sits another square box, this one brown with a pink scalloped lid. Atop that is a round brown cake with pink polka dots. The top cake is a pink box capped by a brown scalloped lid. A chocolate sugar vase filled with handmade buttercream flowers finishes the cake gracefully. (Note that no one used a tacky plastic bride and groom topper, which you can still find in places like the Cake Cottage and Michael's.)

I phoned in my vote for this cake because of my need for a bit of whimsy in my traditions. Pink and brown is a funky, modern color combo, and the shapes are sophisticated, not cute. These are elegant packages, but they're festive, too; they know how to have a good time.

(Okay, if you must know, I voted for it because of a fondness I have for a pair of shoes that got away—a $180 pair of pink and brown pumps in a sort of hybrid style I remember fondly as Spectators–meet–Mary Janes.)

Originally, Leslie produced an all-white version—and mocha might have been on the menu—but the show's producers asked her to make it in the unusual colors, a decision that troubled her. Americans aren't ready for any kind of wedding cake blasphemy; surely a brown cake was some sort of confrontation with the higher nuptial powers. What's next, viewers might wonder: *black* fondant? A pink and brown cake is like the camel's nose under the tent. Let them have this, and brides might abandon trains and veils, choose attractive bridesmaids dresses, give rubber animal nose masks as favors! Leslie was sure that SugarBakers had it locked.

I voted for your cake, Leslie—*because* it was pink and brown.

I didn't tell her to consider the source. At my 1994 wedding, I had no veil or train, my bridesmaids wore sixty-dollar shifts from the White House, and we gave out rubber animal noses from the Nature Company as our wedding favors. Our album is full of candid shots of smiling guests with rats' whiskers, dogs' snouts, and tigers' philtrums. Our own cake, made by Joseph Poupon of Patisserie Poupon, was a masterpiece—five different flavors of boxes wrapped in pink, yellow, gray, and beige paisley, polka dots, and amorphous splotches, with ribbons and braided rope. It might even have been fondant, way back in 1994, but I remember it being far more delicious. Atop the cake was an open-lidded box made of white chocolate. Inside was our topper: Rollerblade Barbie and the Beast (a *Beauty and the Beast* replica). My mom made their gown and tux to match our own. Below the couple stood a plastic dog, his coat painted to match our dog Beowulf's coat; Wulf attended the wedding from a distance.

If it makes me a little odd, it also lets me in on a secret about Americans. We'd rather have fun at a wedding. We might not be able to lighten up for our own party, but we'd give to others what we secretly desire.

SugarBakers is an adorable ice cream parlor of a shop (I want to call it a *shoppe*) on Baltimore's west side. When I meet Jamie Williams there one morning, I learn that she was *told* to do a square cake, though I had already read elsewhere that she'd *chosen* to do it. The dummy of her cake gleams in the window of her Catonsville bakery. She pulls out a photograph of the fresh-made model, as the one in the window has faded in the sunlight. She's like a proud parent showing off her kid's class photo; you expect a halo inches above the precious child's head. It's as glorious as a white wedding cake could be, really: four boxes, in decreasing size, stacked on one another, perfectly centered. The tower of gifts is topped with a fondant ribbon—the fluffy kind of ribbon that you'd find on Martha Stewart's wedding present to you—its four tails draped against the boxes as if they'd fallen there naturally and perfectly. More than a third of each box is lid, demarcated by a single border of pearls and a glittery crust of sanding sugar, into which are pressed small dragées. "We hand-painted the little pearls to pick up the color of the pearls in her gown," Jamie says. The dress was completely beaded, and the sugar was chosen to reflect both the dress and the couple's choice of a beach wedding. It's a traditional cake to be sure, but tight, with considerable logical thought and hard work. Jamie even made a real cake for the samples and says it took about forty hours to complete.

On TV, Natalie Morales referred to Jamie's cake—not one week but *both* weeks—as "Red Velvet PreSENTS." I guess she didn't realize those boxes were actually *presents,* you know, gifts, and that the Red Velvet cake wasn't actually presenting something.

On air, for the tasting of the final entry, that of the Cakediva, Mark, the groom, was blindfolded to prevent him from seeing the cake—formed in the shape of his fiancée's wedding gown—and jinxing their marriage. (No one told these people that the superstition says their marriage is doomed only if he sees his fiancée in the gown before the wedding. Viewing a slouchy, edible, distant replica of a dress is unpleasant but not bad luck.) Sarah is judicious—more so than Duff, who said the Cakediva's cakes "look like they fell off the back of a truck." "It was not beautiful," Sarah says, describing the gown as "short and squatty" and the whole cake as domelike. "Maybe they were rushed," she says, searching for the right words. The cake "looked as if it had already begun falling apart," she admits gently.

The bride's cake wasn't the only one vying for first prize. Before the competition began, Leslie suggested that everyone submit a groom's cake as well. These are generally more kitschy, more like a child's fifth-birthday cake. She was told that everyone had to consent, or *Today* would scrap the idea. But it went over.

Leslie's offering, which I ogle in person, is a faux wood crate—like the kind you'd find filled with apples at produce stands in the country—made of hand-painted fondant and filled to overflowing with realistic-looking crabs, their black beady eyes perhaps a little less sad and pleading. On a fondant-covered cake round, that foil-covered circle all bakers use, are mallets, buttered ears of corn, a single crab, and a tin of Old Bay (Maryland's famous seafood spice)—all made of the rolled marshmallow stuff. It's perfect in every detail.

The groom's cake submitted by Duff's crew is a giant black dumbbell to reflect Mark Dale's interest in weight lifting. Jamie's is a two-layer, square cake topped with a brown Jeep and a pair of Scottie dogs. The rest is a beach scene—shells, boat, seagull, rocks, docks— along with a body builder and his weights. It depicts "everything that he's into," Jamie says. It's no bushel of crabs, frankly, but it's cute enough. What I like best are the little piles of graham-cracker-crust sand everywhere. I can't stop thinking about how clever that is—more clever than the dirt cake (made of cookies, Cool Whip, and pudding) in a flowerpot, Gummi Worms poking through a topsoil layer of crushed Oreos, which is served to delighted five-year-olds via garden trowel. The Cakediva's offering is shaped like a squatty version of the groom's tuxedo.

Meet the Contestants: Duff Goldman, Charm City Cakes

"I have the palate of a four-year-old," said Duff Goldman in a telephone conversation before we met the first time, before he did my cake. He's not kidding. The night before, he had a chicken Parmesan sub and a bag of Gummi Worms. At nine, my daughter is already beginning to grow out of food that wiggles. Duff became a pastry chef because he is, plain and simple, a sugar freak. If he was looking for the cure, Velma Haywood's plan didn't work for him.

But his answer is different a week later, when he addresses a crowd assembled beneath a huge tent at the Baltimore Book Festival, where he is master of ceremonies for the anniversary cake contest. (Hey, they might not have picked my recipe, but there are no sour grapes where free cake is concerned.) "The philosophy store wasn't hiring," Chef Duff explains. It's not as big a stretch as it may sound. After all, many a fine mind has contemplated cake and Kafka or enjoyed Sartre and a slice. Remember Rousseau scrounging around the dark streets for something sweet to go with his wine and book? But with Duff, the connection was clearer.

As a high school kid in Boston, Duff, given his nickname by a

child who couldn't pronounce Jeff, was already a competent graf-
fiti artist when his art teacher suggested a switch to something less
freedom-threatening but equally dangerous: welding. (I wonder for a
moment if he's the one spraying CAKE in red and yellow all over the
trees and water pump in Herring Run Park, where I walk my dogs.)
He had a tag, he admits, but he never vandalized. He liked welding
enough—and it didn't hurt that his teacher let students smoke in the
supply room—but when it came time to choose a college and a major,
he found himself a bit too much of a redneck for the blue-haired,
pierced-nipple art crowd, and went for a physics and philosophy double major at University of Maryland, Baltimore County. He'd never
been to Baltimore and chose it because it was unexplored territory.

"Cake is chemistry," he tells the audience waiting for the names
of the cake contest winners to be announced. (Well, we are not really waiting for that. We want to eat the winners.) "It's science," he
says. "You have to know about gravity. . . . For example, if you want
to bake a cake in the shape of a guy running, you have to know it's
going to fall," which is why half of the cake has to be made of inedible
armature.

Cake is home economics, too. And it's shop. "At my bakery, for
example, we have an arc welder, a band saw, a bench grinder, a belt
sander—some things that you wouldn't necessarily find in a bakery."

Goldman was chosen to emcee this event not merely because he
is all doughy youth and charm and ad lib—at least at this moment;
he has street cred. He's a media darling, with half a dozen Food Network appearances, including the one on *Roker on the Road,* airing
the day before my forty-third birthday. He tells the audience that Al
Roker is "a maniac; he's insane. . . . He came in, grabbed the knife
out of my hand. . . . [He was] eatin' cake all the time. Dude, didn't
you have a gastric bypass?" His hit reality show, *Ace of Cakes,* was set
to debut in April. (He will swear, later, that the show's title is *Fuck
You, Let's Bake*. And for the record, I didn't believe him.)

While the judges—a food editor, an events manager, a neighborhood representative, and an advertising sales manager—inspect and

taste and, shamefully, leave wasted portions on the plates in front of each creation (the confection critics' answer to the wine tasters' spittoon), Duff leaves the jury-rigged Ikea kitchen to take questions from the audience.

"Why do I still have batter in the middle of my cake?" a gentleman asks. "Birthday" by the Beatles plays in the background.

"Cook it lower and longer. Unless it's a thick cake," Goldman tells him, "then you want it faster and higher." He asks the audience if we know why the cakes poof up in the middle. He looks at me. (He really does look at me. I am wearing a glamorous hat, which, when I wear it, makes *everyone* look at me.) I know the answer has to do with the perimeter cooking faster than the center, but instead of the answer, I volunteer a solution disguised as a question.

"What about Magi-Cake strips?" I call out. Since bringing these temperature-regulating strips home from Cake Cottage, I've hardly had to trim any misshapen tops.

He thinks for a moment, a resounding no on his lips from the start, then admits "they actually do work." But when you're baking with giant pans and sculpting many of your creations, you do what the professionals do to get a flat-topped cake. "Every cake bakery throws away a quarter of the cake," he says, adding that it's "where MoonPies came from."* Duff is happy to donate the scraps to Our

---

* But that's not actually where MoonPies come from. According to the author of *The Great American MoonPie Handbook,* Ronald Dickson, they were invented by Earl Mitchell, Sr., a salesman from the Chattanooga Bakery. He asked coal miners what they might like for a snack; they wanted something satisfying. And big. Mitchell asked how big. Legend has it that the moon had risen at that exact moment (accompanied, no doubt, by that Old West five-note whistle), and a miner cupped his hands around it to show the proposed snack's desired circumference. Meanwhile, back at the ranch, something was blooming on the windowsills. Assembly-line workers made themselves snacks of graham crackers dipped in marshmallow, which they left to harden. Mitchell had an aha moment; he told them to add a top, dip it in chocolate, and voilà! Nothing whatsoever to do with tops of cakes.

Daily Bread, a local soup kitchen. "Let them eat cake," he says, and the audience chuckles.

It takes a while for the judges to pick the winners; among them are Steve Blair's Lime Sandwich (it looks like it hopped off the pages of *Southern Living*), Chandra Smith's Lemon Crunch Cake, and Alison Sheridan's Carolina Pound Cake. In the moment following the announcement, the audience rises in unison, like a swarm of hungry bees vying for the same flower. Pushing and shoving is involved. I am elbowed out of the way, even in my fancy hat.

My consolation is a clear path toward the podium, where Duff talks with a fan. I eavesdrop, taking anxious glances back at the quickly disappearing cake I want—that lemon thing, with the ample frosting. He tells the woman that she can look up cake sculptors online, and he mentions two artists in particular: "Winebeckler" and his protégé, Mike McCarey. I interrupt, my enthusiasm bubbling over. I tell the two of them that I just interviewed Roland *Win*beckler by e-mail, so his Web address is fresh in my mind. I give it to her. I spell Winbeckler's name, and she thanks me.

When the woman leaves, I extend a hand and introduce myself to Duff as the person who will be visiting him in the coming week to find out about cake competitions. I am effusive and humble at the feet of this cake god. But Goldman doesn't smile; in fact, he looks angry and practically ushers me off the stage. And so I go, confused and deflated, to the cake table, where the crowd has thinned to those interested in thirds and fourths. I snatch a slice of lemon comfort. I ask for the pile of frosting stuck to the knife, and the cutter obliges with a smile. It's her favorite part, too, she tells me, a wink in her voice.

Puttin' the Charm in Charm City Cakes

The next day, I call Duff to schedule my appointment. I introduce myself, and after a brief, uncomfortable silence, he chews me up and spits me out like a judged cake. "Let me give you a piece of advice," Duff says. "Never correct the person you're trying to get an interview with in front of someone else."

That's an awkward sentence, I think. "Huh?" I say. "Did I correct you?"

"Yeah, about that *Win*beckler."

I stumble, attempting to correct the mistake, explaining that I was merely trying to be of assistance to his customer, that embarrassing him was certainly the last thing I intended to do. After more moments of silence, I beg. "Can I still come? I'd offer to bake you a cake, but it probably wouldn't be as good."

He sweetens and softens. Of *course* I can come, he says. I can tell he feels a lot better after having gotten this off his chest. I can tell a lot of other things about Duff Goldman in these few minutes, too: that he likes to talk about himself above all, and that he speaks his mind freely. Dread and worry follow me, even after our firmed plans, and I realize that I am going to see the sour side of the culinary world, that I will learn the sweets we buy from stores to celebrate our milestones are not made with a grandmother's love or hands that rock their children to sleep. They are made by people with bills to pay, axes to grind, something to prove. They are made by men who would be kings of flour and sugar, men who would lord over their subjects with an iron mitt.

Two days before my Forty-third Eating of the Cake (which is the day before we decorate my cake), I arrive at the doorstep of Charm City Cakes. It's a dreary, rainy day, and I am five minutes early. I knock on the door of this unattractive row house on Twenty-seventh Street, a street I know intimately, and since no one's in (and the door has no canopy under which to wait and stay dry), I get back in my car. After a short wait, I notice the door ajar, a bit of light peeking underneath. I knock but can't hear anything over the swish of tires on the wet street and push open the door to shout a tentative hello into the empty room. I am terrified that Duff is back there somewhere, in the bathroom, perhaps, and just waiting for another chance to chew me out—this time for what might be a more legitimate reason. But it's just an employee, deaf to my shouts and knocks beneath the drone of refrigerators and mixers and band saw motors or whatever is humming and grinding in the kitchen.

I wait, dry and comfortable, on an old sofa in the reception area for nearly thirty minutes before Duff arrives, soaking wet, with his bike. He apologizes, blames a flat tire, and then excuses himself for a few moments to take care of pressing business and make himself fully available to talk. He is warm and relaxed, cheerful despite the flat and the weather. I am impressed. The grocery store is two short blocks from my house, and if it's raining, I drive.

Duff toots his own horn, but in a seemingly humble way, speaking of his appearances on the Food Network and the stories about him in magazines, including *Fortune*. "We've had so much press—I'm not saying that in a jaded way. I'm saying it in like an incredibly wonderfully wow-we-are-incredibly-lucky kind of way." So when a contest of the caliber and the exposure of *Today* comes about, Charm City is the name on everyone's lips. "It's very evident just by looking at our work that you know we're very joyful in what we do."

I can't deny that this is one happy place. The drab exterior belies what's inside: a sort of *Cat in the Hat* meets *Alice in Wonderland*. The shelves are full of Styrofoam models covered with fondant and disguised as whimsical cakes, with springs and wires and bobbing antennae. They are shaped like traditional cakes but off kilter just a smidge, or else they feature perfect, lifelike roses. Hanging from the torchiere is a Pillsbury Doughboy necktie. On a dusty coffee table, next to the old zebra-print sofa, sits a bizarre creation with fondant tentacles, bobbing mini sombreros, and giant feathers, something that looks more like a crazy hat than a cake. A dry-erase calendar on the wall announces the dates of Duff's Food Network competition; his own birthday on the seventeenth of December; everyone's favorite festival of food, "Spanksgiving"; and, on 12/25, the word *Xmas* with a drawing of a menorah—one candle lighted—beneath it. A bookcase holds his favorites by Margaret Braun and Colette Peters, two cake artists whose work Duff seems to combine in imitation.

"It's so much fun," he tells me. "Like, you can't not come in here and smile. It's just full of joy."

For a moment, I picture him at his cheerful desk, stern voice chastising me for helping the woman that day of the Baltimore Book Festival.

Because he plays in a band (a droning, spacey, alternative instrumental band called . . . soihadto . . .), Goldman has a reputation as a rock-and-roll baker. He's created edible masterworks for small bands such as Clutch and Biohazard and big dudes like Alice Cooper and Rick Springfield—or, rather, Rick Springfield's behind. "[Rick's manager] sent me a picture of his ass naked and [said], 'This is his ass; make a cake of his ass.' . . ." (Despite several professional e-mails to Springfield's management, no one would respond to the matter of the butt cake.)

And then there's the story of Hollywood actress Lucy Liu. Her personal assistant called Duff to ask for a cake of a dolphin jumping out of a river. So he calculated the costs of first-class plane tickets for him and a helper, a hotel for three nights in L.A., an SUV waiting at the airport to transport all the stuff he'd need to bring with him, and the cost of the cake and his time. That didn't sit well with the Lucy party. " 'You should be doing this for free,' and I was like, 'Excuse me?' 'Lucy Liu is an A-list star, and that's how we do things out here.' " She went on to say that once Duff spent this small fortune in order to be honored to bake Lucy's cake, his business would take off. "I'm in Baltimore. If Lucy Liu wants me to get on a plane and do an incredibly complicated cake, a cake for some stupid party she's having in Hollywood—if she doesn't want it, tell her to find some baker in L.A. to do it, and tell them to do it for free, because they're the type of people that will do a free cake for an A-list star. I don't think she's A-list."

But look at all the work Duff does for a potential prize or for publicity: the Baltimore Book Festival, for instance, and oodles of competitions on the Food Network. Perhaps at this point in his career—a time when the Food Network uses shots of Duff carrying a cake atilt across a stage to garner publicity for its Iron Chef competitions—he doesn't need any gigs that will cost him; after all, if *this* A-list celebrity won't pay, what A-list celebrities will?

Charm City Cakes has its big, vocal front man, but behind the scenes are a few folks doing some amazing work. Jeff, the engineering-minded 3-D guy, used to earn his keep by building architectural models. Sherry was a sculpture major in college and is now building a bride, a groom, and camels out of gum paste for a cake featuring a couple riding off into the desert for a Moroccan-themed wedding. (Gum paste isn't as gross as it sounds; it's the same stuff used to make the candy message hearts at Valentine's Day.) A former pastry chef for the Vail Cascade Resort and Spa in Colorado (as well as bread baker at Todd English's Olives in D.C., and *stagiere* at French Laundry in Napa Valley), Duff explains why he got out of that business. "It was just bullshit, you know? . . . And I am a very sensitive person, and so I was working in all those places and also, you know, I'm above average intelligence . . . and I'm like, you know, 'if I was running this place, I wouldn't say that. . . .' "

Meet the Contestants: Leslie Poyourow, Fancy Cakes by Leslie

Leslie Poyourow's shop in a suburban complex in Gaithersburg, Maryland, is clean and spare and decorated mostly with sample cakes. Beyond a half-wall, two ladies shape sugar leaves, while a news anchor on television talks quietly in the background. Since it's only Tuesday, and most of the work at cake boutiques is done at the end of the week, the place isn't bustling with the usual staff of seven assembling weekend party cakes. We sit at a consultation table in the corner farthest from the door in a small area in front of the kitchen.

When you look at Fancy Cakes by Leslie's body of work, you can't help the audible awe. Even the few samples on her Web site show a sense of artistic talent. But the leopard-print hatboxes, poodles, satin swags, dogs, purses, bejeweled and beflowered and besparkled cakes never reveal Leslie's lack of art background. Growing up, she loved baking and sewing and made her own clothes and curtains. And she's sure her love of textiles has informed her design sense, but she thinks art is in her blood. Her sister, who paints and does stained-glass work, is a graduate of the Corcoran College of Art and Design, and her first cousin is a sculptor. "I don't even know, honestly, how I do some of it because I was never trained or had any interest. It just surfaced one day."

We have plenty in common. When she talks of baking as a kid, I remember my own experiences with my grandmother and neighbors. "One of my favorite classes was home ec, which dates me." Cough. I had home ec, too, and sewed some pretty awful fashions before I got this cool.

She decided, well into her thirties, to try some cake decorating, just for fun, because she loved to make cakes from scratch. "They tasted good, but they always looked like a mountain of mess." I resemble that remark. Before my own foray into the moist white underbelly, you may remember, I was hauling the "Ugly" sign to every party.

Leslie took some Wilton classes—available at craft and cake supply stores—and loved it. She became so good at cake decorating that neighbors were asking her to bake for them. She worked in federal marketing for over twenty years (her degree is in business), but she chucked it all for cake. Her story is similar to that of CakeLove owner and *Sugar Rush* host Warren Brown, who gave up a law practice for cake perfection. Of course, a middle-aged Jewish lady doesn't have the sex appeal of a young black man with braided hair and a soft voice. Leslie built her business up slowly over the last decade, never thinking she'd be on the *Today* show. "It was never a goal. My goal was always to produce a gorgeous product that tasted good, and that was it."

Most of Leslie's clients come from Washington, D.C., which is, in general, less funky and more traditional. It's why, she says, Duff can get away with what he does in a place like Baltimore; D.C. is starched white collar, while Baltimore is "very blue suit. It's a different crowd." Maybe it's a pink-and-brown, Spectators–meet–Mary Janes crowd.

Meet the Contestants:
Jamie Williams, SugarBakers

On the day I first meet Jamie Williams, owner of SugarBakers, I dress in my one semiprofessional outfit: brown-and-pink pinstripe trousers; a white T-shirt; a striped, button-down blouse in brown, pink, and white; and a pale pink blazer. I look good. But I realize I am dressed in the colors of Leslie's cake. Aware that this could create a subconscious animosity (a problem that didn't even occur to me as I dressed for my interview with Duff Goldman), I change to brown cords, a dusty-rose-and-rhinestone print T-shirt, and a red corduroy jacket with sparkly buttons. I am now in the appropriate attire to meet the creator of an all-white, red velvet fudge cake.

I arrive half an hour early. Cake gluttony usually extends to other things, too—in this case, punishment. I started the Atkins diet, yet again, eleven days, four hours, and thirty-two minutes ago and have lost eight pounds, one ounce. Spending any time at all in the presence of cake—even fondant-covered Styrofoam cake—is, for a person like me (addicted, neurotic, weak-willed), just plain insane. But I am early because this place has what the others don't.

SugarBakers is on Frederick Road in Catonsville, Maryland, a quaint town with a one-lane main street lined with all kinds of retail and service goodies. (The sign for local musicians' favorite hangout, Bill's Music House, is visible from the window where the *Today* show cake sits on its pedestal.) This differs from the shops of the other contestants in some important ways. First, it's the only retail establishment among the four choices. Second, it's the only one that's really *decorated*—from the sparkling tin ceiling to the black-and-white checkerboard tile floor. In a previous life, Williams was an interior designer.

The store has two rooms: a main room, where locals come for a muffin and a hot cup of coffee or tea; and a consultation room, a galley decorated in dusty-rose floral wallpaper and coordinating border, granite-topped café tables with cake-dummy centerpieces, and white metal ice cream parlor chairs. The room is nearly literally dripping with romance—some stuffed hearts hang on the wall, and a floor lamp dangles its crystals with Victorian bordello charm. By the front window is *the* cake, resting on a Corinthian column marked with a sign denoting it as such.

The walls of the main room are covered with a dark green floral (mixed fruits, actually, hanging from a swash of leafy vine) wallpaper above a chair rail; a beige-striped paper is on the wall below. Even the top panel of the commercial refrigerator holding drinks, which usually has some pithy slogan like "ICE COLD" on tacky, backlighted Plexiglas™, is covered with wallpaper. A coffee cart holds Kona, Kona decaf, and water in thermal airpots, and a wire basket holds oodles of white sugar packets. The bakery manager offers me a cup of coffee while I wait, and I think about it. But a closer survey of the cart does not reveal the slightest hint of pink, blue, or yellow packets. I wonder if this is some sort of message: you're in a bakery, lady; this is *Sugar*-Bakers, not *Splenda*Bakers. But I don't want to start trouble asking for Sweet'N Low, so I amble around the store with my pad, writing things like "out-of-place mirrored disco ball," "nothing like the college dorm décor of Charm City," "pink and brown cake on counter."

At every turn, I cannot help but think of Duff Goldman. Even the gumball machine—a glass Pillsbury Doughboy with fabric hat—reminds me.

A customer has just come in for something, and she's talking to the bakery manager, telling her about some expensive cupcakes she saw at a Federal Hill bakery. "They were beautifully decorated, but the cake's just not that good." She wanted to get them for a class of schoolchildren; she thought they'd enjoy a treat. But when she found out the cupcakes were five dollars each, "I almost had a heart attack! I don't like the kids *that* much!"

I watch from the service counter as an employee spreads buttercream on a small cake, using a pastry cutter to smooth the finish. I must look as though I am desirous of some puppy in a cage, as she asks me several times if I'm sure I don't want something. I do. I want *that*. I point to the spot in front of her. It's amaretto raspberry, she says, with German buttercream. There's a *German* buttercream?

At noon on the button, after I've noticed everything—the glass block counter with hand-painted mural of Catonsville's fire station (also across the street) and the copper molds and friendly staff—Jamie comes in smiling. I introduce myself, and without missing a beat, she asks, "Have you had a sample of cake yet?"

On my right shoulder, a devil is saying, "It's your *job,* damn it! Eat the cake!" But the angel on my left shoulder wins. I politely decline and promise I will return for a tasting soon. I don't mean to launch into a litany of maladies, but the cake I've eaten in the name of research has gone to my head (and other areas of my body). I want it, but I pass. She's not offended; in fact, she suffers from lupus and doesn't do well on sugar herself. Still, she's going to give me samples to take home and freeze. (I think of the home page of Charm City Cakes: "Always Fresh Never Frozen." Shut up.)

Everyone at SugarBakers is professionally trained—in *baking,* rather than sculpture or structural engineering. I tell her about the class I took at the Cake Cottage, and she laughs, a little too boisterously. "Oh! *These* people actually have degrees in it." It's not as if I am asking for a job. (Alcoholic in a bar, pedophile across the street from a school, sugar freak in a sweets shop: these are bad ideas.) Anyway, Leslie Poyourow isn't ashamed to admit her career began at Michael's.

When the firm for which Jamie worked was bought out by a huge corporation, she wasn't happy anymore and left. She did some freelance work and then wound up going to L'Academie de Cuisine, in Gaithersburg, Maryland—right next to Fancy Cakes by Leslie—to be a chef. She didn't do pastries but wound up doing her internship with the Elkridge Furnace Inn and was put, for some reason, with the pastry chef, who got injured, making Jamie head of the department. Not exactly what she planned, but okay. A decade ago, she and her husband took advantage of an opportunity and bought a dessert company called Happy Endings. And as usually happens just about anywhere in or around Baltimore (aka Smalltimore), Jamie and I discover a mutual acquaintance; I'd gone to college with the former owner. Fancy wedding cakes were really starting to take off at that time, so Jamie took the little cookie and muffin company and turned it into SugarBakers, a joint so classy that Martha Stewart knows about it.

But Jamie's not the competitive type. She didn't expect to be in this sort of contest, and she's not much concerned about her baking competition either. "Everyone's doing a different thing. Duff does his wild things. . . . We're definitely an upscale kind of an artisan-type bakery, and I don't ever want it to become a factory." There's room, she says, for everyone to do what he or she does.

I don't know if that's necessarily true. While I am no stranger to the ACC (American Crafts Council) and life on the wild side, there's something classy about a cake that doesn't look like it's going to topple over on the guests. And Jamie has a wild side, too. Her amaretto-raspberry mosaic cake is both fine and funky, as is the almost-black chocolate fondant cake at our table, with its dramatic peacock feathers and gold-leafed nuts. Do brides really *know* to prefer one over the other? I have visions of a cake parade, long-legged women beneath cake costumes, prancing by. Beautiful cake is beautiful cake. It's as hard to pick a favorite as it is to pick the prettiest Rockette; when you see legs, your eyes glaze over.

"My brides tell me differently, though. . . . Some people just want a cake from Duff because they love that look. I mean, he does some really beautiful, outstanding things. Not that we can't do the same thing, but we're a little bit more, um, maybe middle-of-the-road. . . . We're more like a Martha Stewart kind of design."

I haven't been convinced, by any of these superlative bakers, that a wedding cake is going to be as delectable as a Capital Grille crème brûlée or even a Vol-ca-noooooo! from my daughter's favorite haunt, the Rainforest Café. They hold back too much. These cakes are never sweet enough, never moist enough, never enough of a delightful surprise. (Pumpkin chocolate chip is probably a surprise, but, to me, not delightful.) "That's why I wanted you to taste ours," Jamie says. "When I started the company . . . my concept was to make cakes as beautiful on the inside as they are on the outside. And I think that we've pretty much succeeded in that. People do *love* our cakes."

Every cake boutique owner says the same thing, and I am always tempted. I want to love Jamie's cakes right here and now. I want to, but I resist.

SugarBakers makes *everything* in their retail bakery: not just a multiplicity of cakes with decadent fillings and frostings, but muffins, at least five types of brownies, cookies (including a gigantic black-and-white, which I snag for my daughter), and bear-shaped pops. And the chocolate tops, cookies that usually have a Hershey's Kiss–shaped squirt of chocolate dabbed in the center, are elegantly swirled, with chocolate spread across most of the cookie. With people sampling your wares right off the shelves, it would be hard to hide the fact that your cakes suck. I'm guessing SugarBakers' cakes don't.

Before I leave, Jamie slips behind the counter to prepare a sample for me, while I fog up the glass case displaying gorgeous carryout slices and whole cakes. I assume I will be getting a bite or two of the most popular offerings. Instead, Jamie returns with a giant catering tray. In it, arranged around a floral centerpiece, as if they were bicycle spokes or, better, numbers on a clock, are eleven—eleven!—different types of cake, each slice about an inch square by four layers. Spaced evenly around the wheel is a fancy dollop of each of the three butter-creams. Imagine: a different flavor for each hour of the day and some frosting at midnight. "This is what I give my brides," she tells me. My daughter's cookie is on the house.

I thank the folks at SugarBakers for their hospitality and leave with my front-seat passenger, the hulking catering tray. I wonder whether I have the fortitude to lock it in the freezer the moment I get home. There's a quiet humming. I turn off the radio and listen. For twenty slow, rainy miles, the cake slices serenade me with Beethoven's "Ode to Joy," each inch-square-by-four-layer piece imitating a differ-ent instrument. I remember my own wedding on a beautiful sunny day, a day with all my friends, really good beer, and lots of cake. I miss two exits.

Big Apple Cakes

Dummies in hand, all four Hometown Wedding cake competitors were off to New York City; it was the day Hurricane Katrina hit. They were each called at about eight or nine at night and told they'd not be on TV the next day because of hurricane coverage. "I was having a *hem*orrhage!" Leslie said, as her sister-in-law, who was minding the store, had to leave to watch her grandchild being born.

The four didn't socialize with each other, and it wasn't exactly a celebrity experience, either. If *I'd* trekked all that way with a tower of fondant-covered foam adorned with crystals and flowers, festooned with pearls and bows, I'd want *something* from Katie and Matt. It wouldn't have to be fawning attention, but maybe they could walk out into the lobby and say, "Hey, thanks for those fab cakes! You rock!" Al Roker has paid Duff Goldman a few visits and learned a few tricks, yet none of the on-air personalities so much as winked at them. Most of them were elsewhere.

"Katie was not there—she was on vacation," recalls Jamie. "We saw Matt, didn't meet him; Al was on vacation; Ann was gone; everyone was kind of gone that week, so we didn't really see—we saw the travel guy. I talked to him for [laughs] quite a while."

She is lucky Matt Lauer didn't bump into her in a mad dash for makeup.

"They're assholes, man," Duff Goldman, self-censor off, says of the folks at *Today*. "Matt Lauer was a dickhead. . . . He like stiff-armed me on the way in and didn't even say excuse me, and I didn't even know who he is, and I was like, 'Fuck you, pal!' "

I am incredulous, of course. How could you not recognize Matt Lauer? And then, in a moment of self-actualization, he adds, "Because that's me. And as . . . you've found out, I have no compunction about opening my mouth and saying whatever I feel like saying."

My innocent question about his treatment by the *Today* staff seems to have riled him. "He stiff-armed me," Duff continued. "And I was like, 'Fuck you, dude,' and he kinda turned around and looked at me for a second, but obviously he had to get to makeup or something. I was like, 'Who the fuck's that,' and they were like, 'That's Matt Lauer,' and I said, 'Who's Matt Lauer?' 'He's the host of the *Today* show.' Fuck that guy!"

I am making my way out of Duff's shop when he says, "I could snap that guy in half. He's a pissant."

"No," says Leslie, making clear that she believes there was no way this could have happened. I had a feeling.

And the Winner Is . . .

Once the spot was done—all the cakes were displayed and voting had commenced—everyone went home. Sarah, who's a confessed dessert junkie, was disappointed with the quick on-air tastes she and Mark got. She couldn't savor the flavor, which is the way she is with cake and pie and cookies. (My eating style is more like the Ronco Food Vac: snort, inhale, snort, look for more.) She needs to mull over every bite, so after the segment, she said, "Can I eat some more?" The staff put the cakes in to-go containers, and the couple took them home to Sarah's parents' house and invited the neighbors for a tasting. She doesn't remember who liked what; it was just a happy time with lots of people eating cake.

The competitors were told that someone would usually take the lead pretty early, and the producers would call whoever it was to bring the cakes back up on Friday. They all figured they'd get phone calls on Wednesday, so the winner would know and arrange transportation and coverage.

Leslie didn't hear anything by five o'clock that day, so she assumed she hadn't won. "My husband was saying, 'You shoulda had a

white cake!' " Leslie laughs. She and her husband went rounds on it.
• The next morning, Thursday, the call from the producer came.

"She said, 'I need to talk to you, but I want you—is anyone in the
room?' " Leslie was told to leave the room immediately, so she went
into the hallway, where she was given the good news. "No one was
supposed to know, period, exclamation point, no matter what! She
says, 'If one person finds out, they're gonna tell another person, and if
I hear that you have told anyone and it gets back to us, it goes to the
next person.' They were adamant!" She laughs.

But Leslie had to tell someone. It was Thursday, and she was
working on her weekend cakes. She had no one else to drive the winners to New York and would have to get her husband to do it; the
producer agreed, then told Leslie how to return to the room where
everyone was working. "She said, 'Turn everything down ten notches
to normal, and enter the room.' " Leslie's husband was out of the shop
within one minute.

And how did *Today* tell the others? They didn't.

"That night," Leslie says, "Duff called me, and he said, 'Have you
heard anything?' And let me tell you: I'm not a good liar, don't really
lie to my customers . . . but I had to lie to him. . . . And I talked to him
for like an hour; we just kind of recycled everything, and that's when
I heard all of his feelings—about *every*thing!" She laughs. "That's
where I heard the whole nine yards," she says, alluding to Duff's un-
restrained opinions.

"Anyway, the next day, Duff called to congratulate me. He saw it
on TV like everyone else. And that's how everyone found out." She
apologized, told him they'd threatened her life if she told anyone,
and he completely understood. "He was very nice about it. He said,
'I'm glad you won; if anyone was gonna win, I'm glad you did, and it
wasn't SugarBakers.' " She laughs. "I said, 'I understand your point;
that would be very painful if they were to win.' "

If it sounds stuck-up, there's a little more to it. Fanciful cake
decorating is a trend sustained by customers; if there's no longer a

demand for it, if America's statement is that real people don't want whimsy and prefer the staid, common, all-white cake, decorators like Duff and Leslie, on the cutting edge, might have to go back to more traditional work.

But okay. There's some snootiness. There's a hierarchy of bakeries, and Jamie's place—with its carryout cakes, brownies, cookies, and pastries—could be considered a step below the wedding cake *boutique,* a place that does one thing and charges a small fortune. But neither Duff nor Leslie is aware of Jamie's repertoire, for her shop is filled with wild, funky, and glamorous fondant-covered cakes that are every bit as finely crafted as those found in the boutiques. But her client base tends to be more traditional. And her cakes are *sweet.*

Losing Isn't Everything

Say you love football—I mean *love* it—and you think Peyton Manning is poetry, a Shakespearean sonnet. And say he lives down the street, and you can knock on his door and ask him how he does it. You would. Your nerves might get the better of you, but eventually, after a bit of stalking, you'd knock.

As a cake lover on a quest for the perfect cake, I stalked and then knocked. I ate up press about the Hometown Wedding. I watched the episodes as they aired, then went back to the Web site to look more closely at the cake porn. (The online video wasn't yet compatible with my Mac, so I had a friend download it and give me the play-by-play until I could find a local PC.) And when it was all over, behind-the-scenes facts began to conflict with each other. It was starting to look like the *Rashomon* of cake! I felt a little like Snidely Whiplash, twirling my moustache with glee. What could be racier than bakery villains?

"They both said they like our cake best," Jamie says. It could sound like sour grapes if you hadn't heard Sarah Raley and Mark Dale say it on national TV when asked which cake they preferred.

And I hadn't. In fact, Mark, who could eat a pumpkin pie all by himself, said, *clearly,* that Duff's pumpkin chocolate chip was his favorite flavor of the lot. And Sarah's choice for taste was the white raspberry cake made by Leslie. What she did say about SugarBakers was that she preferred the *package,* mostly because of the groom's cake, which took Mark into consideration.

Jamie says, "They wanted our cake when they—you know, when they chose it at the end, they said, 'Whose cakes did you like?' and they both said SugarBakers all the way. They liked the taste of the cake and the look of the cake, and then of course—" they had to abide by America's choice.

When I talk about the couple's choice and the way Jamie interpreted it, Duff Goldman is offended. "Bullshit! They're *shoe*makers," he says. "The wedding couple made the winning person bake the cake that *we* made. Fancy Cakes by Leslie. They called Leslie and said they want Duff's cake, the pumpkin chocolate chip."

"But her design," I say. It's not really a question. But it is.

"Yeah. No, but they wanted *our* design, and they wanted our cake." He continues, "SugarBakers . . . Because—SugarBaker's cake was very pedestrian. It was lame."

I admit to him that it looked like an ordinary wedding cake when I saw it on TV, which really isn't such a bad thing (as long as it didn't *taste* like one!).

"It did. *Ours* was incredible. It had flowers on it. It was a mosaic. It was incredible." I can do nothing more than sit back and let him have his say. "The pictures were awful. The *Today* show people were awful. I'm never doing anything else for the *Today* show ever again. They were horrible. They were absolutely horrible. They treat you like you're in an exalted presence or something. . . . They treat you like garbage. . . . They just talk to you like you're just a second-class citizen. Listen, I understand the exposure that I'm going to get from

being on your show, and I appreciate it, but at the same time, you
need to understand that we are all busting our asses to make your
show really awesome and not getting paid a dime for it, so fuck off."

Apropos of nothing, I say, "And you did a lot of work." I sit back
and nod, prepared for the onslaught of opinion.

"SugarBakers' cake was just . . . very pedestrian. Leslie's cake
was really cool looking. . . . The Cakediva is insane. An insane
person. And her cakes are awful. They photograph well . . . you see
it in person, you see the shoddiness of the craft that she does. . . .
And she called me for a booty call that night." He raises his voice
a little, gives himself an accent, and holds his arms a little more
womanly. " 'What's up, Duff? I'm in room 304; you wanna come
get some drinks?' . . . Maryland represented," he adds. "Cakediva
was definitely fourth."

The day Duff made my birthday cake was the day *after* our discussion of the Hometown Wedding competition. On that second day,
while he covers my cake with fondant and sparkles, I bring up the
subject of the pumpkin cake again because I'm just not convinced
that it went down the way he said it did. Did Leslie tell him? "Yeah,
she called me and said, 'Before you hear it from anybody else, I'm
telling you.' "

"And so did you give her the recipe, or—?" I ask.

"I told her how I did it."

"Yeah?"

"I mean, I told her like basically how—I was like take a high ratio
of yellow cake, put some pumpkin in there, put some chocolate chips,
and bake it up. I didn't give her *my* recipe for it." I register a little
more surprise, and Duff adds, "The whole thing was just disgusting."

No one talks for a few minutes. Duff sings the words to some
ethereal Pink Floyd–ish music playing so quietly in the background
it might as well have been off. And then he says, "Leslie was really
cool. . . . She's nice."

I don't want to let the *Today* thing die just yet and poke around a little further, asking whether they had aired the wedding yet and whether Duff had seen the final cake.

"And it was essentially your cake?"

"No, it was Leslie's cake!"

"It was her cake," I say, confused but finally grasping it. "But she just changed to pumpkin–chocolate chip."

"I guess; I don't know the whole story," he says. "Those guys are chump change. . . . They weren't cool. They weren't nice to us."

I commiserate. It's TV.

"Water under the bridge. If they called me up tomorrow and said, 'Hey, you wanna come over tomorrow and do a five-minute spot? I'd have to say yes." (What happened to "I'm never doing anything else for the *Today* show ever again"?)

"Wait," Leslie says calmly when I ask about it. "I will tell you what happened. Because I got the whole story because I was the one at the end to hear it. What happened was the bride liked the taste of my cake, the white with the raspberry, which is what we did in the cake. The groom liked the pumpkin cake. So I said, 'What are we doing? I need to know what we are doing for the flavor of the groom's cake.'" The producers told her that the couple wanted a pumpkin cake inside, so that's what Leslie baked.

So Duff didn't tell her how to make the cake? And it wasn't in the pink and brown cake? And?

"He made it sound very good for himself, and that's not what happened. And I called him beforehand, and I said, 'I want to tell you—before you read it somewhere . . .'" She told him what would be in the crab cake and how it all transpired. "And that's it! No! It was my own recipe. I tasted his pumpkin cake."

"Was it good?"

"I'm not gonna have any comment. But that's what happened.

There's nothing mystical. The girl wanted one thing; he wanted another. So she got it in the bridal cake; he got it in the groom's cake. It was my recipe."

I ask Leslie if she was treated okay by the *Today* crew, and she says, "Oh, yeah! Everyone. I have no complaints at all." She laughs as if she knows what I'm thinking—about Duff's experience. "I won, so it's all—beautiful! If I didn't win, maybe I'd be like, well—"

"Duff said your cakes were beautiful," I tell Leslie, hoping not to have started anything and wishing to keep the peace. (Okay, I wish to *appear* to wish to keep the peace.) And it's true that Leslie was one of the few to have earned Duff's praise.

"Thank you, Duff." She laughs. She laughs a lot, and it's a contagious, good-spirited laughter. I like it. "He was glad that I won and not SugarBakers, because that would've given him a thorn in his side. And vice versa! If he would've won, it would've been a thorn for her."

"I think she thought it might have been a shoo-in," Leslie tells me when I ask how she felt about Jamie's cake. "Because the truth of the matter is, I was very surprised that I won. I didn't have a white cake, and America's vote . . . " She really thought that an all-white cake would win. "And hers was the most standard, ordinary cake that I thought the general public would like."

Leslie does not mean this as an insult, though perhaps she uses the word *beautiful* less easily than I. Jamie's cake *was* beautiful; its color—or lack of—was probably its downfall. "Everyone said to me . . . *every*one said, if you're gonna lose to anyone, it will be to Sugar-Bakers, because their cake was so ordinary, traditional."

Jamie was energized by her appearance on *Today*. "We were fine about it. It was a win-win situation, either way. It was wonderful to receive all the publicity, and the trip was a lot of fun. It put us in a different sort of level in the business, I guess."

* * *

Before Duff learned of the country's decision, he told a reporter, "There's really no accounting for taste in America." That line would cover his back, win or lose. Afterward, Duff told his book festival audience, "If Middle America actually approved of what I did, I might be offended." But the truth is that he wanted to win, and he didn't. Otherwise, why the hard feelings, the explosion about his treatment during the contest?

In the kitchen at Fancy Cakes by Leslie, where two women make leaves for a customer's cake, the Final Jeopardy! theme song plays, and I crane my neck to glance at the TV to see the question while Leslie talks about the energy of all her competitors. They all wanted so desperately to win. "That's one of the happinesses: that I could say to my husband, 'My pink and brown cake won!'"

As America's choice, Leslie also got to attend the wedding. She shows me the photos that prove she was there. "That's me and Katie. That's me and Al. This is the live cake."

See *The* Cake, Live! Cake truly is the star of the wedding. Forget the bride's breathtaking gown, the hideous bridesmaids dresses. Forget the bouquet you never catch and the centerpiece you never get to take home and the cover band that butchered Bruce Springsteen. Forget the dry chicken made memorable only by the open bar. Remember the cake.

Remember the Cakes

Sarah and Mark got close to their wedding and groom's cakes twice. The first time, they cut into Leslie's pink and brown creation for *Today*'s cameras. The taste they fed each other—they did not engage in obnoxious cake smashing—was one of two bites, their second coming during a repeat cake cutting for the guests. The groom's cake was cut then, too; Sarah remembers the basket was thick and difficult to get a knife through. They set aside one crab claw each for later but never got it. That pumpkin–chocolate chip cake that caused such a fuss never crossed their lips.

The couple left immediately for their audience-chosen honeymoon in the Maldives, so the two cakes were cut up and dished out. What didn't go with guests—who loved both cakes—went home with Sarah's parents, who fed those lucky neighbors once more.

But there was more cake in the newlyweds' future. The airline, Emirates Air, presented a Happy Honeymoon cake on the plane (sometime before they lost Sarah's luggage, which remained lost for the honeymoon's duration), but the couple had so much other stuff to carry off the plane, including several bottles of champagne, that they tossed the cake—gasp!—into a trash can upon their arrival. While they were describing the missing luggage, some of the airport personnel pulled the cake out of the trash and ate it. They didn't look like the type of folks who'd regularly eat food from the garbage. They were clean people, working people. "Maybe they wanted cake that day," Sarah says, laughing. I've eaten my share of trash cake. I know about wanting cake that day.

Lest you think the couple saw cake no more, their honeymoon resort had prepared another for their bonus island ceremony. It was a fruitcake. "There's a picture. . . . You see me eating it, and I think he got my first reaction to it," Sarah tells me on the phone. I can hear her face scrunch up. "Yucky fruitcake," she says. The major thing fruitcake has going for it is its moistness, as it's usually soaked in some sort of liquor. But this cake was dry. She and Mark didn't eat it, and the hint wasn't taken; the spa staff brought it to the room for them, where it remained uneaten. Even the hotel staff would not have fished this stuff out of the trash. Don't be surprised if you receive this very cake during *your* honeymoon in the Maldives.

For their first anniversary, Sarah was going to order a small pumpkin–chocolate chip cake from Leslie, as a surprise for Mark, since he didn't get to taste his own groom's cake. But they were going on another trip (they got a lot of vaccinations and were trying to get their exotic travel over with before the immunizations expired). So they pulled the small top of Leslie's wedding cake out of the freezer, invited her parents over, and ate pizza and cake for dinner.

My favorite dinner.

"Tell me about it!" says Sarah. Since they were leaving the next day, the cake went home with the folks and, again, fed those neighbors. It was still good a year later, Sarah says, though it had lost a lot of its original moistness. She was bummed not to have had the original cake. A wedding video revealed Leslie the morning of the wedding preparing the extravagant dessert, so she knew how fresh it had to taste. "The icing on the top [fondant] was thick, so, you know, the guts of the cake were the best."

At this moment, Sarah scores big marks with me. This is a girl who knows the importance of frosting, who recognizes the wedding cake's job but prefers, when all is said and done, a simple cake, yellow, with white buttercream frosting.

Me, too. Now about Piggly Wiggly: The Safeway a block from my house has begun offering wedding cakes. A many-tiered foam dummy towers above slices of misspelled and never-picked-up birthday cakes in the bakery section. It's plain white with some nondescript piping and some prosaic roses—perfectly centered, not off-kilter, not funky glam. But I can guarantee something: it's going to *taste* like a party.

Tiers and Jeers

On a bookshelf in my kitchen, sandwiched between *The Art of the Cake* and *The Cake Bible,* is Colette Peters's *Cakes to Dream On.* The cover features a tower of teacups, a pot at the base, all squiggly and swirled and dotted. The pages are glorious—pillows and flowers and ivory sculptures, truly the fluff of dreams, right down to the cake shaped like six mattresses and topped with two gum-paste sheep. Nothing is cooler, really, than a cake in the shape of something else: a camel, a pair of shoes, a T-bone steak (the whole have-your-steak-and-eat-it-too idea is perfect for vegetarians).

But it's a study best done with pictures. Face it: wedding cakes really don't deliver on their promise. They're always dry and crumbly, or else they're some awful flavor, like strawberry shortcake with vile whipped cream, a frosting gyp outdone only by fondant.

Duff Goldman says wedding cakes *don't have to be* horrible. There's a "misconception in the cake community where cake needs to be, structurally, a certain consistency to be a wedding cake." But if you build it right, he says, they will come. "You can make the moistest, most . . . delicious wonderful cake, and it'll be just fine, if you know what you're doing."

Does Leslie Poyourow know what she's doing? When we talk about our favorite cakes, the winner, hands down, is the carrot cake—wait, *the* carrot cake—from *The Silver Palate Cookbook*. Make a cake out of *that,* I tell her. But she can't! It's too moist!

Even some professional bakers don't make their own cakes from scratch; they use a mix or a combination of them, like my decorating instructor does. Or they farm the job out to other bakers. You can order a stack of 12-inchers, 10-inchers, 8-inchers, square or round, from people who do only that. But while only some upscale cakeries make their own cakes, hardly any make fondant. It's too heavy and time consuming. And while Charm City Cakes is famous for its band saw, it's not equipped with a bagel mixer, which Duff says is tough enough to handle fondant.

Fondant: The smooth canvas that makes magic happen, the ingredient credited with the rise of anything-goes cakes, is also at least partially to blame for the blech. It's the antifrosting—uncreamy, unfluffy, unmoist, undelicious. Even Duff, who loves the way his cakes taste, doesn't like it. Guests who feel that way can pull the fondant off. "It's reminiscent of Easter candy, and I'm Jewish, so I don't like Easter candy." I'm thinking Jesus wasn't keen on it, either, but what do I know. Easter—with its marshmallow chicks and chocolate bunnies—has always puzzled us Jews.

Suppose people want cake decorated with buttercream? "We tell them to go to Safeway," Duff says. I can feel a lecture coming on. *"Why?* Why do you want something gross?" My eyes glaze over as he compares butter to shortening, the former's melting temperature being 87 and the latter's being 110. When a bite of *his* cake goes in your 98.6-degree mouth, it melts. "When you eat one of those grocery store cakes, you get that film you feel over your mouth. Your body isn't warm enough to melt the shortening, so you actually have to wait until your saliva breaks it down." I'm willing to wait.

SugarBakers is not a fondant-only shop. Of course, they use a high-quality fondant, like everyone else. (Leslie calls her own fondant tolerable.) But if you don't like marshmallow, what good is gold-plated, diamond-studded marshmallow?

Jamie's place offers three types of buttercream (American, French, and German), and she piles it on. At the very least, she uses the same quantity under the fondant that you'll find on a fondant-free one. What makes the frostings different is the amount of sugar and butter and that the French recipe uses only the whites of eggs. I want the overly sweet, billion-sugar-crystals-in-every-bite fluff. Which one's that? Jamie says lots of people prefer the American "because that's what they've been raised with and don't know any differently." But I *do* know. I choose it still.

What I want more than anything is to watch Duff bake. Here is a guy who talks a good game. He's all vigor and vim, guts and gusto. You know he's going to have fun with it, drop things, dance around, show some finesse, sift flour onto his shoes. He might do it on purpose to get a rise out of you. But there's not much of a cake smell in his shop. It didn't waft under the front door like it does at decorating supply stores or even in my own kitchen. Every so often, there's a whir or clap in the background—something being sawed or holed, metal landing on metal, a bit of music that momentarily sneaks over the din of old-building hum. Once in a while, a person slips by us or a phone rings, but the serious business here today seems to be all talk. Duff won't let outsiders watch him bake. "It's taken me ten years to figure out how to bake cakes."

Is he guarding a secret?

"I've done a lot of work to make my cakes what they are, and I'm not about to—"

"But you use all fresh stuff?" I ask, trying to squeeze drops from him.

"Eggs, butter, sugar, flour."

"But no milk? Or do you?" I tell him about my personal pound cake bake-off and how the winning recipe was the one with the most milk.

"Dairy products are really good for holding in moisture and retaining moisture." He barely pauses before adding, "Know what else is really good at holding in moisture? Potatoes."

"Potatoes? In the *cake*?" I ask, accentuating my crow's feet.

"That's all I'm saying," he says, arms folded, playful smile dancing on his face.

"Potato starch? Potato flour?" I'm pressing my luck.

"Potatoes. Mashed potatoes." Duff is cute now, boyish. He's teasing me. "If I were to bake a cake," he says, "I might maybe think about putting mashed potatoes in."

I know Duff's stand on sheet cake. Dare I press my luck inquiring about cupcakes? Does he know what I learned at the Cake Cottage; does he follow the Cupcake Wars in New York, a cause heralded by Amy Sedaris, among other foodies? "What? Bullshit! Bullshit! No way. . . . I don't make cupcakes."

Leslie does, but only her way. On a display shelf is a set of adorable mini-cakes covered in fluorescent orange and green and decorated with purple and yellow swirls and stripes, then topped with a daisy. But don't get her started on the whole cupcake fad. "Cupcakes are good for *birthdays*." People who order them are, in her experience, expecting to pay two bucks apiece, then throw 'em on a stand, and wah-lah (hey, if they're buying one of those tacky wire stands for their daughters' weddings, would they recognize *voilà*?). "And you know what it looks like? Nothing!"

But what about the amazing ones you see on TV—bugs and birds and crazy flower sculptures sticking out of a pile of cupcakes? "That's not reality," Leslie says. She has a point. Who can afford to buy that stuff? It's like the fashion designers' new spring lines: a thousand bucks for a blouse that buttons only at the navel, $800 for an original pair of pink and brown Mary Janes. "The average person could not afford that, and it's really the average person that's gonna keep the trend going.

"The other issue," she adds, is that "you have a big wedding, say at the Four Seasons. You do a cupcake cake, and people have spent maybe one thousand dollars to come to your wedding. They've bought a dress, they've bought a gift, they've flown from California, they're staying there, and you're giving them a cupcake that . . . is very difficult to eat and sloppy on their dress."

You can't expect those in the wedding cake biz to *want* to do cupcakes, but when they do, the cupcakes should *not* look like Warren Brown's. (Brown wouldn't do those for weddings.)

"He is a good example of how I don't want mine to look," Leslie says. "You know, if that's what you're giving, and you have this big, elegant seventy-thousand-dollar wedding, and you've got something that looks like your niece did it, it doesn't go together. It's not a good match."

Leslie is a perfectionist. While Duff will put together fantastic creations with gum-paste figures riding hand-carved cake scooters (Leslie won't use gum paste; she wants even the noses of her little creatures to be soft and edible), one thing is missing when the cakes go out to customers. Under each order in his shop is a shiny gold or silver cake board. And if there's a single perfect use for fondant, it's the cake board. Leslie covers every single one. "And I put a ribbon on it. It's a complete package; you've paid two hundred dollars."

Partying Shots

Leslie Poyourow is not driven in the way regular Food Network competitors appear driven. But she *is* lucky. The *Today* competition fell into her lap and helped her with her other two goals: more business and more money. With the exception of winning the French culinary Olympics, what could be a better honor? "What am I gonna do beyond that?" she asks. So she'll simply add this to a résumé. Her different track will take her, sometimes chugging, sometimes full speed ahead, to retirement in about seven or eight years.

It's different for the thirtysomethings in the business, Warren Brown and Duff Goldman. "They're just, like, energized up the wazoo!"

Shortly after Brown landed his *Sugar Rush* gig, Poyourow predicted it wouldn't last long. "The show is good, but he's not like some of the other people who've come in—their persona." He's a nice guy, but perhaps he was pushing it.

* * *

"I'm a libertarian," Duff tells me, by way of explanation for his frank words ("pedestrian," "lame," "normal," "they have no imagination," "not very good") about the cakes of some superstar chefs, nice and cool people who simply don't deserve the praise heaped upon them, who don't rise above the hype. "I believe in a meritocracy."

To give an example, Duff tells me of one of his first meetings with attractive, charismatic Warren Brown, nearly three years ago. He and Brown were invited by the French embassy to do a cake for Bastille Day. "So we make this cake, and it was this seven-tier, five-foot-tall cake. . . . We marbled the frosting so it looked like jade, and it had velvet ropes with gold inlay, and it was [an] absolutely, over-the-top beautiful cake. . . . They put me and Warren next to each other. . . . It takes us an hour and a half just to set up.

"Warren shows up, pulls five Bundt cakes out of a box, puts 'em on the table, and was gone. And everybody's talking about Warren Brown. Oooh! He was on *Oprah*! Oprah. Oprah. I was standing there, and I was like: it's a *Bundt* cake!"

Whenever Duff calls someone a "cheese dick" or an "asshole," I cringe. But the next moment, he tells me of his three influences, one of whom is Colette Peters, "one of the funniest, nicest, sweetest, most wonderful people you're ever going to meet. . . . She's the queen." He says this after a filming of one of the Food Network's cake-decorating contests, which she won. The theme was sporting events, and both Goldman and Peters, separately, came up with the idea to do sport fishing. Peters did a trademark cockeyed cake, with a gorgeous fish splashing out of the top. Her cake was traditional, tiered, decorated (as opposed to sculpted), and the result was clever and refreshing. Duff's cake was a fishing boat, complete with flying bridge, fisherman, pole, and huge fish coming out of the water. He called it the S.S. *Colette,* in the spirit of playful, friendly competition, because Peters would be riding his wake when he won the contest.

Unfortunately, his cake did not make it to the table for judging. "Our cake completely disintegrated in the last thirty seconds. . . . It looked like somebody put a bunch of M-80s in it. . . . We came out lookin' like the winners; you'll see. We were as gracious as we could be. We laughed it off."

Not exactly. Despite the fact that he spent much of the competition smugly declaring his superiority over his competitors, Peters, the winner, looked like the winner. She was sweetly sympathetic to Duff's plight. You could tell that her sadness over his failed effort was genuine.

His other two idols are Mike McCarey and Margaret Braun, author of *Cakewalk*. "She was a judge at the last competition. I tried to get with her," he says, half kidding.

It's not as though Duff is only lavish with criticism. He is simply effusive. We gossip about other cake people he respects, like Joseph Poupon, my baker of choice. "He's a mensch," Duff says. "He has a lot of integrity as a pastry chef, as a human being, as a business owner, as an employer. . . . You won't hear anything bad about Joseph. You won't hear that he screwed somebody out of something or that he did less than his best work on something. . . . Every pastry chef in this town has worked for him except for me." He reminisces about the taste of his *fraisier,* a concoction of strawberries, puff pastry, cream, cake, and marzipan. "Oh, my God. Just go and tell them you need a *fraisier*." Have done, will do again. It is, indeed, a fine bakery. But in many ways, SugarBakers is on par; Duff wouldn't want to hear that.

Generally, Duff is a good guy. He has a nice sense of humor, and while he's not modest, he's certainly appreciative of all his good press. His cakes are stunning to behold. They display wit, talent, sensitivity, and even elegance. Maybe he's cocky to compensate for insecurities. It's true that sometimes the better we are at something, the more we have to keep proving, the more we have to defend our territory, stay number one. Even if it means pissing on a bigger dog's leg.

With his friends in supporting roles, he has created the "awesome" environment of his dreams, a place, he says, that is "based on mutual respect and understanding."

"I don't hear any yelling back there," I admit.

"There's no yelling; there's never any yelling; there's never any freaking out."

It's hard to imagine constant calm at such a busy shop. When Duff moved to this 2,000-square-foot space in 2003, Charm City Cakes was baking eight cakes a week. When we meet, they are baking twenty-four and have to move to a 6,000-square-foot space because they are on top of each other.

Duff calls himself "the softest sell in the world," but I doubt it. Braggadocio has to account for something. Ninety percent of the people who call him find out what he charges for the smallest, single-tier cake, and "they're aghast. . . . You called me because you saw these cakes, and you saw how beautiful they were, and you saw the amount of love and joy that goes into them." That doesn't sound like a soft sell to me, despite the number of times he shrugs. To the people who think he's crazy, who aren't spending more than fifty bucks for a cake, he says, "Okay, here's the number for Safeway bakery, and have a nice day." Hmmm. What's that number?

If you think two hundred dollars for a small cake is reasonable, depending on the event, imagine an event like a wedding, which often requires a cake that can feed hundreds. One of Duff's regulars buys two or three cakes from him each year. Every time she calls, "we just up the price a little bit to see, 'cause it's like this billionaire widow. . . . I'll just throw out this number and see what they say, and . . . I've never even gotten a hiccup. . . . We're up to like, I dunno, thirty-five hundred dollars" for a cake that feeds one hundred people. "She don't care. She knows that we'll do a good job, she knows that whatever she orders from us is going to be absolutely awesome, and that peace of mind to her is worth whatever."

It's hard to reconcile that Duff with the one who speaks, moments later, about the atrocities of the wedding industry, a billion-dollar entity he describes as "so gross" that the brides can feel how so much of it is "geared towards sucking your wallet dry, and so much of it is a scam." He cites fifteen-dollar-apiece chair covers as an example of the obscenity. He deals with these people all the time, he says. "Tons of people that I know . . . are wedding planners, and they're just the vilest breed of person ever to exist."

But it doesn't sound like Duff is less dollar focused. "What we try to do here is let people know that . . . yes, our cakes are expensive, but you don't have to buy one." So by not pressuring the bride into choosing Charm City Cakes, Duff isn't contributing to the greed-driven industry? Perhaps a soft sell is less stressful for the bride, but it doesn't expiate his contribution. Duff insists he's not getting rich; he's paying the bills and keeping his friends in an enjoyable job that pays them.

He knows what the industry is like and doesn't want to contribute to the obscenity of it, and because he's just not a guy who's steeped in tradition, his own wedding would be off the charts in a different way. "Shit, if I get married, I'm gonna have a party in the field with kegs and a roasted pig, and it's gonna be potluck, and everybody's gonna camp out. . . . I'm gonna buy a big bag of disposable cameras." (His girlfriend at the time, the sister of a pastry chef, was born and raised in France. He brings her cake all the time. I can see the blessing of that—and the curse.) But if they get married, it's a "bacchanalian disgusting orgy" all the way. Forget the catering, the flowers. Forget the tux. "I'm gonna dress just like this," he says, spreading out his Billabong sweatshirt.

"Think about your mom!" I say, horrified that my daughter might eschew the frilly white gown that makes me cry and choose, instead, the camouflage pants with the zip-off bottoms that she wears nearly every day. But his mom knows all about Duff's ironic disdain for ritual.

"Thank God there are people who don't think like me in the world." Those people are his bread and buttercream.

Since we're casual and cozy now, and I'm feeling like a distant Jewish relative, I dare to ask a question that I know will elicit a powerful response. Would he ever endeavor to create a low-carb cake, for people like me who shouldn't—or can't—have sugar but who deserve to celebrate whatever success or milestone?

"Fuck that shit. If you need cake, eat the cake. If you can't have cake, have an apple. Or a steak. . . . It's one of those things I just don't want to get into. . . . There's cake, and then there's stuff that's not cake. It's something else, and that's not what I do."

Such Sweet Sorrow

Before I leave Fancy Cakes by Leslie, she quizzes me. Why do I have all this interest in cake? Am I going to be a decorator?

"I'm addicted to cake," I tell her. That's it. And she immediately calls into the back for the girls to cut me a sample of each of two flavors. Because that's what you do, right, when someone says she has an addiction to something fun? Were I interviewing a bartender about his sublime cocktails and admitting my fascination is based on a dependency, he would *not* have his senior mixologist prepare a miniature martini and a shorty of Tom Collins. This is cake. Cake is a *party* in your mouth. It is safe for children. How can it be *serious*?

"That's a chocolate fudge cake," she says, as my tongue admires the tiniest piece of it, and guttural noises of approval emanate from deep within. The other is a piece of the white raspberry that won the contest. I ahhh and oooh over the delicate portions on the fork that move daintily to my mouth, but this is the kind of cake that calls for quantity, much bigger bites. "This is better than Costco," I tell her, but do I believe it? I'm embarrassed to admit that a Costco cake floats my boat. My big-ass boat.

Whenever two women talk of food, the subject of weight is bound to arise. Leslie's about my height, about my size, and only slightly older. As it is with us Jews, our religion can be boiled down to a pretty simple slogan: They tried to kill us, we overcame, let's eat! But afterward, we'll feel really, really guilty.

Cake *is* a party. It's the sweet part, the part that you're supposed to feel good about. But you're not supposed to eat so much of it that you become one of the party balloons. That's the sorrow. And it's a feat I have not yet mastered, a feat rendered impossible by a decision to search for the perfect cake, a cake I do not find at some of this country's finest and most respected bakeries. And this is yet another sorrow.

Your good friend has just taken a piece of cake out of the garbage and eaten it. You will probably need this information when you check me into the Betty Crocker Clinic.
—Cynthia Nixon's Miranda,
character, *Sex and the City*

Cake Fanatics
SIXTH TIER

Cake Jobs

I consider myself one of cake's biggest fans. I haven't made my living from it. I don't have serious dreams of owning a bakery (I just like to imagine how mine would be better), and I don't watch *Ace of Cakes* or Food Network Iron Chef competitions each week. Ever, really. And it's not so much that I *like* to eat cake—oh, I do! I do!—it's that I am *compelled* to eat it. I can't keep from eating it when it's around. And I have to make a conscious effort to *quit* cake, frequently, as so many people find they have to do with cigarettes, the urge being too strong to overcome, especially in social settings.* So this is a little like a junkie's excuse to stay close to her addiction.

---

* In a French study, rats were determined to prefer sweet water to IV cocaine—which they were accustomed to receiving on demand—and it didn't matter "whether the drink was sweetened with saccharin or sugar." In another study, rats became dependent on sugar and experienced both cravings and withdrawal. "Excessive sugar in today's diets may overstimulate the sweet receptors in the brain, leading to a loss of self-control mechanisms and the risk of addiction," says Rachel Dvoskin in *Scientific American*.

Every now and then, my ears perk up when I hear about other cake fanatics or when cake is spoken about on television. On *All My Children* today—not that I watch it—Tad Martin (not that I know him well enough to call him that) said, "A house full of kids, cake—what could go wrong?"

When it's a contest between cake and pie, I am there, cheering on cake. I've even begun using "cake hole" instead of "pie hole."[*]

I know a few others like me. Warren Brown is surely a cake fanatic. Roland Winbeckler, the sculptor of life-size cakes, is a fanatic. Mike McCarey, his protégé, who was one of the first to make a cake that looks like a steak or a Thanksgiving dinner, is nuts for the stuff. Martha Stewart. Duh. And Rose Levy Beranbaum must think she's a prophet, having the nerve to call her book *The Cake Bible*. But the cake lovers who do something *else* with cake fascinate me most.

Lindsay Reed,
author of *Gâteau*; Baltimore, Maryland

When a cake and one's hunger for cake meet, we all know how it will turn out: a plate of crumbs, a dirty fork, remnants of guilt for having broken a diet or for having lived to eat—rather than eaten to live—or for having partied alone.

But who are we fooling? "You don't want me," says a *gâteau au chocolat* in Lindsay Reed's ten-minute play *Gâteau*. It insists, in a

---

[*] Not that I watch it, but on another episode of *All My Children*, Gigi's son, Shane (who is also Rex's son, but he doesn't know it, even though his new wife, Adriana, does and is attempting to keep it from him), is asked to judge a pie bake-off between Moe and Noelle at the restaurant where Gigi waits tables: "I didn't like either of them." Had I been sitting at the kitchen table working while the show was on, my eyes would have moved to the television set just in time to see Shane as he continued, "I don't like pie. I like cake." With that, my right arm would have shot up in a victory cheer.

crusty French accent, "You want love or understanding or comfort or something else."

"Listen, I'm not that complicated," says the plain, twentysomething girl with the ponytail. "Cake tastes good. I wanted some." She bought the cake "for the same reason everyone buys cake. I was hungry. I walked into the bakery, looked around, and there you were."

The cake knows better, of course. Who eats cake *sans soirée,* without a party or even a birthday?

Eventually, the girl admits she is going through a divorce, but she fights the cake at every turn.

A cake life will never be enough, the *gâteau* tells her again and again. By play's end, the girl has attacked the cake (who never says "ouch") and devoured the entire thing in a violent frenzy, as if having rapturous sex. The audience, the play's author assures me, laughs uproariously over this, despite the fact that most of the play is bittersweet.

Lindsay Reed attended the University of New Hampshire because she was "too chicken to go to NYU." When I meet with her in the most likely of places, Edelweiss Bakery—one of those old-world German walk-ins with an old-world German in an oven mitt—we find this to be just the first of our common bonds. (I was accepted by NYU, but my mother didn't want me to leave town, so I was bribed with a car—and grateful; I, too, was scared.) An English major, she studied under Charles Simic and had a great passion for writing. But it got derailed. She skipped the writing MFA to become an Old Testament scholar, having found Judaism much more fascinating than her parents' religion for most of her life. In grad school, she met Sam, a Conservative Jew; once they married, the two kept a kosher home.

Maybe her illicit love affair with cake did not cause the demise of her marriage, but it was certainly the impetus for her play, which originally opened with a scene from Reed's life. "For my thirtieth birthday . . . I asked for a divorce; that was my thirtieth birthday present, which Sam responded [to] by buying me something [instead]." She told him, "Then I want *two* gifts."

Lindsay Reed met someone she calls "a boy," which you can say when you're thirty (but not when you're forty-four without seeming to be a pedophile). And she eventually made her way to Maryland and discovered the Creative Alliance, a place where writing and art coexist. Angry with her current "boy," she signed up for a Thursday-night, ten-minute-play writing course, just to get away from him on the one night of the week that they saw each other. She had no delusions. She was a poet, after all; if she didn't produce something glorious, it was simply because she was out of her genre. But the brilliant *Gâteau* was born.

We two self-professed, to-others-confessed cake addicts sit at a small table in this bakery eating a savory lunch, rather than a sweet one; mine is a chicken salad sandwich (which has grapes), and hers is "dropped egg on toast," some sort of New Hampshire concoction made by breaking, or "dropping," an egg into boiling water. We talk about cake in a language that is punctuated with gasps and sighs and moans, all ellipses and exclamation points. I'm more than a decade older and feel it here, with her talk of the "boy" she loves and her tiny, 110-pound body. No one would ever guess she's a binge eater with a sweet tooth who once weighed 165 pounds.

Though she can't pinpoint an exact moment when that love for cake began, she can recall an early sleepover with a best friend. The pair had scraped together some change and gone to the store for a can of Duncan Hines frosting, which they devoured that night.

We both like cake for the frosting. Though Reed prefers to top her cheap white sheet cake with vanilla ice cream ("I like the cold . . . the mix of textures"), we observe the addict's utensil protocol: "Oh, fork! It's totally a fork. . . . And it has to be a metal fork . . . ; a plastic fork isn't man enough of a fork for me." She describes the way the tines pierce the ice cream and then the cake, and our eyes glaze.

It's not shameless, this display of ours. We are back and forth with cake stories; it's pretty much porn for us. When she waxes poetic and nostalgic about the very moment the plastic lid from a supermarket slice pops open, and you can hear that crackle and smell that sweet air waft your way, you know she's not making this up. Only a fellow junkie could pinpoint that as a moment in time.

She divorced Sam for her own reasons, and though she doesn't say it exactly, I'm sure cake is one of them. "Because he was there, I couldn't eat a whole piece like I wanted to. I was mad at him for being in the way." Sam kept a kosher house, and nonkosher cake is *tref* (from the Yiddish word for "unclean"), so Reed couldn't bring it in, couldn't even let it touch the silverware. But sometimes she'd sneak in those plastic containers from the grocery store and eat in secret while he was out. Then she'd discard all the containers so he wouldn't notice.

"I get really annoyed if people get in the way of getting cake," she says.

"I don't care if your name is on the center of the cake; the corners have *my* name on them," I reply. We nod.

Both Lindsay Reed and I have anticipatory anxiety about cake. When a cake is cut at a party, there's a slight flutter of panic in our chests about getting there before it's all gone. We both plan our meals around dessert. Reed says hers stems from the days of keeping kosher, when she had to concern herself with mixing milk and meat, but you know this is a fellow junkie talking. "I love cake displays," she says. "The case that's mirrored and goes around—I would walk in, walk directly to that octagon cake thing," which she calls a "revolving beauty of cake." Cake-loving comedian Jim Gaffigan talks about it, too: "I love when you go in a truck stop or a diner. They always have dessert in that rotating glass jewel case, like it's some artifact or something. . . . Yeah, I don't feel like dessert, but when I see pudding at *that* angle!"

We talk about the lengths to which our addictions send us, like smokers standing outside in a snowstorm, the temperature twenty below. We talk about how we can eat until we are sick. She recalls how she and her partner in sugar crimes once played poker with a king cake from New Orleans. "I'll raise you two end slices and some more pink frosting," they would say, and they'd eat so much that it was only a matter of time until one of them threw up, which ended the game. Once, she and a friend at work took notice of an uncut cake in the faculty lounge. "What are we going to do?" she asked the friend. It was a cue for the standard line, developed for times when they were attempting to exhibit self-control: "There'll always be more cake. You don't need to eat this one. It's not your last cake." And then she said, a bit incredulous, "But, damn it, it always feels like your last cake."

In all these years our bodies have evolved—to such an extent, for instance, that we no longer need the tonsils or appendix—we have never evolved out of the starvation mentality *or*, much to our detriment, the starvation metabolism. Is there really something in us that believes we won't ever have cake again? That we suffer a subconscious knowledge of Vlad the Impaler of Romania, who locked a whole town in a great hall to partake of a big feast, then burned the hall to the ground while they were inside? There *will* always be another cake, probably too soon for us to have quite recovered from the last.

Reed says she got the idea to add cake to the play on a trip to Pennsylvania to meet the parents of that "boy" she was dating. There was a huge cookout, and she made a pig of herself with cake and cookies and gave herself an awful stomachache, which forced her to stay home from an outing later that evening. The idea popped into her head that she would write her play about cake. But just as ex-smokers find it difficult to write once they quit, she found it tough to compose without a too-much-cake stomachache. "I almost had to be sick to write the play," she says. Before writing, she'd get a slice of chocolate cake and some vanilla ice cream. "I'd have to eat obscene amounts of food to write it." This was sort of ironic, considering she was writing it because she felt awful after eating obscene amounts of food.

Just before the play was performed—along with seven other ten-minute plays acted by people from the Mobtown Players, a Baltimore theater group—Lindsay made 150 cupcakes to hand out to the audience. She had just lost the six pounds she'd gained writing the play, and here she was, in her kitchen, with frosting for the red velvet cupcakes all over her hands. She must have been in serious denial, she says, if she thought she wasn't going to eat it. I tell her about my experience in cake-decorating class, that I was the only one in the whole class eating the frosting; she gasps.

In one hour, we have compared frosting habits and utensil use, reminisced about Entenmann's chocolate-covered doughnuts (oh, the moment at which they become stale is a moment we relish!) and our favorite frosted Pop-Tarts (the white with colored sprinkles or the pink with red sprinkles). We've spoken of the frosting colors that taste bad (red and black, probably because you have to use so much colorant to make them, as white dilutes everything), and we've shared our cake secrets and sad stories. And she has put in my head the need to locate a Bruster's Ice Cream parlor, where they have Birthday Cake ice cream, vanilla ice cream filled with pieces of birthday cake *and* "frosting ribboned inside." She discovered it after she and her boyfriend had arrived at his parents' place in rural Pennsylvania, the day before the great *Gâteau* revelation. She was nervous about meeting them, and it was 10:30 at night. The boyfriend put her in his car, and they traveled thirty miles to Bruster's for this cake ice cream.

By the end of our lunch, Reed and I have regressed to whining about why we can't be addicted to something like celery or broccoli, and, usually, when the conversation goes to this level of inanity, it's time to move along. She leaves empty-handed, even after a perusal of the display case, while I select a pair of almond horns for my husband, whose muscular build and activity level allow him regular indulgences like these, while I endure the emotional and physical results of excess followed by deprivation followed by excess followed by deprivation. Because when you are a sugar freak with a sluggish metabolism, this is the price you pay.

Why can't we be addicted to broccoli? Moving right along.

Philip Rosenthal, producer and head writer,
Everybody Loves Raymond

Larry David once devoted an episode of *Curb Your Enthusiasm* to a
black penis cake. *Seinfeld* had that antique cake, as well as a chocolate
babka. Countless shows depict birthday parties and cake eaters. But
not a single situation comedy in the last twenty-five years has been as
full of cake as *Everybody Loves Raymond*. Producer Phil Rosenthal
estimates about 90 percent of the episodes feature a cake of some
sort. Made by Ray's mother, Marie, the ubiquitous chocolate cake,
as I can't help but call it, is a tool designed to elicit love, inflict pain,
instill guilt, and evoke joy. When her daughter-in-law, Debra, makes
it, cake is little more than an object of ridicule. In an episode after
Ray's brother, Robert, was gored by a bull, he was not feeling up to
celebrating his birthday. Regarding the cake Debra brought to Robert's apartment, Marie said, "If Debra really understood people, she
wouldn't serve that cake!"

Although art does usually imitate life, and comedy is often au-
tobiographical, the meddling, cake-baking character of Marie is not
a member of Rosenthal's family. "Marie's abilities are but a fantasy
of mine—that is, the mother who can cook," he tells me. If cake is
an instrument of emotional blackmail, in Rosenthal's house it was
a weapon. "Especially at holidays such as Passover, when cake flour
was replaced with matzo meal, reminding us how horrible our fore-
fathers had it, slaving in the hot sun, making bricks."

If Rosenthal had to pick a favorite cake, it would probably be a
variation of Marie's: "chocolate, with chocolate filling and chocolate
icing, maybe some chocolate ice cream on the side. With chocolate
sauce." And it would definitely be cake, not pie, chocolate pies being
less easy to come by. "If it's not chocolate, it's not dessert."

Donna Stamps worked on sets for the show and tells me the "prop
master ordered the yummy chocolate cake from Holly's Bakery in
Glendale." I wonder whether Holly's is taking full advantage of the

PR possibilities. I imagine boldface-display-font encouragements to order the cake that played Marie's Ubiquitous Chocolate Cake in *Everybody Loves Raymond*. But I'm unable to find the correct Holly's, and the only phone number I get rings and rings.

But don't think Rosenthal's wife is any more adept in the kitchen than his mother. "I don't bake, and I try to discourage my wife from further attempts. There are already so many wonderful bakers in the world that need our support."

Bunny Koppelman

My mother was visiting her friend Judy, when I called her cell for something of little importance (like "Hi, where are you?"). I tell this story again and again, using my best Pikesville Jewish accent, which is a little like Brooklyn Jewish, minus the Brooklyn, plus some Fran Drescher whine. Judy got on the phone. "Leslie, I told my friend Bunny about you. Bunny is crazy about cake. While everyone else is at the museums wherever they travel, Bunny goes to the bakeries. So I told her, I said, my friend's daughter is writing a book about cake. And she said, 'I want to be in it! Why am I not in it? Did you tell her about me?' "

I smile. A lady wants to be in the book. But is loving cake enough? Has she ever eaten it from a trash can? In a minute, I learn that Bunny's daughter, Jennifer Hutt, cohosts a radio show with Martha Stewart's daughter and that Bunny's husband is Charles Koppelman, chairman of Martha Stewart Living Omnimedia. "Well, of *course* she can be in the book!" I say. And while I'm sure Bunny is full of great stories about cake, her proximity to Martha is the icing on it. I daydream about my interview with her, wonder how I will be able to save my best question for last, knowing that it could mean the end to our talk: Had she ever thought of having someone bake her a cake with a file in it while she was in the clink? What kind of cake would it be? I bet Martha could even find a tasty way to keep that sucker from showing up on an X-ray or setting off a metal detector!

Bunny returns my call and tells me (not verbatim, but close), "Judy said her friend's daughter was writing a book about cake, and I said, 'She's writing a book about cake, and she didn't call me? I love cake! Did you tell her about me? I want to be in that book!' " She tells me that she has a gigantic baker's rack in her kitchen, which, I believe, is the size of my whole first floor, which she fills, every Saturday, with "one of everything I like" from five different bakeries. She has to take a bite of everything. On Sunday, her daughter, who lives on the grounds (compound, probably; it's a Stanford White house), spends the day baking cakes for her.

It's great to have the means, I tell her. But Bunny is convinced that it's *desire* more than *means*. Right now, cake may be just what the doctor ordered, literally. She has been battling pancreatic cancer and spends far too much time being too sick to eat. But when she's not, one of her favorite cakes ever is a chocolate cake from Bergers,[*] a better-baked-goods company (like Entenmann's, as opposed to Tastykake) known for its delectable chocolate-topped cookies that are more chocolate than cookie. These are not the same as chocolate tops, which have the trademarked Hershey's Kiss–shaped, fluted mound of chocolate atop a crumbly white cookie. No, these are enormous smears of chocolate (like the thick, sloppy mess of frosting on a Cake-Love cupcake) on a moist cake of a cookie. And their cake is nearly the same, but bigger.

---

[*] Bergers, without an apostrophe, was started by Henry Berger, a German immigrant who moved to East Baltimore in 1835. His son, also Henry, took over his bakery, while the other two sons each had their own. They merged in the early 1900s. The bakery is no longer owned by relatives of the Bergers, but the products are the same.

If you look over the years, the styles have changed—the clothes, the hair, the production, the approach to the songs. The icing to the cake has changed flavors. But if you really look at the cake itself, it's really the same.

—John Oates, musician

The U.S. of cAke
SEVENTH TIER

LAYER THIRTY-NINE

Journey Cake

A journey is often most fulfilling—spiritually, emotionally, and intellectually—because of the side trips, as long as you make it back on course. So before I visit the cakes of small-town America and the back roads of Appalachia (where all the roads are back roads), I have to plan my itinerary. I'll be skipping a few towns that host standard-fare cakes, avoiding those whose dessert histories are a little dull, and passing on the Big Apple, where the namesake cake is not really cake. The regionals featured here, then, have scored high marks in my book for originality.

Regarding the origin of anything, there are two schools of thought: that there is nothing new under the sun, and that you can't step in the same river twice. The first idea goes at least as far back as the Bible. Ecclesiastes, 1:9–14, holds that "what has been will be again, what has been done will be done again; there is nothing new under the sun." The tendency to see this in everything, besides being an ironic justification for evolution, is why it's impossible to pinpoint the moment of conception for so many desserts. Sure, our cakes evolved from crackers and honey, but squishy sponge cake with fluffy frosting is *new*.

Lynne Olver, a New Jersey reference librarian, created the Food Timeline, one of the most amazing bodies of food research I've ever seen. She seems to disagree with me, subscribing to a strict interpretation of new. "Very few (if any) foods are invented," she says. "Most are contemporary twists on traditional themes." To make her point, she compares corn dogs and Wiener schnitzel, fries and fritters, and Hershey's chocolate Kisses and Incan cocoa.

As for who gets credit for inventions, or, as Olver would put it, *conventional twists,* it's usually less about getting there first than getting the most publicity about having gotten there at all. It doesn't matter if your grandfather brought the first Dobos torte with him from Hungary when he fled in 1922 if Beulah Ledner starts to sell a whole bakery full of Doberge cakes to Louisianans. And it's not too far-fetched to figure that lots of people at around the same time are making similar original recipes in their kitchens. You find this in all endeavors. While the Beatles were getting credit for changing the sound of music, other bands were bopping up and down in abandoned warehouses and family garages and barrios and jungles all over the world. Even the Golden Rule has dozens of variations in every religious or philosophical body of work, phrased in various ways, and composed between 5,000 BCE and the present day. It's quite possible that your great-great-grandmother in Lansing, Michigan, passed down her recipe for crepes layered with apples and honey, even though the state of Kentucky earns the credit for it.

The second idea—that your having set foot in it alters a river—is a matter of semantics. That river now has your foot germs, the plant matter from your shoes or soles; perhaps you stepped on a minnow on its way to mama, caused a bigger fish to miss a meal, a fisherman to miss the bigger fish. But to really alter a river, you must do more than bless it with your presence. You must dam it, redirect it, drain it, pollute it in order for your having been there to have an effect on its future.

Likewise with a recipe. You don't make it original by sticking your sweet finger into it—or by adding a half cup of walnuts. (If anything, you shortchange your recipes by not using the more flavorful pecans!) "Cooking is not considered inventing; rather, it evolves," says Joyce Gemperlein in *The Washington Post*. A list of ingredients, even in a particular order, cannot be protected by copyright law. The instructions are another matter; they are protected as literature. While it's courteous, and even ethical, to attribute your recipes to their sources, the only recipe police are working at Pillsbury, where Bake-Off contestants are subject to " 'originality' searches." (Still, if you do the honorable thing and ask permission to use recipes as they appear, you will be charged a fee.)

Chowhound, the online bulletin board for foodies, sparked debate when someone wanted to know if Floridians could claim the sour cream pound cake for their own. I pointed out that one of the earliest American recipes for pound cake came from New Englander Amelia Simmons in the 1700s.

An expert in food history, or so he or she appears, someone called "Making Sense," had a problem with this, claiming the Simmons book was too limited in reach. Pound cake probably didn't travel *to* Florida, since "St. Augustine was founded in 1565, 55 years before the *Mayflower* even landed in 1620." Still, it's more likely that it did travel to Florida by the same method it traveled to New England— by Englanders and other Europeans settling the colonies. Who gets the credit depends on who gets it in print first.

"Toodie Jane," the original poster, later asked a valid question about whether these recipes are from here or whether they came from across the pond. Both. Making Sense said that it's logical to believe "baking styles would be based on the traditions that immigrants brought with them to America." This is exactly what makes a recipe new—this reinterpretation for different times and places. Climate, making some new and old ingredients available in place of others, is a catalyst for regional favorites, as are customs and traditions and advances in equipment.

Making Sense intimidates me with his or her formidable knowledge of baking history. I got a D in my one college history course, Survey of English History to 1783, though I was making A's in Shakespeare's Tragedies and Victorian Literature.* (To this day I have recurring dreams that my absence from Dr. Blumberg's history class, which I need in order to graduate, has gone entirely unnoticed. I show up for the final and can't answer a single question.)

The cakes I explore here are the result of both reinterpretation and invention. In this game of telephone, where our cuisines travel through time and space, the pound cake is reborn into the maple-walnut cake; the crepe becomes the dried apple stack cake; and the German chocolate cake morphs into the Texas sheet cake. Even most recipe writers agree that they needn't write "adapted from" when the recipe has been *significantly* altered. So while additions of sour cream or milk might *enhance* or *improve upon* an old recipe, they don't change the original enough. The sour cream pound cake doesn't become the Seminole cake. But add some coconut, too, and cover it with sliced oranges, and then we'll talk.

Greg Patent, author of *Baking in America,* agrees, noting that in our short two hundred years of baking, we have developed a repertoire matching those with thousands of years of history. He recalls spending some time in the rare books section of his library with Eliza Leslie's 1828 book, *Seventy-five Receipts, for Pastry, Cakes, and Sweetmeats,* where he read about Indian Pound Cake. Nearly identi-

---

* In case anyone checks my transcripts, I also got a D in General Psychology that first semester of college. A boy who sat behind me used to kick my chair and make fun of the way I dressed. He was later arrested, along with a friend, for the murder of his father, from whom they were stealing drug money. Five dollars.

cal to the English recipe, this cake contains two important changes. It "had been transformed into something new by the substitution of an authentic American ingredient, cornmeal, known at the time as Indian meal, for the flour. And it was flavored with an entire nutmeg to boot."

This said, most every local cake has its roots in our ancestors' traditions, but the cakes that follow put such a new twist on the combination of flour, sugar, butter, and eggs as to make them unique, local-yokel creations.

As a young cross-country camper—"young" is the only *sane* kind of camper, as far as I'm concerned—I wasn't a culinary adventurer. For example, my goal one summer was to have pizza in every stopover town in the 4,900 round-trip miles between Baltimore and San Francisco, traversed via un-air-conditioned Ford Escort Wagon (which is how you can tell we were barely twentysomething). That meant lots of Pizza Huts and a few gems like Mile-High Mountain Pie (Jackson Hole, Wyoming) and Beau Jo's (Denver, Colorado).

Now, though my tastes have matured, and I'm sleeping *exclusively* in beds surrounded by walls made of something other than rip-stop nylon, a cake vacation is *still* out of the question. Yet it doesn't stop me from dreaming about what my Kentucky host might bake for me if she knew I was coming. Perhaps it would be some bizarre combination of dried apples, ginger, and molasses. My girlfriend Lysandra has been begging me to visit her on the island of Oahu, in Kailua, where she could feed me chantilly-cream-filled chocolate chiffon cake (she looks great in a bikini, but of course she avoids that kind of food).

Wherever you go in the United States—and I dare say the world, too (Asia excluded)—the cake will likely taste heavenly for one or more of many reasons, including: someone else baked it; you are on vacation; it is cake. The one exception I have found is the Norwegian

Cruise Lines buffet, where the only edible dessert is ice cream. Not a single baked confection is worth its metamorphosis into the eight-pound average cruise weight gain.

Though many of the cakes of the United States have much in common with one another (for example, the Hawaiian Dobosh cake and the New Orleans Doberge cake are pronounced similarly and are both descendents of the Hungarian Dobos torte), their stories are unique and as colorful as maraschino cherries and pineapple chunks in coconut fluff. Best of all, you aren't likely to find these desserts in your own local diner's revolving jewel case, and that keeps them special. The braided king cakes of New Orleans, in which a plastic baby Jesus is baked, are legendary, yet Kentuckians won't serve you one at Epiphany; instead, you might get mint julep cake, which you won't find in Charleston, South Carolina, where they're eating Lady Baltimore cake—with chopped nuts, candied fruits, and fluffy frosting—which they're not eating in Baltimore, where, if it's summer, someone is eating a peach cake. Just over the Bay Bridge, however, they're eating a towering cake filled with crushed candy bars.

During outdoor soccer season, moms gather at the base of a hill adjacent to my daughter's school. Most will stay for the games or practice, but at least one of them each week will have to leave early to bake something for this or that bake sale or kid's birthday. Sometimes it'll be a novelty, like dirt cake. (One year, my daughter requested the most foul novelty ever, a cat litter cake, made in a litter box and topped with crushed mint Oreo cookies, then dotted with Tootsie Roll turds; I refused.) Usually, though, on the baking agenda is some regional mystery—milk or soda cake—some down-home recipe that rarely appears in upscale cake compendiums but can probably be found in the cookbooks of Wives of the Knights of Columbus or the Randallstown Hadassah or even snobby food forums, where native cooking is always hip. The same sort of snobbery that excludes the regional cakes from other-than-regional publications affects me a little. In this regard, Baltimore is closer to Paris than it is to Smith Island,

Maryland; I'm more likely to have had *gâteau au chocolat* than I am to have tasted the Smith Island Ten-Layer Cake, which commands official notice.

Smith Island Ten-Layer Cake, Smith Island, Maryland

The more cosmopolitan eaters among us might turn up our noses at instructions that call for cake mixes and Cool Whip and the layering of crushed candy bars between thin cakes baked in ten individual pans. But our secret thoughts betray our good breeding: Mmm . . . Snickers and cake!

Smith Island is a tiny dot of land in Chesapeake Bay, a community with fewer than four hundred inhabitants, yet it has its own cake. Depending on whom you ask, the cake is composed of seven, eight, ten, or fourteen layers and is filled with thick chocolate or cream or crushed candy bars. All the recipes seem to agree that it's a yellow cake with chocolate frosting, but it is common for filling compositions to include strawberry, coconut, and fig. *Saveur*'s recipe calls for *eight* layers and floured peanut butter cups, along with a box of Duncan Hines cake mix and some traditional additions like condensed milk. Each of the four eight-inch-round cakes is sliced in half to create the eight layers.

Frances Kitching, author of *Mrs. Kitching's Smith Island Cookbook*, is sometimes credited with the creation of this kitschy cake, but the dearly departed "Grand Lady of Smith Island" wasn't so sure of that when she was seventy-five, telling Midge and Dave Patterson, in the summer 1993 edition of the *Crisfield and Smith Island Newsletter*: "Well, I don't know who made the first one. . . . I could've very well been [*sic*] I don't know." The recipe promoted by the Crisfield and Smith Island Cultural Alliance uses no cake mix (which wouldn't have been invented when Kitching made this for her kids) and calls for cooked (but not boiled or scorched!) frosting and everything cake ought to have (flour, sugar, butter, eggs, baking powder, vanilla, and a pinch of salt, in case you've forgotten), plus milk and water. Bakers of Kitching's published version are instructed to put "three serving spoonsful [sic] of batter" in nine-inch pans. These are baked three pans at a time, and each is finished "when you hold it near your ear and you don't hear it sizzle." Instructions like these delight me but irritate cookbook editors and bakers, who want exact times and measurements, even though it's impossible to say how long baking will take in *your* oven with the amount of batter from *your* serving spoon. This is the way we all should be learning to bake: by sound, by smell, by touch. These sorts of instructions come from grandmothers and neighbors; professional recipe writers do away with them and leave us wondering why we entrust them with our ancestors' culinary treasures when they can't conjure up the spirit of the baking, too. They literally take the sizzle out of recipes.

Each of the layers of Mrs. Kitching's version (some say the cake began as four normal-size layers, thin ones being rare in the early to mid-1900s, when this cake might have first appeared) is probably about a half-inch thick and assembled with liberal frosting between, along with randomly sprinkled crushed or chopped candy (your favorite—though I imagine mine, the Peppermint Pattie, might not fly). The finished cake (no candy on top) is frosted, top and sides, and is as big as the top hat you might doff to the Grand Lady in appreciation.

Such appreciation has now been mandated by the Maryland state legislature. The Lower Eastern Shore Heritage Council wanted Mrs. Kitching's cake to become the official cake of Maryland. Owners of the Sweet Shop, in Crisfield, Maryland, are preparing to emphasize their point by sending their version of the cake to state delegates.

Jean Marbella, columnist for *The Sun,* asks: "Does this sophisticated state, home to such floury celebrities as Duff 'Ace of Cakes' Goldman, want its official dessert to be one whose recipe includes as an ingredient, 'one 18¼-oz. box yellow cake mix, preferably Duncan Hines'?" But it's not uncommon for professional bakers—especially those known primarily for their outlandish decorations—to use box mixes, doctored or not. Places that do a large volume are more likely to rely on commercial preparations.

Are we, collectively, too snobbish to crown a cake that is the "ordinary-folks dessert"? Or are we just more grammatical? In Marbella's column, "Assembly May Rise to Just Desserts," island native Mary Ada Marshall regards the varying numbers of layers in the cake: "Some does 10, some does 12, some does 9." I doesn't make this cake at all. Never has.

"You know the role Smith Island plays in the English language, don't you?" asks my friend and fellow dog walker, Kirk Osborn, one morning on the field. Kirk's a snooty foodie who has just finished telling me about a coffee tasting around the corner, where people sampled a blend brewed from beans rescued from the poop of Indonesian civets (he is still waiting to get a cup). So I couldn't tell if he was full of shit when he told me that Smith Islanders are one of the last links to ancient British dialect. The island's inhabitation by English-speaking peoples and its physical isolation have combined to keep modern English—or American—dialects out. Islanders, though their numbers are fewer because of the dwindling crab economy, seem to be maintaining their unique speech. It's possible that the remaining islanders demonstrate their stubbornness by staying and holding fast to the old ways.

On Tuesday, January 22, 2008, legislators get their taste, as hundreds of slices from thirty cakes are delivered to Annapolis. Delegate Page Elmore is the bill's sponsor. The other delegates—with slot, cell phone, smoking, budget, and tax concerns—need to get their priorities in order. Baltimoreans need to get us a rival peach cake lobby. I make a call.

But spring arrives, and the legislature is worried about the way it looks to designate a state cake, what with all the other troubles, including where our budget will come from now that the computer service tax has been nixed. In early April, the bill is stalled in a committee that has been asked to make soybeans the state crop and walking the state exercise, but, at last, the bill passes, and the tacky candy-filled cake belongs officially to Maryland.

Peach Cake, Baltimore

If you ask a local for the name of Baltimore's signature cake, he or she will look at you the way a dog looks when it thinks you've said "walk," with a mixture of joy (cake) and confusion (signature). Nineteen out of twenty have never heard of peach cake. Local blogger and foodie Barrett Buss says he's never "seen a Baltimore specialty (other than Natty Bo) that didn't involve . . . crustaceans." So he was surprised to learn that the peach cake is a city tradition.

This single-layer cake is light on shortening and heavy on milk. It is baked in a jelly roll pan and topped with sliced peaches, sprinkled with cinnamon sugar, and drizzled with melted butter. Sounds like breakfast. And sometimes it actually is. When my friend Kirk was a kid, his family attended mass at St. Dominic's, a church up the road from our neighborhood. Because you couldn't eat before receiving communion, "after mass, everyone would line up at Hergenroeder's Bakery on Hamilton Avenue, famished for their luscious peach cakes, éclairs, and other goodies. Then Dunkin' Donuts opened across the street from the church. It was novel and quicker than the bakery. Within a year, Hergenroeder's went out of business." While Kirk was dating his wife, Jane, he waxed nostalgic about those wonderful peach cakes, and she told him to try the one at Woodlea Bakery, which sits on Belair Road, not two miles from where Hergenroeder's used to be. He was pleased to find it named Woodlea Hergenroeder's Bakery, even if thirty years later. "Same peach cake, same old German baker."

When the news of a Smith Island cake coup d'état hit the papers, I placed a call to Delores Pomles of Woodlea. Delores's father, John Hergenroeder, opened the Belair Road bakery in 1943, leaving her grandfather's Harford Road shop. When I ask if there was a falling-out, Delores tells me, "Goodness, no! He just had more kids than one bakery could support." Twelve children in all. Her father began working in her grandfather's west side bakery when he was in the sixth grade, riding the bread wagon to work after school.

Though she doesn't know for certain, it's likely that her grandfather was the first local baker to make the peach cake. A German immigrant, John Hergenroeder returned frequently to Germany by boat, taking his car with him. In the late 1940s, he bought a peach orchard so that he could make this special cake, which is really rather Danish-like, a slab of bun dough dotted with butter and graced with fresh peaches, peaches that are both the success of this creation and its failure to place in Annapolis. January is not the ripe time.

Cake, Clockwise

Dried Apple Stack Cake, Southern Appalachia

If ever a cake reflected its region, it's the mountainous stack cake of Kentucky. The pioneers' wedding cake, the Dried Apple Stack Cake is composed of heavy layers of ginger- and molasses-flavored cake, not so sweet, with spiced apple filling in between.

But Appalachia is not the only region reflected in the cake. Mountain weddings, shotgun or not, were typically potluck dinners, and guests would donate a layer of the wedding cake—sometimes just heavy dough rolled flat, other times a thin cake cooked on a griddle in a cast-iron pan—which would be filled by the bride's family with dried apples that had been cooked and spiced. The height of the cake sometimes reflected the popularity of the bride. But because this cake took a coon's age to assemble (three hours, to those unfamiliar with the ages of raccoons), the more popular brides had to settle for a twelve-layer cake. You can cheat and use applesauce or apple butter, but why?

Fred Sauceman, who writes extensively about southern cooking, especially Appalachian foods, says that he is "deeply familiar" with that cake, his wife being the only family member in her generation to keep her grandmother's century-old recipe alive. In April of 2005, *Southern Living,* which my friend Kirk calls *Southern Trailer* (I can't use this slur; my husband's a direct descendant of the Hatfields, and we have at least one mongrel under our porch for much of the summer), published a version of Jill Sauceman's recipe, with the note that her "grandmother used a less spicy filling during the Depression because spices were hard to come by." Sauceman says his wife's version doesn't even contain vanilla. The traditional dessert is *still* baked in a cast-iron skillet.

The recipe in Fred Sauceman's book is considered authentic. "If you ever try making it," he tells me, "use White Lily flour. A flour such as Gold Medal will not work in the amount specified." The people at White Lily explain that you'll need an additional two tablespoons of their flour for every cup of all-purpose called for in a recipe because White Lily is lighter. (Likewise, subtract two tablespoons of all-purpose flour if a recipe calls for White Lily—or any other bread flour.) It's lower in gluten than all-purpose flours, which is probably why people prefer the crumb of southern cakes and biscuits; less gluten makes baked goods less chewy or tough. (Bread flour does the opposite.)

Pig Pickin' Cake, North Carolina

Pig pickin' is a southern—North Carolina, Tennessee—term for pulled pork, usually smothered in pig pickin' BBQ (not barbecue) sauce. And the perfect cake to follow your meal and ensure that you become what you eat is the Pig Pickin' Cake. Like the Smith Island cake, it's one of those junk food concoctions that are more faux-made than homemade, with boxed cake mix, instant pudding, and whipped *topping* (one of my favorite words; it's not quite *cream*). Add some canned mandarin oranges and pineapple, eggs, and oil, and Joe Bob's your uncle.

Lady (and Lord) Baltimore Cake,
Charleston, South Carolina

A white cake with fluffy white frosting laden with chopped fruit and nuts, the Lady Baltimore Cake has birthed a few legends about its origin, but none include the theory that it's quite possibly a theft of the older Lane cake. The most popular legend holds that one Alicia Rhett Mayberry served this cake, when she worked at Charleston, South Carolina's Lady Baltimore Tea Room, to novelist Owen Wister, famous for *The Virginian* (which is famous for the line "When you call me that, smile"). Wister is said to have been so inspired by the cake that he named his 1906 novel *Lady Baltimore* after it and even gave it top billing.

Lady Baltimore is set in Kings Port after the Civil War, where the rich protagonist, John Mayrant, is engaged to a gold digger who feigns poverty to the point that she can't make her own wedding arrangements, leaving John to order their cake, the Lady Baltimore, from the tearoom of the Women's Exchange. And that's where he meets his true love, the cake's baker.

As Julia Reed wrote in *The New York Times,*

> It is no wonder that this cake plays such a key role in the novel. It is really, really good, a fact the narrator, a Yankee who eats a piece for lunch almost every day, comments on with frequency. ("Oh, my goodness! Did you ever taste it? It's all soft, and it's in layers, and it has nuts—but I can't write any more about it; my mouth waters too much.")

Of course, tracking down the real Lady Baltimore is like finding out for certain who said "Let them eat cake." Reed says it's Joan, George Calvert's second wife. Maryland Public Television says it was Anne Arundell, who married the second Lord Baltimore, Cecil Calvert (George's son), in 1628, when she was thirteen. I believe I was still eating frosting out of a can and singing into a spoon at thirteen, but times were different when life expectancy was short. Baltimore's *City Paper* says that Anne and Joan Calvert were the first and second wives of George Calvert and that both were Ladies Baltimore, which would make Anne Arundell the *third* Lady Baltimore.

How the Baltimore barons were linked at all to South Carolina remains the story's biggest mystery. Cecil, Calvert, Anne Arundell, and Baltimore are all Maryland counties now. The Old Foodie says that neither Lord nor Lady Baltimore ever lived in the colonies over which they lorded and ladied. However, several sources find George sending his second wife, Joan (sometimes called Joann), to warmer Jamestown, Virginia, from the too-cold Newfoundland, where she suffered from *illnesses*. George joined her there, but, as a Roman Catholic, he was poorly received.

But scrounging around beneath all that questionable, conflicting history has taught me only that you can't trust the textbooks anymore, especially today's. But you can trust the cake. It is always what it appears to be. The Old Foodie has tracked down the first published version of this recipe, from *The Daily Gazette and Bulletin* of Williamsport, Pennsylvania, on Christmas Eve, 1906:

Beat the whites of six eggs. Take a cup and a half of granulated sugar, a cup of milk, nearly a cup of butter, three cups of flour and two teaspoonfuls of good baking powder. Sift the flour and baking powder together into the other ingredients, adding the eggs last of all. Bake in two buttered pans for fifteen or twenty minutes.

For the frosting: Two cups of granulated sugar and a cup and a half of water, boil until stringy, about five minutes usually does it. Beat the whites of two eggs very light, and pour the boiling sugar slowly into it, mixing well. Take out of this enough for the top and sides of the cake, and stir into the remainder for the filling between the two layers, one cup of finely chopped raisins and a cup of chopped nuts. This is delicious when properly baked.

Of the Lord Baltimore Cake, little is known. Patricia Bunning Stevens, in *Rare Bits: Unusual Origins of Popular Recipes,* writes that it was just a matter of time before someone created a cake that uses the leftover egg yolks not used in the Lady's cake. A 1951 ad for Karo Syrup calls the *Lord* Baltimore Cake's boiled white icing the "Aristocrat of Frostings." Often made with toasted coconut, pecans, almonds, and maraschino cherries, it might have given the walnuts, raisins, and figs of the Lady's frosting a run for their money; it certainly made for a more colorful Karo ad.

While visiting with CakeLove owner Warren Brown, I discovered that he was working on a new project, *United Cakes of America,* which would do something similar to what I've done in this chapter, only Brown's goal would be to make a cake for each state out of indigenous ingredients—maybe do a Lady Baltimore Cake for Maryland. I realized that he was not quite into the research phase yet, so I was only a little surprised when he added my phone number to his PalmPilot, after asking if I'd mind helping him out with his book. "You seem to know a lot about cake," he said. (Later, I wrote to him suggesting he do a peach cake or maybe something he could name after me.)

Lane Cake, Alabama

I had never heard of Lane Cake and got the lead from someone at Chowhound. The first recipe I found had lots of exclamatory instructions and musings, "along with all the directions in the world! YOU COULD MAKE THIS CAKE EVEN IF YOU'VE NEVER BEFORE MADE A 'SCRATCH' CAKE! I felt this was perfect for a 'cake' Web page! I have made this cake many times. It is so delicious!" The instructions also make use of the single quotation mark for emphasis. The recipe is from "some very old cookbook" and is "at least 60 to 70 years old," from a time "when people baked in 'uncontrolled ovens' . . . re: wood stoves."

"LET'S BEGIN OUR 'LANE CAKE,'" the author says. (As I write, local meteorologist Norm Lewis is telling viewers that the cold front is like a layer cake, the top of which will be passing over us tomorrow.) The writer warns us to read the entire recipe before beginning and to make no substitutions. No whipped or sweet butter. No packing flour once it's sifted. The entire recipe is written as though the baker is a ten-year-old boy or a Martian. "TO FROST CAKE Spread frosting between layers and on top and sides of cake. Frosting on sides may slide off. Lift with spatula and spread back on sides. Repeat if necessary." You mean it might fall off again?

Harper Lee, a native of Monroeville, Alabama, wrote about this most famous, most luxurious, most difficult regional cake in *To Kill a Mockingbird*. Miss Maudie, the neighbor vigilant over her azaleas, ". . . made the best cakes in the neighborhood. When she was admitted into our confidence, every time she baked she made a big cake and three little ones, and she would call across the street: 'Jem Finch, Scout Finch, Charles Baker Harris, come here!' Our promptness was always rewarded."

Later, when Aunt Alexandra comes to take care of the Finch kids, Scout says, "Miss Maudie Atkinson baked a Lane cake so loaded with shinny it made me tight," "shinny" being slang for *moonshine* and "tight" being slang for *liquored up*. I'm not averse to getting tight. There's even an inch of shinny, a gift from a friend, sitting on our bookshelf in a Mason jar. It's clear as water, but when the gold lid is unscrewed, those stinky spirits fill the room. Comedian Jim Gaffigan thinks the cake-booze combination makes perfect sense. "You know, 'cause we've all been eating cake and thought: 'You know what this needs? Booze! Shot o' liquor. I don't have time to eat *and* drink. I only got two hands, buddy, and one of 'em's holding a cigarette. Meet me halfway, will ya?'"

Miss Maudie is fictional, but the cake is not, as any Alabaman can tell you. And if you visit there or Georgia at Christmas, it's likely someone will slave over a Lane Cake—or Prize Cake, as it was called when Emma Rylander Lane self-published it in her 1898 recipe book, *Some Good Things to Eat*—just for you. It's often a test of the true Alabaman cook. Even those who know their way around a kitchen, like *Southern Food* author John Edgerton (who spent three hours baking this), find their mettle tested with the making of this laborious dessert. Fred Sauceman, who tracked down information about Lane while writing about the cake for Auburn University's *Encyclopedia of Alabama,* says, "The baking of an elegant, scratch-made, laborious Lane cake is a sign that a noteworthy life event is about to be celebrated." It came to be called Christmas Cake because its difficulty required a special occasion.

There's nothing special about the cake part; it's a typical sponge. But the filling—made with egg yolks, sugar, finely chopped raisins, and a glass of bourbon or brandy (and sometimes coconut, pecans, and maraschino cherries, all chopped fine)—leaches through those layers of cake, drenching them with a sweet, liquory goodness that was an exception from sin in dry Alabama. The original frosting is made with corn syrup and sugar—a typical boiled, fluffy frosting. Some more modern versions, which use a lot of optional ingredients, use the filling as the frosting, too, and this gives the cake a look of sophistication to match its difficulty. Some Alabamans and Georgians treat the Lane Cake as a fruitcake, wrapping it in a bourbon-soaked cheesecloth and keeping it in dark storage. Everyone agrees that it tastes better after it ages. Rylander Lane's cookbook, *Some Good Things to Eat,* seems to exist only as a title in historical records. It's on the wish list of a few food writers, including Jean Anderson, the Recipe Doctor. The late Jewell Ellen Smith had her hands on one she obtained much like the way one experiences an urban legend, through the FOAF (friend of a friend). Smith says,

Recently, through a friend of a friend who has a friend living in Clayton, I obtained one of the last copies of the 1976 revised edition of THE ORIGINAL MRS. LANE'S "Some Good Things to Eat" COOKBOOK. In it, Lane tells readers: "Do not raise a family without making tea or ginger cakes for the children once a week. Otherwise, you rob childhood of one of its rights, also one of its chief joys.

Smith agrees, and opines on the rights of children. Unfortunately, she allows copyright laws to keep her from reproducing Lane's original recipe, as it was written in the cookbook—though it doesn't stop her from quoting other parts of the book! All of this can be found in a column, "Sunbonnet Soliloquy," which she wrote regularly for the Fort Rucker Officers' Wives Club's magazine, *Hedgehopper.* In it, she offered practical homemaking advice and stories. Smith, who won the Alabama Mother of the Year award in 1987, died in 1998. And who was the lucky heir to the original Mrs. Lane's cookbook?

Mrs. Lane died on April 25, 1904, in Guadalajara, Mexico, where she had lived for two years; the death announcement appeared the following day in *The Atlanta Constitution*. It didn't mention the cookbook or the cake.

Red Velvet Cake, the South

The South claims an overwhelming number of butt-widening favorites, like caramel, coconut, carrot, chocolate, and blueberry cakes. Perhaps it's simply that Southern hospitality demands a cake for every occasion, and its climate is certainly hospitable to all kinds of fruits and nuts. But even the name of the Red Velvet Cake conjures an image of Rhett Butler.

The history of the Red Velvet Cake seems to be decorated with legend. In fact, the first time I'd ever heard of it was 1998, ten years ago, when I got my first e-mail address. With it came all kinds of loathsome virus warnings and urban folktales, including one about an expensive Neiman Marcus cookie recipe. But that legend is merely an updated version of the 1948 legend of the "$25 Fudge Cake," which morphed into the one about the Red Velvet Cake at New York's Waldorf-Astoria Hotel. The story, in case you have never had an e-mail address, is that a woman dined at the hotel's restaurant and loved the dessert so much that she asked for the recipe. With it, the waiter brought a bill for $350, and the woman's lawyer concurred with the restaurant. She had to pay it. To get even with the hotel, the woman mailed the recipe to everyone she knew, with instructions to pass it on. The tale has taken on many confectioners and their sweet comestibles, yet it's never been true.

Like anything that's much talked about, the Red Velvet Cake has its detractors. For one thing, the amount of red dye necessary—up to three ounces!—makes this unappealing to most people, especially when we know what red dye does to the system. Others complain about the amount of oil—up to two and a quarter cups! Few people complain about the traditional frosting, which is not, as many believe, made with cream cheese. Instead, it's a milk-based icing with butter, sugar, vanilla, and a bit of flour.

King Cake,
New Orleans, Louisiana

As a Jewish child, I found those all-lit-up Santa-in-the-manger scenes to be a sinful visual delight, like so many of the adults around me, who declared the cacophonous lawns frightful, yet still oohed and ahhed as we drove past on our annual tour of the goyim areas, sort of like the poor kids trick-or-treating two neighborhoods over. I guess it's the same way I feel about the annual Mardi Gras tradition, the

King Cake. The Sno-Ball of neighborhood bakery items, the King Cake, garishly smeared with many colors of frosting, is made even tackier with the surprise inside: a plastic baby Jesus. No offense. It's not the Jesus (well, maybe a little) but his plasticity. My husband, a Catholic school social studies teacher, is often presented with some hideous expressions of students' faith: Jesus clocks, mugs, ties, and ornaments, all of which have given us entrée into any number of bad-gift-regifting parties at Christmastime. There's a reason you don't find Jews giving each other a Torah clock or a 3-D postcard of Moses parting the Red Sea. Taste.

A well-made King Cake resembles a frosted ring of braided challah, one of the most challenging baked goods I've ever made. A traditional cake has no filling, but it's now come to resemble a Danish, with fillings that include strawberry, cream cheese, and pineapple. Long ago, the King Cake was baked with a bean representing the baby Jesus, but this is the modern world, and kitsch makes us smile. And what happens when your slice contains the replica of the Christ child, be it porcelain or plastic? You are obliged to provide next year's King Cake.

During Hurricane Katrina, when all eyes were on New Orleans, NPR ran a story about David Haydel's bakery, one of the few to survive the hurricane, where customers stood in line to order gift cakes to send to families who helped hurricane victims. Haydel gave radio listeners an audio tour of the creation of a King Cake, narrating each step. He fills a "modified French bread machine" with 125 pounds of dough. It's an assembly-line process, but it's not hands-off. The dough rises, gets divided into units by weight, then each is rounded and dropped into a proofing unit, where it rolls around a few times. Finally, the ball falls through a chute, where rollers flatten it a bit, and a waiting baker grabs the dough, sprinkles it with oil and cinnamon, and folds it in half. Soon it's braided, left to rise again, then baked twelve minutes. Once a cake is cooled, it's turned over, and the baby's shoved into an unfilled area of the cake. "No baby is in the same spot," a baker says. An icing machine pours just the right amount of two hundred pounds of liquefied sugar on top of the cake. Haydel calls it fondant icing, but it is different from the thick, opaque, rolled fondant found on novelty cakes. (Recipes for this are available everywhere but usually consist of a huge proportion of confectioners' sugar and a small bit of water, corn syrup, and almond extract, cooked on the stove until pourable but still thick.) "Without purple, green, and gold sugar, you just have a cinnamon roll," Haydel says. The colors are actually symbols of justice, faith, and power, respectively.

You might be inclined to think that this cake is all about the Jesus, but the kings referred to here are the Magi, the three wise men, "we three kings (of orient are)," those who brought gold, frankincense, and myrrh (a camphorlike balm that needs no explanation, thanks to Monty Python's *The Life of Brian*) to the Christ child. It is traditionally served at Epiphany (also known as Little Christmas), a day especially important to me for the birth of my own epiphany, my daughter, Serena. It's not too late to start our own tradition.

One of the oldest cake traditions, this cake is known by many names, among them King's Cake, Dreikönigskuchen (Three Kings Cake), Twelfth Night Cake, Rosca de Reyes, and Le Gâteau des rois. It's eaten by the French, the Spanish, the Portuguese, the Cubans, the Filipinos, the Puerto Ricans, the Argentineans, the Belgians, the Mexicans, and other Christians around the world. Just about the only European place that doesn't partake of the cake is England, where they eat Christmas cake. Since the thirteenth century, bakers have been burying a single bean or pea or coin in this cake and its finders given the royal treatment. The king—or queen—for the day is entitled to order the party guests around.

The Mexican King Cake, Rosca de Reyes, is similar, a wreath of sweet bread decorated with dried or candied fruits. A bean or candy once was used to represent *el niño Dios,* but some say Mexicans were sneaky—and smart—swallowing their obligation to return the hidden prize to the nearest church on February 2,* Día de la Candelaria. Now, a proper choking hazard has replaced the edibles.

My friend Ed is the Chilean-born son of a Mexican mother. He takes the time to prepare traditional dishes like tamales while here in America, but when he asked his mother why she never did, she said, "Why make this by hand when there are perfectly good people out there making it for me?" Their Rosca de Reyes was baked with a glass baby Jesus, which was reused each year. Though Ed is Hispanic and a Catholic, he isn't familiar with Día de la Candelaria, the holiday on the second of February, when the recipient of the now plastic Jesus is to return to church as a godparent for the re-creation of the baby Jesus' baptism, presenting him with a christening gown and throwing a dinner party, where the traditional dish is tamales.

La Galette or Le Gâteau des Rois (wafer or cake of the kings, depending on your region), is a puff pastry filled with frangipane. A 1774 painting, *Le Gâteau des Rois,* by Jean-Baptiste Greuze depicts the tradition. A dramatic interpretation of the painting, which bears the cracks and scratches of centuries, can be heard at the National Gallery of Australia's Web site. A commanding voice tells the story of both cake and painter:

> Jean-Baptiste Greuze painted the poetry of everyday life
> with a grandeur and heroism that made him welcome in
> intellectual and revolutionary French circles. He worked
> primarily in a genre known as "morality painting." His

---

* February 2 is also the day designated as the end of the Christmas season, and decorations are usually taken down that day. I like Epiphany (January 6) for that tradition, having been scarred by an event in the mid-1990s. One of the few times we decorated the front of our house with *tasteful* white Christmas lights, someone in the neighborhood got tired of them around February 3 and decided to tell us by phone, anonymously, at midnight—and before Caller ID and *69—that she objected. "Don't you think it's time to turn off your Christmas lights?" she screeched.

complex scene penetrates the emotions of a humble peas-
ant family celebrating the Epiphany, a Catholic holiday
that falls on the sixth of January. The traditional three
kings cake is being served. Only one person will find the
bean that's been baked into the mixture. The father holds
slices in his serviette and patiently holds them out for
the young boy to choose. Everyone else waits somewhat
anxiously for their turn—everyone, that is, except for the
young girl, who appears to be sulking behind her father's
chair, and the mother on the left, who takes advantage of
the moment to embrace a child. The lucky one who finds
the bean will become a king for the day.

Jacob Jordaens, a Flemish artist, painted *The Feast of the Bean King*
(1640–1645), one of six Twelfth Night festival paintings, which
shows, among other things, a little girl drinking wine. In *What Great
Paintings Say,* Rose-Marie Hagen writes that "pieces of Twelfth Cake
were cut not only for the guests, as . . . Sebastian Franck observed: 'To
honor God,' he wrote, pieces were kept for Jesus, the Virgin Mary
and the Magi."

Once containing a hidden broad bean, or *la fève,* the pastry now
holds any small object at all. If you buy one at a French bakery, you'll
get a paper crown, so that you can be king for a day. The cake is to be
divided evenly among the guests, with one extra piece for God, Mary,
the poor, or, possibly, Elijah.

"Leslie Miller's Fantastic Lemon Cake Creation!!"

As always happens when I sit down to write, someone needs a cake.
Two weeks ago, the writing subject was a concert survival guide
for parents of 'tweens, and the occasion was my daughter's birthday,
for which I baked a dark chocolate Town Cake with cream cheese

frosting (which Serena's friend talked about to other parents). Yesterday, while the subject was Smith Island cake, the occasion was a visit from the chaperones of our Costa Rican exchange students. The cake was a lemon layer cake, with a recipe from *America's Test Kitchen,* one of the best true-blue cooking shows around.

I was a kid when I started watching PBS on Sunday afternoons on the sofa. Jeff Smith's *Frugal Gourmet* was my favorite cooking show, but I'd watch all of them. When I grew up, I wrote down everything, planning to make chicken potpie with homemade crust and Mexican wedding cookies. I rarely made any of those dishes but shoved all my handwritten notes in a file box anyway, where they stayed, crumpled, for twenty years.

The lemon cake haunted me. Two days was all it took before I found myself shirking my writing duties to cook some lemon curd. The cake was an all-day affair, with pesky instructions to add frozen half-inch cubes of butter to the dry ingredients, cutting them in as one would make a piecrust. (This is evidence that Harold McGee's choice of cold butter works!) Milk and eggs had to be at room temperature. Honestly, I don't know if any of that junk makes a difference. I seem to make the best cakes at the last minute, when I microwave the butter to soften it and mix in wet ingredients just out of the fridge. Even this time, when I didn't want to make a mistake, my butter wasn't frozen enough, so my flour had lumps, rather than that damp sand look from the TV show; my milk and eggs, on the counter for two hours, were still cold.

Why didn't I make the Smith Island or Baltimore peach cake, if I wanted to present something traditional to our Costa Rican guests? I guess making one would have been pretentious. It's not, after all, a tradition here in this house. Peaches aren't in season, and candy bars aren't particularly special. But it didn't make too much sense to choose the lemon cake, either, as I'm not a huge fan of fruit desserts. (I generally want my sweets to be devoid of those poster children for good health: apples, bananas, strawberries.) I couldn't shake the lemon cake. I knew making it would teach me a thing or two about chemistry. I was in learning mode.

One trick is the way to properly slice a cake into two layers. It took a demonstration on *America's Test Kitchen* to click: Using a serrated knife, simply score, halfway between the top and bottom, around the entire perimeter (a lazy Susan is a must). Next time around, go in a little deeper. On the next turn, you can slice the cake all the way through, with no unevenness.

The other thing I learned is that Swiss meringue is not a good enough frosting for any cake, especially for those of us who dislike marshmallow. And I learned that I'm pretty good at making things up, at this point; I added a stick and a half of softened butter, cut into cubes, and turned the meringue into Swiss buttercream.

Marta and Monica joined Miss Renee (REE-nee), the first-grade teacher at our school, for cake at our house. Though we were all stuffed full of crab cakes, crab dip, and crab soup, no one rejected the offer. I cut seven slices for the six of us, miscounting, and my daughter and I didn't wait for the others to pick up their servings before digging in. As the syndicated noon news guy, Mr. Ford, would say, "Ooooh, it's so good!" I couldn't get over how perfect the lemon curd tasted with the cake, whose crumb was delicate. And even though it spent twenty-four hours in the refrigerator (I had let it come to room temperature for three hours before we ate it), the cake was moist. Everyone agreed the cake was terrific, and Miss Renee, who's all of five feet and 100 pounds, went for seconds, while Marta and Monica gave me a lesson in the Tres Leches, or Three Milks, Cake, which they claim originated in Nicaragua.

The lemon cake stayed in the refrigerator for several days, despite the *Test Kitchen*'s note that it can be made a day in advance. Most recipe writers would rather you toss a perfectly good cake after a day than blame them for a stale, week-old slice. But I think we're capable of figuring out certain things: that plastic wrap suffocates babies, that the contents of a coffee cup are hot, and that cake doesn't taste as good when it's been in the fridge (or on the kitchen counter) for a week. I take one piece to a park dog walker and two to the administrative assistant and the counselor of the school. I give a slice to my neighbor, and I nibble slivers. But when I offer a piece to my daughter—several times, in fact—she turns me down. She turns down cake! I find myself becoming the typical Jewish mother (worse, *grand*mother), my bottom lip quivering with hurt, my eyebrows rising, the ends of my mouth turning downward. "Mom! I love the cake; I just don't want it right now," she says. And I don't understand. Who wouldn't choose a homemade cake over a Hershey bar?

On Friday morning, Miss Renee brought me a thank-you card. "I have to say though that Leslie's creation lemon cake was beyond the beyond! My all-time favorite dessert used to be ice cream but I have to say my new #1 choice is Leslie Miller's Fantastic Lemon Cake creation!! It is truly awesome!" See, there's nothing better than that. Tell me I look beautiful, and that's nice of you (I don't believe you, but it's nice). Tell me I'm funny, and I thank you, though you state the obvious. But tell me I'm a good cook, that you love my meat loaf and my lemon layer cake, and you are loving *me*. Food is love.

Pastel de Tres Leches, Texas (Austin et al.)

Literally translated, the pie or pastry of three milks is a favorite cake in Austin and other areas of Texas, primarily because of the state's proximity to Mexico, where the recipe is said to have migrated from Nicaragua. My Costa Rican guests (Marta is in her late forties) had not heard of this cake until recently, when a Nicaraguan restaurant opened in San Juan.

Lots of sleuthing has turned up little recorded evidence. The cake itself is perforated and soaked in a mixture of three milks, two of them evaporated and one sweetened condensed. At this point, lesser detectives would throw up their arms and declare this a recent culinary invention, as canned milk couldn't have been around for too long. But Nestlé was manufacturing canned milk (in Mexico!) from 1875. And the recipe for this cake was, indeed, published on one of their milk can labels. Patricia Quintana, Mexican food expert, says the recipe came from Sinaloa.

Most likely, as food writer MM Pack discovered, this recipe evolved from some older, European-influenced milk-soaked breads and cakes, including Torta de Leche and *antes,* a nineteenth-century soaked bread.

Whether it came here by way of Miami from Cuba or Texas from Mexico is less important than the fact that it's here and that, through some miracle of chemistry (as so much of baking is), the milk-soaked cake doesn't become nasty mush. It is traditionally a one-layer cake, its moistness probably hindering support of a second layer.

Texas Sheet Cake, Texas

Texans claim another single-layer cake for their own: the Texas Sheet Cake, sometimes called a Texas *Sheath* Cake. Karen Haram believes like I do that "someone had bad ears and didn't hear right." When I taught college English, I did a lesson on what I dubbed *mishearance,* common phrases like "butt naked" and "dressed to the nines" that made it into our language because someone didn't know what was naked about a buck (someone who's obviously never seen a male deer's ass) or what part of the body was "thine eyen." Regardless of the name, the two cakes are undoubtedly the same: an inch-thick (or thereabouts) chocolate-frosted chocolate brownie, reminiscent of the German chocolate cake, but only in the way that every cake is reminiscent of something older.

Dobosh Cake, Hawaii;
Doberge Cake, New Orleans

Recipes for the chocolaty cakes popular in Hawaii and New Orleans can be found in dozens of recipe books and on hundreds of
cooking Web sites. Both recipes have a puddinglike frosting made
with cornstarch. No one knows for sure where the recipes originated, but two key bakers seem to have brought the idea home from
Europe. Wanda Adams of *The Honolulu Advertiser* traced the cake
for a reader, who believed the original chef of King's Bakery, Robert
Taira, told her mother that he had discovered the cake on a trip to
Europe. The now defunct King's Bakery was famed for its Dobosh
Cake and its sweet breads. Robert Taira died in 2003, and the bakery,
which was left to his son Mark, is also gone. A little bit of detective
work may have turned up Mark in Los Angeles at King's Hawaiian,
where he sells sweet breads (not sweetbreads) to big-name supermarkets all over the country, but he's not talkin'.

The New Orleans version is similar to the Hawaiian but was the
creation of pastry chef Beulah Ledner, whose early 1900s cake began,
according to *New Orleans Classic Desserts,* by Kit Wohl, as a white
cake with chocolate custard filling and chocolate frosting, just like
a famous predecessor, the Hungarian Dobos Torte. Robert Portnoy,
now a resident of Houston, Texas, says he remembers eating Ledner's Doberge Cake for his third birthday in 1951. His mother and
his aunts were friends with the baker and were her patrons "during
World War II, when, due to shortages and rationing, you had to
bring your own butter and sugar to the bakery to have it converted
into a dessert." Portnoy remembers her sugar cookies with particular
enthusiasm and regrets not having gotten her recipe for the cake. "I
guess we never looked ahead to a time when it would not be there for
us." He also laments the quality of the imitators of her recipe at New
Orleans bakeries—so much that his family stopped buying the cakes.
He can't be sure whether anyone has the true recipe, since her cook-

book has been out of print for so long. But the Doberge Cake is so etched in his memory that he can describe the flowers—pink, green, and yellow—that she piped on the cake. "Instead of roses, which are so common, she always did sweet peas, which made her cakes very distinctive." Had I not taken the cake-decorating course, I, too, might have seen this as distinct. But as a total failure at the rose—and a success at the sweet pea—I can only imagine poor Beulah at the kitchen table in 1910, cursing the frosting roses in the middle of the night.

Because the Hungarian pronunciation of the creation is do-BOSHTORTah, it's easy to see how *torte* became *cake* and *Dobos* became *Dobosh*. It's like the game of telephone: the name evolving less out of an attempt to conceal the cake's history than from a simple misunderstanding that the history lies *within* the name. What's not easy to see is Ledner's relationship to the original cake. It does not resemble what's thought to be her original inspiration in many ways besides color.

According to George Lang, author of the 1971 book *The Cuisine of Hungary,* the St. Sebastian Kaffee-Conditorei, the first pastry shop, opened in the middle of the eighteenth century. From that moment on, the torte and other pastries seemed to accompany so many historical events and love affairs. One involved the invention of something called the Indianer (perhaps the precursor to a Berliner), a doughnut filled with cream and covered with chocolate. It was named to promote a poorly received East Indian magician and promote Count Ferdinand Palffy's theater production. The Indianer took off, and pastry shops made it nearly exclusively for a while. "Since that time Hungarian chefs and housewives have made a sport out of creating new tortes, and you are likely to find in cookbooks or on your plate a Cotton Torte, a Potato Torte, a Potato Layer Cake, a Water Torte, or even—believe it or not—a Carrot Torte."

Lang tells the story of a Gypsy violinist, Rigo Jancsi, who eloped with a princess in 1896. Their romance inspired both a cake and a torte, both called the Rigo Jancsi. The torte became an international sensation. In 1918, a similar star-crossed love was born between an English countess and a Gypsy leader, and with it came another cake. The Jancsi Kiss Torte was a flop. The author's poetic flair led him to say, "The second batch of moon astronauts cause hardly a ripple and a shrug. . . ."

But it's the Dobos Torta, created in 1887 by its namesake, Jozsef C. Dobos, that inspired some similar cakes in the United States. Dobos opened a gourmet shop where he sold his cake and even "devised a packaging for sending this delicacy to foreign countries. Soon everybody started to imitate this cake, mostly with very bad results." He decided to publish the recipe, and it became one of the most celebrated cakes in the world, so much so that its seventy-fifth birthday was honored by the Hungarian Chefs' and Pastry Chefs' Association, whose members placed a wreath on Dobos's grave in commemoration. Lang says, "The world remembers the anniversaries of battles and the birthdays of great composers. But what city other than Budapest would stage a full-scale festival to commemorate the seventy-fifth birthday of a torte?"

Something in my blood connects me to this particular pastry. It's a coincidence, surely, that the anniversary took place in 1962, the year I was born, but it's no coincidence that my grandfather was born in Budapest. He was one of the most devoted eaters of cake, despite the fact that he ate with the gentleness of a well-mannered aristocrat. My grandfather was always trim and small, my grandmother always giving him the look of "put that down" as he reached for a slice, a "how dare you" look as he attempted to reach for a second. I never got the chance to talk to my grandfather about cake, but I know how he felt.

Gooey Butter Cake,
St. Louis, Missouri

We used to tease our Urbana, Illinois–born friend that he probably even buttered his butter. He could turn the most good-for-you meal into six clogged arteries. Maybe he came by it honestly, as the Gooey Butter Cake is said to be the result of a German baker's ingredient mistake: too much buttah. The legend has been floating around on the Internet at least as long as Linda Stradley's 2004 discussion of the "History of Gooey Butter Cake." It was, at the end of 2006, corroborated by someone with intimate knowledge of the event.

> In late 1942 or early 1943, Johnny Hoffman of St. Louis Pastries Bakery was working on a Saturday and made what eventually turned out to be Gooey Butter Cake. You're right, it was a mistake! He subsequently called Herman Danzer, my dad, and told him he thought he may have something and asked to come to my dad's shop on Spring & Gravois to see if they could duplicate it.

Experiments ensued, with Danzer adding glycerin to achieve the right consistency. Danzer's wife, Melba, exclaimed something like, "This sure is gooey!" (She did not, upon eating the stale cracker creation, exclaim, "This sure is toast!" Credit for Melba Toast goes to Helen Porter Mitchell, an Australian opera singer who went by the name Dame Nellie Melba. She also lent her name to the Peach Melba.)

More like a coffee cake than a dessert, it is usually composed of a buttery bottom layer of yellow cake topped with a gooey batch of egg, cream cheese, butter, and sugar. Paula Deen's recipe calls for a box of yellow cake mix with a stick of butter and an egg.

Boston Cream Pie, Boston

Legend has it that the famous pudding cake was derived by the owner of Boston's Parker House Restaurant from a recipe published in New York. It's hard to keep your claim to a recipe when even a small alteration by a chef, this time a French one named M. Sanzian, makes it original. It's probably called a pie because many cakes were baked in pie tins, the cake pan being hard to come by at the time, and because the layers are filled with a traditional pastry cream, which resembles a pie filling.

The Parker House, which opened in 1855 (about the same time the recipe for pudding pie was published in a New York newspaper), still calls itself the "Birthplace of the Boston Cream Pie." The Parker House has many claims to fame. Ho Chi Minh worked in the kitchen for two years, and Malcolm X was a busboy. Its patrons included Charles Dickens. The Boston Cream Pie has been the official dessert of Massachusetts since December 12, 1996. The bill was sponsored by Norton High School's civics class, but it did not go unchallenged. Both Indian Pudding and the Toll House cookie (which came from the Toll House Restaurant in Whitman, Massachusetts, in 1930) were in the running. The cookie became official in 1997. And the Boston Cream Donut is the official state doughnut. What does a doughnut bill look like?

PART I. ADMINISTRATION OF THE GOVERNMENT

TITLE I. JURISDICTION AND EMBLEMS OF THE COMMON-WEALTH, THE GENERAL COURT, STATUTES AND PUBLIC DOCU-MENTS

CHAPTER 2. ARMS, GREAT SEAL AND OTHER EMBLEMS OF THE COMMONWEALTH

Chapter 2: Section 51. Donut of commonwealth

Section 51. The Boston Cream Donut shall be the official donut of the commonwealth.

"Donut of the commonwealth!" Note to self: lobby for Maryland's state doughnut.

The Boston Cream Pie is not a difficult cake to bake or assemble:

the cake is a typical sponge; the filling is a typical cooked custard; the frosting is a chocolate glaze. Not a bad choice for a state dessert.

Blackout Cake,
Brooklyn, New York

When some desserts are in the room—or in this case, in the city—no one is on a diet. The famous Blackout Cake, which is chocolate on top of chocolate with chocolate on top, has an old and romantic history. Molly O'Neill wrote about this cake in 1991 for *The New York Times,* when a man named John Edwards attempted a spectacular kind of torte reform.

This cake, composed of the most devilish of devil's food, chocolate pudding, chocolate frosting, and a generous sprinkling of cake crumbs, was born at Ebinger's Bakery, and Brooklynites' memory of it seems to make them weep. In 1898, the Flatbush Avenue bakery opened, and, like furry *Star Trek* tribbles,* grew to fifty-four locations. O'Neill says, "Anybody who lived in Brooklyn lived close to an Ebinger's. The unstinting quality and consistency of its 200 German-style pastries made them shrines." Sometime in the fifties, the Blackout Cake, said to have been named for wartime blackouts, was concocted and became an instant obsession.

After Ebinger's went bankrupt in 1972, a few bakers and patrons tried to bring back the name and the cake that made them famous. Dick Forman, a patron, became obsessed with re-creating the Blackout recipe, using brownie mix and chocolate syrup, eventually giving up and passing his file to *Cake Bible* author Rose Levy Beranbaum, who believes the memory of the cake is probably better than the cake itself. Those indoctrinated by Ebinger's say it's nonsense. So do I. Memories of the gigantic amusement park you visited as a child are

---

* Actually, tribbles grew to 1,771,561, according to Spock's calculations.

better than that run-down place. Memories of standing in a bakery line after church are better than having stood there, fidgeting with the flower on your dress while your mother smacked your hand. But no *memory* of cake is better than cake. Even if it's not the identical cake, even if you can't reconcile its flavor to the one of your youth, it's going to taste fantastic. Hell, it's *chocolate*. Maybe you've been around the block a few times now, and you've scarfed down slices of *Silver Palate* carrot cake and hunks of Mississippi Mud Cake. But unless a re-created Blackout Cake is dry as dust and not sweet enough, fans will associate it with the original.

Resistance is futile when cake is making a comeback. Lou Guerra tried to bring it back in 1982 with what he said were original recipes—right down to the one-day shelf life, which made financial success impossible for Guerra. So John Edwards bought the bakery in 1989, making a commercial version of the Blackout Cake that he shipped to supermarkets in packaging identical to the original. Those who grew up with the cake described the moment of recognition as discovering the Holy Grail. If, as some claimed, the closing of Ebinger's was like the death of God, then the sightings of these boxes in local grocery stores was like Lazarus rising from the dead.

Recipes for Blackout Cake abound, including seemingly authentic ones, but the best probably comes from Molly O'Neill's 1991 *New York Times* story.

I'd heard of Blackout Cake, of course, and assumed it was named for some Con Ed disaster that left all of New York without electricity. The first blackout to affect New York was the Great Northeast Blackout of 1965, after the cake was popular, but *wartime* blackouts are responsible. I've never gone *looking for* such a cake, but while visiting Manhattan, I walked with a friend from place to place in search of a café that served both beer and cake. One would think it's easily done in New York, where, on St. Mark's Place, you can get tattoos and cappuccino. But patisseries had no beer, and bars had no cake. Even an Italian restaurant lacked cake. A third friend joined us and suggested Puck Fair, which sits across the street from the Puck Building, of *Will and Grace* fame. Only one cake was on the menu. "I don't usually eat sweets, but our chocolate cake is incredible," the tattooed (and cappuccino'd) waitress told me. Incredible, yes, but it was more like a brownie in texture—light on flour and leavening, dense, and moist.

Full of pizza, ale, and cake, and exhausted from a nine-hour shopping excursion on foot, we made our way back to my friend's apartment on Twenty-seventh Street and Third Avenue by way of Irving Place, a three-block street near Gramercy Park. I thought I'd take my friend, Teena, a lifelong New Yorker born in Brooklyn, to peek at the Gramercy Park Hotel. I'd stayed there at the end of the 1990s, before it became a posh—no, swanky—piece of real estate commanding six hundred dollars a night. Now I can't even afford a drink at the bar, where you can find enormous paintings by Warhol, Basquiat, and Schnabel. On the way, I spotted Hilary Swank, who smiled at a group of tourists before entering 71 Irving Place Coffee & Tea Bar. Teena wasn't sure it was really Swank and wanted to go in for a closer look. I obliged; I'm not averse to a little celebrity spotting. How *does* an Oscar-winning actress take her coffee or tea at 6:00 p.m. on a Saturday? It was Swank's turn when we got in line, about fourth behind her, but while Teena was remarking on the star's smile, I was captivated by an enormous cupcake called "Faux-Stess." It was a nearly black chocolate mound with the Hostess trademark white squiggle, and above it was a Blackout Cake, the first one I'd ever seen in person. Forget about Swank: I wanted *its* autograph. On my tongue. So how does Swank take her coffee? Mmm . . . cake.

New York Cheesecake, New York

Here is my quandary. As a former college English instructor and owner of the Grammar Police, a company that issued citations to

people who mangled the English language, I used to judge my dictionaries by whether they had an entry for *irregardless*. Dictionaries are, after all, full of words. Nonwords ought to be absent.

Cheesecake is a noncake. That's right; it's *pie*. It's made of crust and filling. It's okay that the crust doesn't go up the sides; that's not a rule with pies. And cakes don't have sides, either, but what's between the layers is called filling. It is, however, a rule that cakes have a good amount of flour, that they have the texture of a bread product rather than custard. Maybe "cheese pie" sounded too savory.

My girlfriend Jennifer König is the great-granddaughter of Arnold Reuben, owner of the legendary Jewish deli Reuben's and the Turf Restaurant in New York. Reuben is said to have invented the Reuben sandwich, though that credit seems to belong to one of his chefs, who told Arnold Jr. that he ate too many hamburgers and created a sandwich just for him. The son liked it so much that it became a menu item. But Arnold Sr. is credited with serving the first "New York–style" cheesecake, which he made from cream cheese (Breakstone brand), rather than the cottage cheese other restaurants were using. It's said that he fell in love with the idea of a cheese pie served by a friend but wasn't enamored of the recipe, so he invented his own.

No one knows why Reuben renamed it *cake;* perhaps he was looking for a distinction from the friend's recipe.

I happen to be gifted in the art of cheesecakes, baking them in a *bain-marie,* or water bath, that helps to keep those flourless, cream-cheese-filled pies from cracking (some of the time—overcooking is really what cracks them). Concoctions include white chocolate caramel with apricot preserves and almonds, white chocolate with dark chocolate ganache, eggnog, and coconut. The best thing about them is that they can be made easily for diabetics using a crust of almond meal and butter and a filling sweetened with a combination of xylitol and Splenda, two sugar substitutes that, when used together, can fool even my husband, who still has no clue about the one in the refrigerator right now.

And So Much More!

Without a doubt, your great/not-so-great grandmother/aunt/uncle/grandfather, one of your parents, your friends, your parents' friends, your friends of friends made the first-ever 1-2-3-4 or Applesauce or Blackberry Jam or Chess or Chocolate Tipsy or Coke (or Dr Pepper or Pepsi) or Dolly Varden or Hummingbird or Italian Cream or Sanders Bumpy or Scripture Cake. Maybe you know the Aunt Ruth of Aunt Ruth's Pound Cake or the Grandma Hill of Grandma Hill's coconut and plain cakes. Maybe your bloodline is responsible for Bourbon Cake, Louisiana Crunch, Mississippi Mud, Peanut and Molasses, or Pineapple Upside-Down Cake. Maybe you are the direct descendant of the namesake of the Queen Elizabeth or Queen Nefertiti Cake. Perhaps your name is Dolly Varden—after the cake, not the Dickens character. Thank you all for your wonderful contributions to American cuisine and my waistline.

Cake Karma

> The most dangerous food is wedding cake.
> —James Thurber, cartoonist, humorist

We have come a long way from the days when a bride wore the least smelly dress she had and carried a bouquet of herbs to mask her stench. At least we like to think so. Yet we're still throwing salt over our shoulders—like my grandmother used to do (and my father and I still do), even when she didn't spill, just for good measure—or avoiding walking beneath a ladder or crossing paths with a black cat.

The wedding, one of mankind's oldest rituals, has no shortage of superstitions and legends. For instance, the beautiful bridal bouquet is nothing more than window dressing, having evolved from its utilitarian purpose. But even that purpose evolved from the ancient Roman custom of a bouquet of wheat sheaves, chosen as a magic charm to ensure fertility.

Everything—from the ring finger (chosen for its spiritual proximity to our heart) to the wedding dress—is shrouded in mystery and myth. Queen Victoria, of the so-many-named cakes, is said to have begun the trend of wearing a white wedding gown. According to some historians, the white dress was a sign that you were wealthy enough to own a dress you'd wear only once, because how practical is an all-white gown—especially after Labor Day and before Memorial Day, and in the hot parts of the country, it's pretty useless in summer months, too. In the Victorian age, the less well-to-do women "would trot out the white dress on special occasions throughout the first year of their marriage." I tried to wear my Stuart Weitzman wedding shoes, bought from Nordstrom's in 1994 for over two hundred dollars, postnuptials, but, ew. Even dyed, who can't tell they were your wedding shoes? But for what occasion could I "trot out" my six-hundred-dollar David's Bridal gown, though perhaps some anniversary ritual, performed at regular intervals, could require the wearing of the dress, which might help some of us keep our girlish figures. I was thirty-two and 140 pounds when I married. I remember my important dates in pounds. "Oh, my wedding? I got married [inaudible mumbling] pounds ago!"

The role of best man takes the cake for worst origin. Leopold Wagner, author of *Manners, Customs, and Observances,* says that when a man would take a wife, he'd literally take her. "[M]arriage by capture was the universal practice in the early eras of civilization, as it still is among primitive races." Some say the German Goths started it; others blame the Scots for enlisting the best man of the clan to help the groom steal a woman from a rival's party.* (Not true.) Philippa Waring, in *A Dictionary of Omens and Superstitions,* says that brides-

---

* Apparently, bride kidnapping is *still* in practice in many countries. It even has a name in Russian: *ala kachuu.* Russ L. Kleinbach, a sociology professor at Philadelphia University, has a spot on his professional Web site dedicated to just that: "Understanding Ala Kachuu and Preventing Non-Consensual Marriage." (He also has pages for other victims: Uzbek kidnapping, "Why Women Stay," and Human Rights Watch.) Below the boldface header, he says that this practice violates the laws of the Kyrgyz Republic and a woman's freedom. He tells the story of Kurmanjan Datka, a stateswoman who "broke with tradition" and rejected the man she was required to marry.

maids, "along with the best man, are actually relics from the days when marriage ceremonies were not infrequently attacked by enemies wishing to carry off the bride, and their presence was to prevent such an outrage." But how? We're talking about big, strong warriors. Maybe this is also where the custom of the bridesmaids dress derives, the object being to stun and blind (or shock and awe) any wedding crashers with electric pink taffeta.

Another theory is that the bridesmaid's job was to trick evil spirits. See, evil spirits lie in wait for your birthday, your wedding, and other days of importance—as you know. It works just like a cold. The moment you go on vacation to relax, to let your guard down, you get sick. Or the prom night zit. Same idea. Just *try* to enjoy some special event, and that's the day the evil spirits will show up at your door. But dress up a bunch of your best girlfriends, and the spirits won't know *which* pretty lady needs her marriage plagued. Why is it that we give them credit for knowing the date, time, and place of our wedding, but we believe them too stupid to figure out which one is the bride?

Similarly, the candles on a birthday cake were supposed to protect children (especially vulnerable because they are children *and* because it's their birthday) from evil spirits.

Of course, no one goes to a wedding *just* to make fun of the bad attire and the wedding singer. It's to see the cake. Like the bouquet, it's about fertility. After the wedding (the Latin word is *confarreatio,* which means to "share a cake of wheat or spelt"), the newlyweds dined on cakes, hoping that all this wheat symbolism would turn to substance in the bride's womb. (Honeymoons were originally times for the couple to spend in seclusion to that end, but if you were a kidnapped bride, you'd most likely be taken to a cave, rather than the French Riviera, where making babies would be far less stressful.)

Christians adopted the Jewish custom of throwing wheat over a bride's head, which the Jews probably got from those wacky ancient Romans, who were not content with a sheath bouquet and a postnuptial cake bite but who also broke bread over the bride's head. Though some say the veil is yet another assertion of male dominance over the female, it was probably the woman who said, "Dang, I just got my hair did!" And we *let* the men think it was their good idea.

In England, cake crumbling was more dangerous. A plate of cake was thrown—not an amount of cake but an actual *plate*—over the bride's head. What mattered was that the plate break into a lot of pieces (obviously a tradition that began pre-Corelle). If the plate didn't break, guests were allowed to help it along by stomping on it. Then they'd go at the cake crumbs like a bunch of birds.

Our modern wedding cake grew out of all these traditions. Tad Tuleja, author of a few books of curious traditions and common-knowledge fallacies, says,

> Meanwhile, the folks who had been provided with wheat cakes (that is, the wedding list) continued to hurl them as before. Some of them were eaten by the young couple; some were taken home by hopeful maidens, who would place them under their pillows in the hope of receiving dreams of future husbands; some were distributed to the poor. The remainder were piled together, to be coated with almond paste or sugar. Eventually this pile of coated cakes grew into the modern, tiered creation—the conferration meal back in spades.

Some sources say that tiered cakes also began in England when wedding guests brought small buns, stacked them up on a table, and invited the wedding couple to kiss over the growing stack of cakes. Doing so without knocking them over was good luck for them, of course (while knocking them over was bad luck for the guy who had to clean up).

Such legends abound, all with different theories of evolution. Emily Post might have had the right idea in her quick and dirty description of the wedding cake's origins:

The evolution of the wedding cake began in ancient Rome where brides carried wheat ears in their left hands. Later, Anglo-Saxon brides wore the wheat made into chaplets, and gradually the belief developed that a young girl who ate of the grains of wheat which became scattered on the ground, would dream of her future husband. The next step was the baking of a thin dry biscuit which was broken over the bride's head and the crumbs divided amongst the guests. The next step was in making richer cake; then icing it; and the last instead of having it broken over her head, the bride broke it herself into small pieces for the guests. Later she cut it with a knife.

As for the kitschy (or tacky, depending) couple lording it over the wedding cake, the topper was a tradition begun sometime in the nineteenth century but not adopted by the upper classes until about 1920. In her 1922 book, Emily Post described the cake: "On the top it has a bouquet of white or silver flowers, or confectioner's quaint dolls representing the bride and groom." Sometimes the toppers were bells or lovebirds or couples in gazebos or hot-air balloons. Robert Reed, in *The Antique Shoppe Newspaper,* says, "The idea of wedding toppers in general and bride and groom toppers in particular had expanded enough in 1927 for the Sears and Roebuck mail order catalog [to] include a whole page of wedding cake ornaments. The following year Slack Manufacturing offered bride and groom figures made of celluloid. The bride wore a paper dress and the groom wore a paper suit. Both figures were about two and a half inches tall."

One would think it easy to find some more remarkable toppers now, and online searches turn up hundreds of offerings—all kinds of displays, like crystal-studded initials and crowns for several hundred dollars, goofy Fimo-sculpted couples designed to look like Jewish cartoon characters, and couples sculpted to look just like the two of

you and made by someone who calls himself Micro-Dwarf. There are clever, comic sculptures of runaway grooms, grooms with a ball and chain attached, a groom on a leash. And there are hillbilly trolls.

Eva Longoria was a guest on Jimmy Kimmel's thousandth episode. Kimmel had gotten her a cake topper made to look like her and Tony Parker of the San Antonio Spurs. Kimmel was thrilled that she used it. "It was such a beautiful wedding, and then you spoiled it with our stupid little [thing]." Longoria explained that her cake decorator was not happy when she learned the tacky couple would sit atop her elegant creation, but Longoria insisted. "Wedding cake tops are hard to find when you're a biracial couple."* Kimmel replied, "Oh! How about that? So, see, I solved yet another of the world's problems."

Most people don't care too much about the topper. They go to Cake Cottage, grab the white couple (if they're white) or the black couple (if they're black) that's the plainest or the funniest or the most nondescript—or they have their cake maker decide what goes on top

---

* They're not *that* hard to find. Hell, on my fireplace mantel, I have a Día del Muerto bride and groom, a pregnant bride in white (her husband in a blue tux), and a pair of ceramic lesbians. A simple Google search for "interracial cake topper" will return hundreds of hits (with hundreds of misses).

(if he's lucky; otherwise, he might have to contend with topping his beautiful creation with a pair of wooden trolls whose faces are shriveled like Raisinets). Our cake, resembling stacks of wedding gifts, accommodated our funky choice—Rollerblade Barbie and the Beast, as you may recall. My mother cut the Beast's hair short except for the rat tail worn by my husband and pasted the rest of it on the doll's face. They sat in a white chocolate box with their dog, a replica of our Beowulf.

Cake has long stood for abundance. The more you have, the better off you're said to be, which is why the word is also slang for money.* A sweet life together, one with lots of babies, begins with cake (maybe that's why the baby-to-be demands it). Always use Magi-Cake strips for wedding cakes, lest you jinx a marriage with a lopsided treat. Remember: those evil spirits who can't recognize that the bride is in

---

* And vagina. Melinda Gallagher and Emily Scarlet Kramer founded CAKE, a group dedicated to empowering women to express their sexuality. Says their site: "CAKE fulfills the evergrowing [sic] needs of a new generation of women (and their partners) who enjoy and want to explore their sexuality. *A Piece of Cake: Recipes for Female Sexual Pleasure* is the first CAKE book published by Simon & Schuster/Atria Books." (Simon & Schuster also publishes Paula Deen and yours truly.) For $75, you get a membership card "embossed with your name in silver," the CAKE book, a copy of *The HOT Woman's Handbook,* some form of limited-edition CAKE Wear, and two comp tickets to CLUB CAKE with "guaranteed access," which makes me wonder if this is Studio 54 all over again. And it's quite possible; membership has to be *approved,* and the question that decides it all? "Why do YOU get the Juice?" Not the Slice, the Frosting, the Icing, or even the Crumb,† but the *Juice.* Juice doesn't even taste good with cake.

† *Crumb,* or *crum,* in case you didn't know, is slang for penis and also, in some circles, slang for what's left of a woman's "cake" after she's already given a slice to someone else.

white can tell if you've trimmed a cake to level it. And never throw the scraps away! Feed them to *someone* (the evil spirits?), but tossing wheat products brings bad luck. And be sure that the cake tester you insert to check for doneness is shaped like a skewer (I use a turkey lacer, which comes in handy for many crafts and for removing splinters and for fastening the Magi-Cake strips when you inevitably lose the hat pin that hold the ends together around the cake pan). "She that pricks bread with fork or knife / Will never be happy, maid or wife. The same applies to cakes." It's also bad luck to count your cakes or breads, to have them split while they are baking (so much for pound cake), or to have them break (I am so screwed). And if you dream of yeast, you'll either be successful, or you've gotten someone pregnant. Or you have taken too strong an antibiotic.

Brides would do well to heed the admonition not to make their own cakes—as if any normal bride would add that to her to-do list. If you make your own cake, it is said, you'll end up working your fingers to the bone. And don't taste the cake, either, before it's served to your guests. And be sure *you* are the one to wield the knife, unless you plan to keep your prepregnancy figure by never becoming pregnant. Abundant wheat will carry its sympathetic magic only so far; when your husband touches the knife, all bets are off. He may *assist* you by clamping his hands atop your own, but you are in control of this marriage. (Until the early 1900s, only the bride cut the cake!) Tad Tuleja says "the groom helps direct the bride's hand," but this is untrue. It's at this moment, in fact, that the bride learns to let the man *think* he's actually helping. She offers her husband the first bite of cake as a gesture of submissiveness, "the gustatory equivalent of her body, which he will have the right to 'partake of' later." Then she slams her mate with cake. This ritual is related to the traditional roles of marriage, and perhaps in the past it did reinforce the dominance of the male (the sloppy mess the bride made on the groom's face only shows that she is incompetent). Maybe it's why many forgo this silly portion of the cake-cutting ritual.

Emily Post describes a ritual I've found nowhere else, which includes favors hidden inside the cake.

> The bride always cuts the cake, meaning that she inserts the knife and makes one cut through the cake, after which each person cuts herself or himself a slice. If there are two sets of favors hidden in the cake, there is a mark in the icing to distinguish the bridesmaids side from that of the ushers. Articles, each wrapped in silver foil, have been pushed through the bottom of the cake at intervals; the bridesmaids find a ten-cent piece for riches, a little gold ring for "first to be married," a thimble or little parrot or cat for "old maid," a wish-bone for the "luckiest." On the ushers' side, a button or dog is for the bachelor, and a miniature pair of dice as a symbol of lucky chance in life. The ring and ten-cent piece are the same.

If you are a guest at a wedding, have some cake, even if it has the aftertaste of a mix and frosting made from marshmallow, and even if you've just started Atkins for the eighth time. To refuse is bad luck for you and the couple.

The groom's cake used to be a fruitcake. Single women were to take a slice of it home, place it under their pillows, and dream of future husbands, though the same is said for wedding cake.

Another way to divine one's mate comes by way of a *dumb cake,* a British Isles tradition. Though it had no sugar or leavening (and no vanilla), the cake was baked on a hearthstone, the initials of the questioner carved in the top. "If all is done correctly and in complete silence," says David Pickering, author of *Cassell's Dictionary of Superstitions,* "the future partner of the person concerned will appear and similarly prick his or her own initials on the cake." Then they eat the cake and walk backward to bed.

If you really want to ensure the nighttime vision of your future

husband, do this: pass a small piece of wedding cake through a borrowed wedding ring (though it's probably bad luck for the lender to
remove her ring) three times, then place the cake under your pillow.
Be sure the shoes you wore to the wedding that day are arranged
in the shape of a *T*, and the ring is placed on your left hand's third
finger.

Or maybe you could just go on eHarmony like a normal woman.

Holy Cake Daze

Not counting the usual suspects, there are plenty of opportunities to say it with cake.

Chocolate Cake Day: January 27
Carrot Cake Day: February 3
Black Forest Cake Day: March 28
Coffee Cake Day: April 7
Applesauce Cake Day: June 6
National Cheesecake Day: July 30
Raspberry Cake Day: July 31
National Sponge Cake Day: August 23
National Dessert Month: October 1–31
National Angel Food Cake Day: October 10
National Dessert Day: October 14
Cake Day: November 26
National Fruitcake Day: December 27

Special birthdays, like the Sweet Sixteen, are not common everywhere. Latina girls celebrate the *quinceañera* when they are fifteen, and their cake is as extravagant as a wedding cake. If you're a bat or bar mitzvah, and your family has big money (like defense contractor David Brooks, who spent $10 million on his daughter's celebration), you'll likely get some weddinglike cake creation, too.

All over the world, birthdays are celebrated with cake. The Finnish like strawberry-banana shortcake with so much whipped cream that the candles are nearly lost. Malaysians eat ribbon cake. Netherlanders celebrate with a candleless cake and pastries, unless you're turning fifty, and then you get cookies that look like Abraham. New Zealanders eat buttered bread with lots of sprinkles. And Mexican kids get three wishes if they blow out all the candles in a single breath.

Cakesongs

Courtney Love sang, "I want to be the girl with the most cake." I know what she means. And I want to be the girl with the most songs about cake. If I could put out a CD compilation, it would include the following:

"Cake," B-52's
"Daria," Cake
"Fan Mail," Blondie
"Out of Your Mind," Jonatha Brooke
"Come on-a My House," Della Reese
"Time's A Wastin'," June Carter Cash
"What Can You Tell Me?" Chuck Prophet
"Round and Round," Bob Schneider
"Jackson Shake," Arty Hill and the Long Gone Daddys
"Piggyback Ride," Billy Harvey
"Cheesecake Truck," King Missile
"Wedding Cake," Damien Jurado
"Wedding Cake," Connie Smith

"Lay, Lady, Lay," Bob Dylan

"My Cat's Birthday," Cheryl Wheeler

"Cut the Cake," Average White Band

"Piece of Cake," Jethro Tull

"Tears at the Birthday Party," Elvis Costello

"Alison," Elvis Costello

"Cheers Darlin'," Damien Rice

"Spirit in the Night," Bruce Springsteen

"Strawberry Cake," Johnny Cash

"Cheese Cake," Aerosmith

"Angel Food," Ani DiFranco

"Wrap My Head Around That," Lucinda Williams

"Chocolate Cake," Crowded House

"Chocolate Cake for Breakfast," Bill Cosby

"Chocolate Cake," Vinyl Kings

"Doll Parts," Hole

"Pound Cake," Van Halen

LAYER FORTY-FOUR

Sweet Dreams

If you're like me (admit it; you are, at least a little), you've probably had a dream you were eating cake. It might not surprise you that some dream dictionaries think cake represents selfishness—you're not getting your rightful piece of the pie, so to speak. A dream of cake could mean you don't delegate work. It can also symbolize your achievements. A cake that's been eaten represents something you didn't explore to its fullest. And if you're buying a cake in your dream, you are reaping a reward for your hard work.

The two or three times I have dreamt of cake were related to attempts to stop eating it, and I would most often go for a doughnut, which, according to the same dream dictionary, means I am not quite whole.

Life for me has been exactly what I thought it would be, a cake, which I have eaten and had too.
—Margaret Anderson, founder and editor, *The Little Review*

The Last Course
EIGHTH TIER

Dessert

How does a book on cake end, when cake is both the end and never ending? A cake, or news of one, lurks around every corner of your life. On your home calendar, you can probably find an occasion for a cake at least once a month.

Every day, my e-mail announces the launch of a new cake blog or someone's extravagant wedding or a new snack cake product. Today, in fact, Jessie Oleson, head Cakespy and cupcake artist for her company, Cakespy.com, announced that she is such a popular writer now that she was able to quit her already-fun day job as art director of a refrigerator magnet company. Also this morning, I got a press release from TAG Heuer, which alerted me to Maria Sharapova's twenty-first-birthday cake. It was described as an "elegant white and pink eight-tier cake" on her Web site but was shown as two round layers of black (black!) surrounded by pink candles on top of a couple of layers of orange-, pink-, and white-topped cupcakes. Go figure. And appearing regularly in my spam folder is an announcement of Oreo's new snack cake.

On Easter Sunday, I awake to find, in my bulk mailbox, an ad for the new Oreo Cakesters, in Original and Chocolate Creme. I'm to click for a complimentary three-box sample. Oreo is the poster cookie for junk food—with hydrogenated oil coming out of the gate and high-fructose corn syrup bringing up the rear. It's also one of the first cookies to ever be sued.[*]

I click out of a voyeuristic fascination, with my daughter standing beside me saying, "Can we try it, *please*?" I have bought Oreos twice in my life, both times to make—you guessed it—that dreaded Dirt Cake.

I am not at all persuaded by the description of "soft, moist, fresh chocolate snack cakes"— how fresh could they be? Nor does it entice me that these are filled with a "thick layer of smooth, one-of-a-kind Oreo creme," which means only that it has *more* trans fat and *more* high-fructose corn syrup. But I do it, just for fun, and I wind up wasting twenty minutes filling out forms, only to learn I have to sign up for all kinds of other special offers.

My daughter groans. She groans again when I toss out the toaster tarts—some generic brand, in cinnamon and brown sugar, yet, not even the glorious pink-frosted, pink-sprinkled, *real* Pop-Tarts—that she brought home, a castoff from another child's lunch.

Writing about cake has made me reexamine the role that cake plays in our lives, especially in relation to other sweets, and especially where my daughter is concerned. Like all addicts, she tries to find ways to get some kind of sugary substance into her body at the end

---

[*]   Ban Trans Fats (bantransfats.com) says it sued Kraft over the Oreo because "we couldn't sue everybody. It was sufficient to establish the point using the Oreo. Once we received a ruling from the court, or Kraft agreed to reduce or eliminate the trans fat in the Oreo, there would be a 'domino' effect with respect to other manufacturers and products." I'm usually opposed to this kind of lawsuit—I like my coffee panty-hose-melting hot—but we should not expect our foods to be laced with carcinogens *deliberately*. Once you know something is wrong, you should stop doing it. Once you know you are *poisoning* people, you should be made to stop.

of every day. And if she's not had something sweet by then (unlikely, with a class of twenty-three sugar-loving kids, many of them crinkling cellophane at lunchtime), she gets a little panicky and tries to make a deal. She'll even accept a sugar-free Popsicle.

I realize now why cake is present at our holidays and our milestones. We could eat a cookie or a doughnut or a cupcake every day. We could have pudding or mini shortcake tarts, muffins, and buns. So why don't we have a slice of cake every day instead? Why is it that you'll buy a bag of cookies to send to work with your husband, but you won't bake—or buy—a cake, slice it up, store it in your 1950s cake keeper, and squeeze a small piece into the Incredible Hulk lunch box your five-year-old daughter had to have?

We have learned to believe that cake is *special*. It is not the cookie you allowed yourself because you ran four miles. It's not the chocolate bar you can have instead of lunch. With cake, if it's not mandated by holiday, you really feel you have to *deserve* it. Cake is a pat on the back, an acknowledgment that you are loved for having been born, that someone loves you enough to marry you, that you have gotten a long-sought-after promotion, that you have finally quit that pain-in-the-ass job so you can travel by trailer eating cake in diners all over the country—every day for lunch, if you feel like it, damn it!—until you die. Cake is for new neighbors and company you knew were coming. It is for Mother's Day, Father's Day, Grandparents' Day, Christmas Day, and Thanksgiving Day. It's for after dinner at a fancy restaurant on your anniversary and Valentine's Day.

Cake is not for lunch. It's not for breakfast like leftover pizza.*

To paraphrase *The Incredibles,* if every day is special, no day is.

And that is what it is about cake.

---

* In theory.

Notes

A Note to the Reader

PAGE

xv   *"You can't have everything":* Steven Wright, "Steven Wright Quotes,"
Brainy Quote, 2008, http://www.brainyquote.com/quotes/quotes/s/
stevenwrig138072.html.

●●●●●

xix   *"All the world is a birthday cake":* "Cake Quotes," Brainy Quote, 2008,
http://www.brainyquote.com/quotes/keywords/cake.html. All chapter epigraphs come from the above source, except where individually
noted.

Introduction

PAGE

1   *1922, when Harry A. Kunkel:* "History," Capitol Cake Company, n.d.,
http://www.capitolcake.com/history.html.

1   *just as Tastykake's Philip J. Baur:* "Company History: Tasty Baking
Company Poised for Growth, Ripe with Innovation," Tastykake,
2006, http://www.tastykake.com/history.aspx.

1   *and Little Debbie's O. D. McKee:* "Brand History," Little Debbie,
2008, http://www.littledebbie.com/about/brief_history.asp.

1   *But Capitol's Shirley Jean:* Ted Kunkel (owner, Capitol Cake Company), in phone interview with the author, Baltimore, September 18, 2005.

2   *imaginary Betty Crocker:* "Our History," General Mills, 2008, http://www.generalmills.com/corporate/company/history.aspx.

2   *"It's Out of This World":* "Shirley Jean Fruitcake," Capitol Cake Company, n.d., http://www.capitolcake.com/oldfruityinspace.html.

2   *An astronaut picked up:* Ted Kunkel, interview.

2   *By the time Ted Kunkel:* Ibid.

First Tier: Cakelure & Cakelore

PAGE

5   *Shrek: Ogres have layers: Shrek*, DVD, directed by Andrew Adamson and Vicky Jenson (2001; USA: DreamWorks Animation, 2003).

Layer One: Lure

PAGE

7   **Low-carb guru and blogger:* Johnny Bowden, "Sugar Addiction," Johnny Bowden Solutions, May 20, 2008, http://www.jonnybowden.com/2008/05/sugar-addiction.html.

7   *except in Asia:* Jennifer 8. Lee, "Food and Wine: My Struggles with the Oven," The Fortune Cookie Chronicles, February 18, 2008, http://www.fortunecookiechronicles.com/blog/2008/02/18/food-and-wine-my-struggles-with-the-oven/.

7   *Super Bowl XLI (Forty-one) VIP attendees:* "Food Network's Duff Goldman Faces Cake Challenge of Super Bowl Proportions in Season Finale of Hit Series 'Ace of Cakes,'" PRNewswire, Press Release, April 6, 2007, http://www.prnewswire.com/cgi-bin/stories.pl?ACCT=ind_focus.story&STORY=/www/story/04-06-2007/0004560970&EDATE=FRI+Apr+06+2007,+10:40+AM.

8   *But those are nothing compared:* "Our Virtual Scrapbook: World's Largest Birthday Cake," Las Vegas Centennial 1905–2005, 2004–2005, http://www.lasvegas2005.org/news/scrapbook/cake/.

8   **Also at the Guinness:* "World Records," Guinness Attractions, 2001, http://www.guinnessattractions.com/worldrecords.aspx.

8   *After all, one of the first specialty*: Alice Ross, "Hearth to Hearth,"

The Journal of Antiques and Collectibles, October 2003, http://www
.journalofantiques.com/Oct03/hearthoct03.htm.

8 *By 1771, colonial women:* Linda Stradley, "History of Election Cake/
Hartford Election Cake," What's Cooking America, 2004, http://
whatscookingamerica.net/History/Cakes/ElectionCake.htm.

9 *Historians have even suggested:* Linda Stradley, "History of Angel
Food Cake," What's Cooking America, 2004, http://whatscooking
america.net/History/Cakes/AngelFoodCake.htm.

10 *"Between bites Isaac gazed":* Michael Pollan, *Botany of Desire* (New
York: Random House, 2001), 18.

Layer Two: Qu'est-ce que Cake?

PAGE

14 *Syrian farmers grew wheat:* Bruce Fellman, "Finding the First
Farmers," Yale Alumni Magazine, October 1994, http://www
.yalealumnimagazine.com/issues/94_10/agriculture.html; "Sci/Tech
First Farmers Discovered," BBC Online Network, October 28, 1999,
http://news.bbc.co.uk/1/hi/sci/tech/489449.stm.

14 *flat bread with honey:* Lynne Olver, "About Cakes," The Food Timeline, April 1, 2007, http://www.foodtimeline.org/foodcakes.html#
aboutcake.

15 *"The original dividing line":* John Ayto, *An A–Z of Food and Drink*
(1994; repr., Oxford: Oxford University Press, 2002), 52.

15 *Romans added eggs and butter:* Ibid.

15 *"Some brede is bake":* Ibid.

15 *Some say the birthday cake:* "History of Birthday Cake," Tokenz: The
Gift Shop, n.d., http://www.tokenz.com/history-of-birthday-cake
.html.

15 *Others believe the tradition:* Kassidy Emmerson, "About Birthdays:
There's More to Adding Another Year on Your Age," Associated
Content, June 1, 2006, http://www.associatedcontent.com/article/35098/
about_birthdays.html.

15 Cake *is an old Norse word:* "11 Results for: Cake," Dictionary.com,
2007, http://dictionary.reference.com/browse/cake.

15 *"something round, lump of something":* entry for "Cake," OED (On-

line Etymology Dictionary), n.d., http://www.etymonline.com/index .php?search=cake&searchmode=none.

15 *it became a loaf:* Ibid.

15 *In the middle of the 1600s:* Lynne Olver, "History Notes—Cake," The Food Timeline, April 1, 2007, http://www.foodtimeline.org/food cakes.html.

Layer Three: Let Them Eat It

PAGE

17 *"It was a callous and ignorant":* David Emery, "Let Them Eat Cake; er, I Mean Brioche. Oh, Nevermind [*sic*] . . . ," Urban Legends, August 29, 2002, http://urbanlegends.about.com/od/dubiousquotes/a/ antoinette.htm.

18 The London Magazine *called these memoirs:* Madame du Hausset, an "Unknown English Girl" and the Princess Lamballe, *Memoirs of Louis XV./XVI* (Boston: L. C. Page and Co., 1899; reissued as a Project Gutenberg Literary Archive Foundation Ebook #3883, 2006), http://www.gutenberg.org/etext/3883.

18 *"Even at the moment":* Ibid.

18 *"took . . . into [his] head to covet":* Jean-Jacques Rousseau, *The Confessions of Jean-Jacques Rousseau,* trans. W. Coonyngham Mallory (New York: Penguin Classics, 1953; e-book), http://philosophy.eserver.org/ rousseau-confessions.txt, 200.

18 *" . . . [T]he difficulty lay therefore":* Ibid.

19 *Jean-Baptiste Alphonse Karr:* Cecil Adams, "Did Marie Antoinette Really Say 'Let Them Eat Cake'?" The Straight Dope, October 24, 1986, http://www.straightdope.com/classics/a2_334.html.

19 *Antonia Fraser says Madame Sophie:* Antonia Fraser, *Marie Antoinette: The Journey* (New York: First Anchor Books, 2002), 135.

19 *"But the most convincing proof":* Ibid.

19 *He thought of her:* Ibid.

19 *Some say this was a sign:* "Alt.talk.royalty," Google Groups, January 24, 2003, http://groups.google.com/group/alt.talk.royalty/msg/6a7b7 6d15c411368?dmode=source.

20   *this was the result of:* Laura Rosen Cohen, "Did Marie Antoinette Really Say, 'Let Them Eat Cake'?" Ask Us at UofT, n.d.,http://www .news.utoronto.ca/bios/askus40.htm.

20   *In 1775 France, peasants were:* Gonçalo L. Fonseca, "Anne-Rogert-Jacques Turgot, 1727–1781," *The History of Economic Thought,* n.d., http://cepa.newschool.edu/het/profiles/turgot.htm.

20   *Turgot "lifted the controls":* Ibid.

20   *In the 1700s, the phrase:* Fraser, *Antoinette,* 135.

20   *But some believe the word:* Lynne Olver, "History Notes—Bread," The Food Timeline, September 7, 2006, http://www.foodtimeline .org/foodbreads.html.

20   *The most far-fetched of the* brioche: Adams, "Did Marie Antoinette."

21   *"I sometimes went out":* Rousseau, *Confessions,* 200.

Layer Four: True Cake

PAGE

22   *"Nowadays hardly anyone makes":* Linda Wolfe, *The Literary Gourmet* (New York: Simon & Schuster, 1989), 90.

22   *The recipe that follows:* Ibid.

23   *ancient Romans made a concoction:* Linda Stradley, "History of Fruitcake," What's Cooking America, 2004, http://whatscookingamerica .net/History/Cakes/Fruitcake.htm.

23   *"One theory presented by an historian":* Marjorie Dorfman, "Et Tu, Fruitcake!" Eat, Drink and Really Be Merry, 2002, http://www.inge standimbibe.com/Articles_p/fruitcake_p.html.

23   *Some believe it was outlawed:* Stradley, "Fruitcake."

24   *Victoria was so popular that:* Patricia Bunning Stevens, *Rare Bits: Unusual Origins of Popular Recipes* (Athens, Ohio: Ohio University Press, 1998), 227–230.

24   *The Puritans, who once banned:* Ken Bastida, "What's the Origin of 'Devil's Food'?" CBS 5, January 25, 2007, http://cbs5.com/food/ local_story_026012428.html.

24   *though it may have looked to outsiders:* Tad Tuleja, *Fabulous Fallacies* (New York: Galahad Books, 1999), 63.

24   *and even Cotton Mather:* Lewis Lapham, "Quarrels with Providence," Yale Alumni Magazine, March 2001, http://www.yalealumnimaga zine.com/issues/01_03/lapham.html.

25   *The fruitcake catapult:* Jacob Quinn Sanders, "Better Run and Hide, Virginia," *Portland Tribune*, December 20, 2005, http://www.port landtribune.com/news/story.php?story_id=33168.

25   *Manitou Springs, Colorado, held:* "12th Annual Great Fruitcake Toss," Historic Manitou Springs, January 20, 2007, http://www .manitousprings.org/ASP/CalendarItem.ASP?NUMBER=94.

25   *"Fruit? Good":* Jim Gaffigan, "Cake," *Beyond the Pale*, CD, 5 min. (n.p.: Comedy Central, 2006; via YouTube), http://www.youtube .com/watch?v=JDfp45Utg5k.

25   *In 2003, Canada:* CTV.CA News Staff, "Fruitcake the Latest Banned Item on Airlines," CTV.CA, December 10, 2003, http://www.ctv .ca/servlet/ArticleNew/story/CTVNews/1071000046020_37/?hub =Canada.

Layer Five: Eatymology

PAGE

26   *Some etymologists believe the term:* Brenden I. Koerner, "Where Do 'Cakewalks' Come From?" Slate, April 3, 2003, http://slate.msn .com/id/2081116/.

26   *One source finds that it:* Sonny Watson, "Cake Walk," Sonny Watson's Streetswing, August 9, 2006, http://www.streetswing.com/histmain/ z3cake1.htm.

26   *The most likely origin:* Ibid.

26   *Eventually, the cake walk:* Sandra L. West, "We Are a Dancing People," Chicken Bones: A Journal, September 17, 2005, http://www .nathanielturner.com/weareadancingpeople.htm.

27   *it appeared at the beginning:* Ayto, *A-Z*, 52.

Layer Six: If I Knew You Were Locked Up, I'd Have Baked a Cake

PAGE

28   *Owner Maury Rubin sold:* Rachel Kramer, "Paris Hilton Nail File Cupcake," Cupcakes Take the Cake, June 23, 2007, http://cupcakes

takethecake.blogspot.com/2007/06/paris-hilton-nail-file-cupcake
.html.

29 *cake was instrumental in the prison:* David Fitzpatrick, *Harry Boland's Irish Revolution* (County Cork, Ireland: Cork University Press, 2003), via Google Books, http://books.google.com/books?hl=en&id=cp8uz dnhT4QC&dq=%22harry+boland's+irish+revolution%22+david+fi tzpatrick&printsec=frontcover&source=web&ots=_4rvemzZqL&sig =6YJWOGvoEu6BYg2bv8lD8iQSl2o, 114; Sean Kenny, "Peter De Loughry—the Kilkenny Patriot and Politician: The Man Who Made the Key That Sprung De Valera from Lincoln Jail," Irish Identity, December 2002, http://www.hoganstand.com/general/identity/extras/ patriots/stories/loughrey.htm; Jason O'Brien, "Historic Collins Letter to Fetch €50,000," Independent.ie, November 23, 2007, http:// www.independent.ie/national-news/historic-collins-letter-to-fetch-euro50000-1227280.html. All historical information about this event comes from these sources, except where noted below.

29 *"The Irish reputation for a sweet tooth":* Fitzpatrick, *Irish Revolution*.

29 *cake was used as a weapon:* JTW/AFP (pseud.), "Beware Inmates Bearing Gifts: Spiked Cake Puts Prison Guards in Hospital," Spiegel Online International, March 14, 2008, http://www.spiegel.de/ international/zeitgeist/0,1518,541540,00.html.

29 *"Normally the guards and the inmates":* Reuters, "Danish Inmates Poison Prison Guards with Cake," National Post, March 13, 2008, http://www.nationalpost.com/news/story.html?id=373083.

Layer Eight: Many Happy Returns of the Day, Cake!

PAGE

35 *We can find the first mention of a lollipop:* Lynne Olver, "History Notes—Candy," The Food Timeline, March 18, 2007, http://www. foodtimeline.org/foodcandy.html#lollipops.

35 *Frosting began as:* Olver, "About Icing and Frosting," Food Timeline, April 1, 2007, http://www.foodtimeline.org/foodcakes.html#icing.

36 *frosting preceded icing:* John F. Mariani, *The Encyclopedia of American Food and Drink* (New York: Ticknor & Fields, 1983; New York: Hearst Books, 1994), 166.

36   *So is 1908 the magic year:* Ibid.

36   *"professional bakers and caterers":* Olver, "Birthday Cake," The Food Timeline, March 20, 2008, http://www.foodtimeline.org/foodcakes .html #birthdaycake.

36   *cakes were inscribed with:* Ibid.

36   *became the world's most popular song:* "Happy Birthday to You," Wikipedia, May 29, 2008, http://en.wikipedia.org/wiki/Happy_Birthday_ to_You.

36   *Once a German superstition:* "Birthday Cake," Wikipedia, May 28, 2008, http://en.wikipedia.org/wiki/Birthday_cake.

36   *The lighting of incense is one:* Kathy Keville, "History of Aromatherapy," howstuffworks, 2008, http://health.howstuffworks.com/ history-of-aromatherapy2.htm.

36   *It wasn't until the late 1800s:* Olver, "Birthday Cake."

Layer Nine: Beefcake

PAGE

39   *Layer Nine: Beefcake:* Roland Winbeckler (cake decorator, Redmond, WA), e-mail message to author, September 12, 2005. All chapter material comes from this source, except where noted below.

39   *It was 125,000 calories:* "Roland Winbeckler's Cake Sculptures— Page Two," A-J Winbeckler Enterprises, n.d., http://www.winbeck ler.com/sculptures2.asp#Marilyn%20Monroe.

Layer Ten: Expensive Cakes

PAGE

41   *"What is nice?":* "The Frogger," Seinfeld Scripts, April 23, 1998, http://www.seinfeldscripts.com/TheFrogger.htm.

41   *"latest acquisition. A slice":* Ibid.

42   *One of the most expensive cakes:* Deidre Woollard, Luxist, "The Diamond Fruitcake," December 8, 2005 http://www.luxist.com/2005/12/08/ the-diamond-fruitcake/.

42   *Another Tokyo cake:* Esther (pseud.), "$2.16 Million Vienna Gold Coin Cake to Commemorate Mozart's 250th Anniversary," Born Rich.org,

March 2, 2006, http://www.bornrich.org/entry/216-million-vienna-gold-coin-cake-to-commemorate-mozarts-250th-anniversary/.

42   *In October 2006:* "Diamond-Studded Wedding Cake," Spluch, October 18, 2006, http://spluch.blogspot.com/2006/10/diamond-studded-wedding-cake.html.

42   *But that didn't stop some New York:* Anna Jane Grossman, "$10,000 for Child's Birthday Party?" CNN.com/Living, April 18, 2008, http://www.cnn.com/2008/LIVING/04/18/lw.pricey.bday.parties/index.html.

Layer Eleven: May As Well Face It: You're Addicted to Cake

PAGE

43   *"true symbol of gluttony":* Gaffigan, "Cake."

43   *"You never hear someone":* Ibid.

43   *more women than men:* "Binge Eating Disorder," Rush University Medical Center, n.d., http://www.rush.edu/rumc/page-P06665.html.

43   *Some say adolescent and young women:* Ibid.

45   *it's the flower's fault:* Pollan, *Botany of Desire*, xvii.

46   *"Food cravings are extremely":* Dr. Bruce Semon, "Bruce Semon, MD," Nutrition Institute.com, n.d., http://www.nutritioninstitute.com/bruce_semon_md.html.

46   *"Addiction results":* Ibid.

47   *A French fry covered with sugar:* Gaffigan, "Cake."

Second Tier: Cake Love
Layer Thirteen: Passing the Wooden Spoon

PAGE

67   *Chocolatetown Special Cake:* Cooks.com, "Hershey's Chocolatetown Cake," http://www.cooks.com/rec/doc/0,176,144189-250195,00.html.

68   *One-Bowl Buttercream Frosting:* Colleen Crosby, "Hershey's One-Bowl Buttercream Frosting," http://www.project-insomnia.com/colleen/kitchen/chocolateglaze.html.

Third Tier: The Moist White Underbelly
Layer Fifteen: Cake Cottage

PAGE

83   *Layer Fifteen: Cake Cottage:* Susan Staehling and Rebecca Cook (Cake
      Cottage employees), in discussion with the author, Baltimore, Mary-
      land, October 20, 2005. All chapter material comes from this source.

Layer Sixteen: Pound for Pound

PAGE

91   *"It'll be richer":* Staehling, discussion.

91   *her pound cakes, dubbed:* Rose Levy Beranbaum, *The Cake Bible*
      (New York: William Morrow and Company, 1988), 25–26.

91   *His traditional* quatres-quarts: Bruce Healy and Paul Bugat, *The
      Art of the Cake* (New York: William Morrow and Company, 1999),
      24–25.

94   *"One pound sugar":* Amelia Simmons, *American Cookery, or The
      Art of Dressing Viands, Fish, Poultry, and Vegetables, and The Best
      Modes of Making Pastes, Puffs, Pies, Tarts, Puddings, Custards, and
      Preserves, and All Kinds of Cakes, from the Imperial Plum to Plain
      Cake: Adapted to This Country, and All Grades of Life* (Hartford:
      Printed for Simeon Butler, Northampton, 1798; reissued as a
      Feeding America: The Historic American Cookbook Project ebook),
      http://digital.lib.msu.edu/projects/cookbooks/coldfusion/display.
      cfm?ID=amer&PageNum=36.

94   *"Work three quarters of a pound":* Ibid.

94   **Earlier cookbooks:* Michigan State University Library, ed., "Sim-
      mons, Amelia," *Feeding America,* May 21, 2004, http://digital.lib.msu
      .edu/projects/cookbooks/html/authors/author_simmons.html.

95   *Simmons, the editor, notes:* Ibid.

98   *"The fat molecules must be fairly cold":* Mark Scarbrough (food
      writer), e-mail message to author, February 16, 2008.

98   *"I believe there's more of the same":* Ibid.

99   *"I'm not sure why more people":* Ibid.

99   *"Baking the almost two-hundred-year-old recipe":* Greg Patent, *Baking*

in America: Traditional and Contemporary Favorites from the Past 200 Years (New York: Houghton Mifflin Company, 2002), 1–2.

Layer Seventeen: Decorating Tips

PAGE

103 *Layer Seventeen: Decorating Tips:* Much of the information in this chapter comes from a cake-decorating course I took at the Cake Cottage in November 2005. All quotes are in-text attributed except where noted below.

118 *In the holiday edition of:* PCD's Cooking Enthusiast catalog, Holiday Edition 2005, 58.

Fourth Tier: Tiers
Layer Twenty-one: Hostess? No-stess

PAGE

131 **Sugar, partially hydrogenated vegetable:* Bill Chapman, "Other Ingredient Lists," Bill Chapman's Classroom Tools, February 9, 2001, http://www.classroomtools.com/foods.htm.

132 †*"In the early '50s, Frank Sinatra":* "About Us: Fun Facts," Entenmann's, 2008, http://entenmanns.gwbakeries.com/funFacts.cfm.

132 *Maybe Anna Ayala:* "Wendy's: The Finger in Wendy's Chili," jose pino.com, March 2007, http://www.josepino.com/real_meal/index .php?wendys_finger.jpc.

133 *"cast a wide net and find":* Steve Almond (author), email message to author, November 29, 2007.

133 *"8 million pounds of sugar":* "FAQ," Hostess Cakes, http://www .hostesscakes.com/faq.asp.

133 *What isn't disclosed:* h2g2 Researchers (pseud.), "Twinkies," BBC, 2002, http://www.bbc.co.uk/dna/h2g2/alabaster/A516836.

133 *how much dextrose:* Ibid.

133 **Of the eighteen ingredients:* Steve Ettlinger, *Twinkie, Deconstructed: My Journey to Discover How the Ingredients Found in Processed Foods Are Grown, Mined (Yes, Mined), and Manipulated into What America Eats* (2008; repr., New York: Penguin Group, 2007), x.

134   *replies at 8:19 a.m.:* Casey DePalma, Linden Alschuler & Kaplan Public Relations, e-mail message to author, March 31, 2008.

135   *"the Gremlin Factor":* h2g2 Researchers, "Twinkies."

135   *The ABC News* Nightline *story:* John Berman and Mary Marsh, "The Secret Behind the Twinkie: A Closer Look at One of America's Favorite Treats," ABC News *Nightline,* May 3, 2007, http://i.abcnews .com/Nightline/story?id=3080425.

136   *Ettlinger thinks Twinkies are fine:* Ibid.

136   **Not even if you're San Francisco mayor:* Carol Pogash, "Myth of the Twinkie Defense: The Verdict in the Dan White Case Wasn't Based on His Ingestion of Junk Food," SFGate, November 23, 2003, http://www.sfgate.com/cgi-bin/article.cgi?f=/c/a/2003/11/23/ INGRE343501.DTL.

136   *" 'Too much' is subjective":* Steve Ettlinger (author), e-mail message to author, April 11, 2008.

136   *"No, not really," he says:* Ibid.

Layer Twenty-two: The Bakeries' Bakery

PAGE

137   *Layer Twenty-two: The Bakeries' Bakery:* Lawrence Crawford, Alvin "Sugg" Eddings, Pearl Floyd, Velma Haywood, Nella Mednikova, Cleveland Milton, and Terry Perkins (Gourmet Bakery employees), Baltimore, Maryland, interview with the author, February 25, 2008.

Layer Twenty-three: CakeLove Love

PAGE

145   *Layer Twenty-three: CakeLove Love:* Warren Brown (chef/owner, Cake-Love), interview with the author, Baltimore, Maryland, March 5, 2008. All chapter material comes from this source, except where noted below.

147   **"any food of such type":* US Food and Drug Administration, "Evaluation and Definition of Potentially Hazardous Foods," FDA, December 31, 2001, http://www.cfsan.fda.gov/~comm/ift4-aa.html.

154   *cake light is the best light:* "Time Flies," *Six Feet Under* (via TV.com), aired June 27, 2005, http://www.tv.com/six-feet-under/time-flies/ episode/418885/summary.html.

Layer Twenty-four: The Acing on the Cake

PAGE

155   *Layer Twenty-four: The Acing on the Cake:* Duff Goldman (chef/owner, Charm City Cakes), interview with the author, Baltimore, Maryland, October 6–7, 2005. All chapter material comes from this source.

Fifth Tier: Competitions

PAGE

167   *Fifth Tier: Competitions:* Duff Goldman (chef/owner, Charm City Cakes), interview with the author, Baltimore, Maryland, October 6–7, 2005; Leslie Poyourow (chef/owner, Fancy Cakes by Leslie), interview with the author, Gaithersburg, Maryland, November 1, 2005; Jamie Williams (chef/owner, SugarBakers), interview with the author, Catonsville, Maryland, March 2, 2006; Sarah Raley-Dale (Hometown Wedding bride), phone interview with the author, February 26, 2007. All material in this tier was taken from these interviews, except where noted in individual layers below.

Layer Twenty-six: Gentlemen, Start Your Mixers!

PAGE

169   *In 1880, Cadwallader C. Washburn:* "Our Heritage," General Mills Flour, n.d., http://www.gmiflour.com/gmflour/ourheritage.aspx.

Layer Twenty-seven: It's the Cakes, Dummy

PAGE

173   *"This spectacular four-tiered pumpkin chocolate":* "*Today* Throws a Wedding 2005," MSNBC.COM, 2005, http://www.msnbc.msn.com/id/8544668/#anc_tdy_wedding05_vote8Cake.

173   **The cake for the wedding of Carmen:* "Celebrity Wedding Cakes," India Wedding Sutra.com, 2002, http://www.weddingsutra.com/planning/celeb_cakes.asp.

173   *Well, they were married:* "Photo Gallery—Wedding Cakes" i-do.com.au, n.d., http://weddingcakes.i-do.com.au/imageview.aspx?image=8126&gallery=25.

173   *Not incidentally, Carmen and Dave:* "Carmen Electra and Dave Na-

varro Split," *People,* July 18, 2006, http://www.people.com/people/
article/0,26334,1183288,00.html.

Layer Twenty-eight: Meet the Contestants:
Duff Goldman, Charm City Cakes

PAGE

179   *Layer Twenty-eight: Meet the Contestants:* Duff Goldman, emcee, Baltimore Book Festival, Baltimore, Maryland, September 25, 2005. All
information for this layer, except where noted below.

179   *"I have the palate of a four-year-old":* Duff Goldman (chef/owner,
Charm City Cakes), telephone interview with the author, Baltimore,
Maryland, September 20, 2005.

181   **But that's not actually where MoonPies:* "MoonPie History," *Moon-
Pie,* n.d., http://moonpie.com/hist_text.asp.

Puttin' the Charm in Charm City Cakes

PAGE

183   *"Let me give you a piece of advice":* Duff Goldman, telephone interview.

183   *"Huh?" I say:* Ibid.

183   *"Yeah, about that* Win*beckler":* Ibid.

Layer Thirty-three: Losing Isn't Everything

PAGE

205   *"There's really no accounting for taste":* Rebecca Logan, *"Today* Show
Just Icing on the Cake for City Business," *Baltimore Business Journal,* September 1, 2005, http://www.bizjournals.com/baltimore/sto
ries/2005/08/29/daily28.html.

205   *"If Middle America actually approved":* Duff Goldman, Baltimore
Book Festival.

Sixth Tier: Cake Fanatics
Layer Thirty-eight: Cake Jobs

PAGE

225   **In a French study, rats were determined:* Rachel Dvoskin, "Sweeter
Than Cocaine: Rats Prefer a Sugary Drink to Drugs," *Scientific*

American, April/May 2008, p. 16.

226 *"A house full of kids, cake": All My Children,* April 14, 2008, confirmed at
http://allmychildren.about.com/od/dailyrecaps/a/bl20080414r_3.htm.

226 **"I didn't like either of them": All My Children,* December 18, 2007,
confirmed at http://209.85.215.104/search?q=cache:E2LjBoGB6swJ:
www.soapoperaweekly.com/recaps/oltl/2007/121707/+%22all+my+
children%22+%22i+don%27t+like+pie%22+%22i+like+cake%22&
hl=en&ct=clnk&cd=1&gl=us.

226 *Lindsay Reed, author of* Gâteau: Lindsay Reed (playwright), interview with the author, Baltimore, Maryland, August 16, 2006.

226 *"You don't want me":* Lindsay Reed, *Gâteau.* Subsequent to my reading the play in hard copy, it was published here: Christine Stewart,
ed., *Freshly Squeezed: A "Write Here, Write Now" Anthology* (Baltimore: Apprentice House, 2008).

229 *"I love when you go":* Gaffigan, "Cake."

232 *Philip Rosenthal, producer:* Philip Rosenthal (producer and head
writer, *Everybody Loves Raymond*), personal e-mail to the author,
April 21, 2008.

232 *"prop master ordered the yummy":* Donna Stamps (props and sets, *Everybody Loves Raymond*), personal e-mail to the author, May 5, 2008.

233 *Bunny Koppelman:* Bunny Koppelman (cake lover, New York), telephone discussion with the author, April 10, 2008.

234 *Bergers, without an apostrophe:* "Berger Cookie History," Berger
Cookies, 2008, http://www.bergercookies.com/history.htm.

Seventh Tier: The U.S. of cAke
Layer Thirty-nine: Journey Cake

PAGE

238 *"Very few (if any) foods":* Lynne Olver, "Food History Research
Tips," The Food Timeline, October 21, 2007, http://foodtimeline
.org/foodfaqa.html#tips.

238 *To make her point:* Ibid.

239 *"Cooking is not considered inventing":* Joyce Gemperlein, "Can a
Recipe Be Stolen?" *Washington Post,* January 4, 2006, http://www
.washingtonpost.com/wp-dyn/content/article/2006/01/03/AR2006
010300316.html.

239   *A list of ingredients:* Ibid.

239   *While it's courteous:* Ibid.

239   *An expert in food history:* Making Sense (pseud.), "General Chowhounding Topics: Regional Cakes," Chowhound, December 19, 2007, http://www.chowhound.com/topics/464253.

239   *"Toodie Jane," the original poster:* Toodie Jane (pseud.), "General Chowhounding Topics: Regional Cakes," Chowhound, November 30, 2007, http://www.chowhound.com/topics/464253.

240   *Even most recipe writers agree:* Gemperlein.

241   *It "had been transformed into something":* Patent, *Baking in America*, 1.

Smith Island Ten-Layer Cake, Smith Island, Maryland

243   Saveur's *recipe calls for* eight *layers:* "Smith Island Cake," *Saveur,* n.d., http://www.saveur.com/food/new-recipes/smith-island-cake-51805.html.

243   *Frances Kitching, author of* Mrs. Kitching's: Midge and Dave Patterson, "A Visit with Frances Kitching, a Grand Lady of Smith Island," Smithisland.org, summer 1993, http://www.smithisland.org/kitching.html.

244   *"three serving spoonsful":* "Smith Island 10-Layer Cake," Museum History: Crisfield and Smith Island Cultural Alliance, Inc. Page, August 11, 2004, http://www.smithisland.org/cakerecipe.html.

244   *The Lower Eastern Shore Heritage:* Kristen Wyatt, "Smith Island Bakers Hope Dessert Sparks Revival," WTOPnews.com, April 24, 2008, http://www.wtop.com/?nid=598&sid=1392806.

244   *Owners of the Sweet Shop:* "Should Md. Have an Official State Dessert?" WTOPnews.com, January 2, 2008, http://www.wtopnews.com/?nid=598&sid=1319325.

244   *"Does this sophisticated state":* Jean Marbella, "Assembly May Rise to Just Desserts," *The Sun*, January 8, 2008.

245   *Are we, collectively, too snobbish:* Ibid.

245   *"Some does 10, some does 12":* Ibid.

245   *The island's inhabitation by English-speaking peoples:* "Smith Island,"

The American Heritage Dictionary of the English Language, Fourth Edition (via Bartelby.com), 2000, http://www.bartleby.com/61/76/ S0497650.html.

Peach Cake, Baltimore

PAGE

246 *Barrett Buss says he's never:* Barrett Buss, "Baltimore Peach Cake," Too Many Chefs, September 11, 2007, http://www.toomanychefs .com/archives/001954.php.

Layer Forty: Cake, Clockwise
Dried Apple Stack Cake, Southern Appalachia

PAGE

248 *Mountain weddings, shotgun or not:* Sidney Saylor Farr, "Dried Apple Stack Cake," Appalachian Heritage: A Literary Quarterly of the Appalachian South, n.d., http://community.berea.edu/appalachian heritage/issues/fall2004/memoir.html.

248 *he is "deeply familiar":* Fred Sauceman (author), personal e-mail to the author, January 11, 2008.

249 *"grandmother used a less spicy":* "Apple Stack Cake," My Recipes, 2008, http://find.myrecipes.com/recipes/recipefinder.dyn?action=display Recipe&recipe_id =106218.

249 *Sauceman says his wife's:* Sauceman, personal e-mail.

Lady (and Lord) Baltimore Cake, Charleston, South Carolina

PAGE

250 *"It is no wonder that this cake":* Julia Reed, "Food; Rich and Famous," *The New York Times,* April 21, 2002, http://query.nytimes.com/gst/ fullpage.html?res=9B03E1D9103CF932A15757C0A9649C8B63.

250 *Reed says it's Joan:* Ibid.

250 *Maryland Public Television says:* Maryland Public Television, ed., "Anne Arundell, Lady Baltimore (1615–1649)," Exploring Maryland's Roots: Library, 2008, http://mdroots.thinkport.org/library/anne arundell.asp.

251   City Paper *says that Anne and Joan:* Brennen Jensen, "Charmed Life: Ms. Mobtown," *City Paper,* June 28, 2000, http://www.citypaper.com/news/story.asp?id=2478.

251   *The Old Foodie says:* Janet Clarkson, "Lady Baltimore Cake," The Old Foodie, March 24, 2007, http://theoldfoodie.blogspot.com/2007/03/lady-baltimore-cake.html.

251   *"Beat the whites":* Ibid.

252   *it was just a matter of time before:* Stevens, *Rare Bits,* 251.

Lane Cake, Alabama

PAGE

252   *The first recipe I found:* "Lane Cake," A Web Page for Cake Decorating Worldwide, n.d., http://members.nuvox.net/~zt.proicer/recipes/laneck.htm.

253   *The recipe is from "some very old cookbook":* Ibid.

253   *"LET'S BEGIN OUR 'LANE CAKE' ":* Ibid.

253   *"TO FROST CAKE Spread":* Ibid.

253   *Miss Maudie, the neighbor:* Harper Lee, *To Kill a Mockingbird* (1960; repr., New York: Warner Books, 1982), 47.

253   *"Miss Maudie Atkinson baked":* Ibid., 131.

253   *"You know, 'cause we've all been":* Gaffigan, "Cake."

254   *Even those who know their way around:* Fred Sauceman, "This Valentine's Day, Bake Up History," WETS 89.5 FM, n.d., http://www.wets.org/index.cgi?&CONTEXT=cat&cat=10152.

254   *"The baking of an elegant, scratch-made":* Ibid.

255   *"Recently, through a friend":* Jewell Ellen Smith, "A Child's Teacakes and Rights," Sunbonnet Soliloquy, February 1989, http://www.missionaryclinicbelize.org/usa/Sunbonnet89-02.htm.

255   *Smith agrees, and opines on the rights:* "Introduction," The Jewell Ellen Smith Homepage, n.d., http://www.missionaryclinicbelize.org/USA/homepage.html.

Red Velvet Cake, the South

PAGE

256   *"$25 Fudge Cake":* Barbara Mikkelson, "(Costs a) Fortune Cookie,"

Snopes, January 3, 2007, http://www.snopes.com/business/consumer/
cookie.asp.

256   *which is not, as many believe:* "The Real Red Velvet Cake Frosting,"
Cooks.com, 2008, http://www.cooks.com/rec/view/0,176,156168-2551
95,00.html.

King Cake, New Orleans, Louisiana

PAGE

257   *He fills a "modified French bread":* Audie Cornish, "A Taste of Mardi
Gras: The Return of the King Cake," NPR, February 23, 2006,
http://www.npr.org/templates/story/story.php?storyId=5228675.

257   *"No baby is in the same spot":* Ibid.

258   *"Without purple, green, and gold":* Ibid.

259   *Día de la Candelaria, the holiday:* Rebecca M. Cuevas De Caissie,
"Mexican Christmas Traditions Posadas," Bella Online, 2008, http://
www.bellaonline.com/articles/art38224.asp; Suzanne Barbezat, "Día
de la Candelaria," About.com: Mexico Travel, n.d., http://gomexico
.about.com/od/festivalsholidays/p/dia_candelaria.htm.

259   *"Jean-Baptiste Greuze painted the poetry":* "Introduction," French
Painting from the Musée Fabre, Montpellier, n.d., http://www.nga
shop.com.au/Exhibition/FrenchPainting/Detail.cfm?IRN=12656
2&BioArtistIRN=17728&Audio=32k&ViewID=2&MnuID=1.

260   *In* What Great Paintings Say: Rose-Marie Hagen and Rainer Hagen,
What Great Paintings Say (Los Angeles: Taschen, 2003; as a Google
Book), 250, http://books.google.com/books?id=e2DvEibWkKsC&pg
=PA250&lpg=PA250&dq= %22feast+of+the+bean+king%22+%22ja
cob+jordaens%22&source=web&ots=D_TrW—sXb&sig=bDhGk—
voZoHpUdw-oWELP6KW6k#PPA250,M1.

Pastel de Tres Leches, Texas (Austin et al.)

PAGE

264   *But Nestlé was manufacturing:* MM Pack, "Got Milk?™ On the Trail of
Pastel de Tres Leches," *The Austin Chronicle,* February 13, 2004, http://
www.austinchronicle.com/gyrobase/Issue/story?oid=oid%3A
196888.

264   *Patricia Quintana, Mexican food expert:* "Tres Leches Cake from Café
       Central, El Paso," Texas Monthly.com, November 1999, http://www
       .texasmonthly.com/food/recipes/9911_tresleches.php.

264   *Most likely, as food writer:* Pack, "Got Milk? ™"

Texas Sheet Cake, Texas

PAGE
264   *Karen Haram believes like I do:* Lynne Olver, "Texas Sheet Cake,"
       The Food Timeline, 2000, http://www.foodtimeline.org/foodcakes
       .html# texassheetcake.

Dobosh Cake, Hawaii; Doberge Cake, New Orleans

PAGE
265   *Wanda Adams of* The Honolulu Advertiser: Wanda A. Adams,
       "Food for Thought: Dobosh Cake's Roots Hungarian," *The Hono-
       lulu Advertiser,* October 10, 2007, http://the.honoluluadvertiser.com/
       article/2007/Oct/10/il/hawaii710100368.html.

265   *but was the creation of pastry chef:* Joy Bugaloo (pseud.), "Finally . . .
       We Celebrated June," Lindsey's Luscious, November 20, 2007,
       http://lindseysluscious.blogspot.com/2007/11/finallywe-celebrated-
       june.html.

265   *Robert Portnoy, now a resident of Houston, Texas:* Robert Pornoy,
       e-mail from Ann Thompson to the author, January 26, 2008.

265   *"I guess we never looked":* Ibid.

266   *"Instead of roses, which are so":* Ibid.

266   *the St. Sebastian Kaffee-Conditorei:* George Lang, *The Cuisine of Hun-
       gary* (New York: Crown Books, 1971), 52–54.

267   *"Since that time Hungarian chefs":* Ibid., 56.

267   *In 1918, a similar star-crossed love:* Ibid., 54.

267   *"The second batch of moon astronauts":* Ibid.

267   *"devised a packaging for sending this":* Ibid., 62.

267   *"The world remembers the anniversaries":* Ibid.

Gooey Butter Cake, St. Louis, Missouri

PAGE

268 *the Gooey Butter Cake is said to be:* Linda Stradley, "History of Gooey Butter Cake," What's Cooking America, 2004, http://whatscook ingamerica.net/History/Cakes/GooeyButterCake.htm.

268 *"In late 1942 or early 1943":* Ibid.

268 *Experiments ensued, with Danzer:* Ibid.

268 *Credit for Melba Toast goes to:* "Melba Toast," *The American Heritage Dictionary of the English Language, Fourth Edition* (via Bartleby.com), 2000, http://www.bartleby.com/61/52/M0205200.html.

Boston Cream Pie, Boston

PAGE

268 *Legend has it that the famous pudding:* Stephanie Jaworski, "Boston Cream Pie," The Joy of Baking.com, 2008, http://www.joyofbaking .com/BostonCreamPie.html.

268 *It's hard to keep your claim to a recipe:* Linda Stradley, "History of Boston Cream Pie," What's Cooking America, 2004, http://www .whatscookingamerica.net/History/Cakes/BostonCreamPie.htm.

269 *It's probably called a pie:* Jaworski.

269 *The Parker House, which opened:* "Parker's Restaurant," Citysearch, 2008, http://boston.citysearch.com/profile/11624987/boston_ma/parker_s_restaurant.html.

269 *Ho Chi Minh worked:* Ibid.

269 *"PART I. ADMINISTRATION":* "The General Laws of Massachusetts," Mas.gov, 2008, http://www.mass.gov/legis/laws/mgl/2-51.htm.

Blackout Cake, Brooklyn, New York

PAGE

270 *This cake, composed of the most devilish:* Molly O'Neill, "The Cake Box from Heaven (Brooklyn, of Course) Is Back," *The New York Times,* June 5, 1991, http://query.nytimes.com/gst/fullpage.html?res =9D0CE0DE1330F936A35755C0A967958260.

270   *Actually, tribbles grew to:* "The Trouble with Tribbles," *Star Trek,* December 29, 1967, http://www.youtube.com/watch?v.

270   *"Anybody who lived in Brooklyn":* Ibid.

270   *After Ebinger's went bankrupt:* Ibid., 2, http://query.nytimes.com/gst/fullpage.html?res=9D0CE0DE1330F936A35755C0A967958260&sec=&spon=&pagewanted=2.

271   *Lou Guerra tried to bring it back:* Ibid.

271   *The first blackout to affect New York:* JTS (pseud.), "Home: Welcome to the Blackout History Project," Blackout History Project, June 27, 2000, http://blackout.gmu.edu/home.html.

New York Cheesecake, New York

PAGE

273   *But Arnold Sr. is credited with:* Cedrick White, "Origin of Cheesecake— It's Older Than You Think," EZine Articles, January 4, 2008, http://ezinearticles.com/?Origin-Of-Cheesecake—Its-Older-Than-You-Think&id=910668.

Layer Forty-one: Cake Karma

PAGE

275   *Queen Victoria, of the so-many-named:* Kelsey McIntyre, "The History of the White Wedding Dress," From Times Past, n.d., http://www.fromtimespast.com/wedding.htm.

276   *In the Victorian age:* Tad Tuleja, *Curious Customs: The Stories Behind 296 Popular American Rituals* (New York: Stonesong Press, 1987), 56.

276   *"[M]arriage by capture was":* Leopold Wagner, "Courtship and Marriage," *Manners, Customs, and Observances: Their Origin and Significance* (n.p.: Omnigraphics, 1995; Ebook), http://www.sacred-texts.com/etc/mco/ml07.htm.

276   *Some say the German Goths started it:* "Enduring Wedding Traditions . . . Customs and Their Origins," Hudson Valley Weddings, n.d., http://www.hudsonvalleyweddings.com/guide/customs.htm.

276   *others blame the Scots:* Woohoo2me (pseud.), "Wedding Facts, Traditions, Superstitions Game," Onewed.com, March 12, 2008, http://

forums.onewed.com/showthread.php?s=686225a4427be8ce355a176
7e6428bde&t=14726&page=2.

276   *It even has a name in Russian: "Ala Kachuu," Wikipedia, April 1,
       2008, http://en.wikipedia.org/wiki/Ala_kachuu.

276   *Russ L. Kleinbach, a sociology: Russ L. Kleinbach, "Bride Kidnap-
       ping," Russ L. Kleinbach, n.d., http://faculty.philau.edu/kleinbachr/
       ala_kachuu.htm.

276   (Not true): Melanie and Mike, "From D.K. Shaw," Take Our Word for
       It, issue 120, p. 2, http://www.takeourword.com/TOW120/page2.html.

276   bridesmaids, "along with the best man": Philippa Waring, A Dictio-
       nary of Omens and Superstitions (1978; repr., London: Souvenir Press,
       1997), 42.

277   Another theory is that the bridesmaid's: Allie McComas, "Why We
       Throw Rice at Weddings, and Other Nuptial Origins Revealed,"
       Buzzle.com, 2008, http://www.buzzle.com/articles/why-we-throw-
       rice-at-weddings-other-nuptial-origins-revealed.html.

277   After the wedding (the Latin word: "Marriage and Customs and
       Roman Women," Classics Unveiled, n.d., http://www.classicsun
       veiled.com/romel/html/marrcustwom.html.

278   "Meanwhile, the folks who had been": Tuleja, Curious Customs, 63.

278   tiered cakes also began in England: A. S. Manji, "Food of the Gods:
       The History of Cake," Manjicake, n.d., http://manjicake.com/
       index2.php?tag=fog.

279   "The evolution of the wedding cake began": Emily Post, "The Day of
       the Wedding," Etiquette (New York: Funk & Wagnalls Company,
       1922; Ebook), http://www.bartleby.com/95/22.html.

279   "On the top it has a bouquet": Ibid.

279   "The idea of wedding toppers in general": Robert Reed, "Bride and
       Groom Wedding Cake Toppers," The Antique Shoppe Newspa-
       per, June 2006, http://antiqueshoppefl.com/archives/rreed/Bride%20
       and%20Groom.htm.

280   Eva Longoria was a guest on Jimmy Kimmel's: "Eva Longoria on
       Jimmy Kimmel's 1,000th Episode," Entertainment Jam, April 4,
       2008, http://entertainmentjam.com/?p=89.

281   *Melinda Gallagher and Emily Scarlet Kramer: "About," Cake: Enter-
        tainment for Women, 2005, http://www2.cakenyc.com/about.

282   "She that pricks bread": David Pickering, Cassell Dictionary of Super-
        stitions (London: Cassell, 1995), 41.

282   And if you dream of yeast: Ibid., 19.

282   Brides would do well to heed the admonition: Pickering, Cassell Dic-
        tionary, 41.

282   "the groom helps direct": Tuleja, Curious Customs, 64.

283   "The bride always cuts the cake": Post, Etiquette,

283   "If all is done correctly and in complete silence": Pickering, Cassell Dic-
        tionary, 89.

Layer Forty-two: Holy Cake Daze

PAGE

285   Layer Forty-two: Holy Cake Daze: 123 Greetings, n.d., http://
        www.123greetings.com/cgi-bin/search/search.pl?words=cake+day&
        action=Search&fpage=HPsearch; "Special Days and Holidays," Home
        schooling, n.d., http://homeschooling.about.com/library/bljan27a.htm;
        "Food!" Bizarre Food Holidays, http://library.thinkquest.org/2886/
        foo.htm.

286   like defense contractor David Brooks: Anthony Lappé, "Updated:
        50 Cent, the War Profiteer and the $10 Million Bat Mitzvah,"
        Guerrilla News Network, December 1, 2005, http://www.gnn.tv/
        articles/1915/50_Cent_the_War_Profiteer_and_the_10_million_
        Bat_Mitzvah.

286   The Finnish like strawberry-banana: Mary D. Lankford (Il. Karen
        Dugan), Birthdays Around the World (New York: Harper Collins,
        2002),

Layer Forty-four: Sweet Dreams

PAGE

289   some dream dictionaries think cake represents: "Cake," Dream Moods
        A–Z Dream Dictionary, n.d., http://www.dreammoods.com/dream
        dictionary/c.htm.

Layer Forty-five: Dessert

PAGE

294   *"*we couldn't sue everybody*": "The Oreo Case," Ban Trans Fats, 2006, http://www.bantransfats.com/theoreocase.html.

About the Author

Leslie F. Miller is a writer, graphic designer, photographer, mosaicist, mom, wife, daughter, and cake lover. She has written for such publications as *Weigh Watchers* magazine, the *Baltimore Sun,* and *Baltimore City Paper*. She lives in Baltimore with her husband and daughter, where she tries to resist the constant urge to eat cake.